PHILOSOPHI

Philosophical logic addresses fundamental questions about truth and meaning. Often considered one of the most intellectually demanding of subjects, it provides a basis for much of what is discussed in philosophy and other fields. This book provides a first introduction to the subject. Lucid, up-to-date, and comprehensive, it is based on over twenty years of lectures given by the author at Oxford University.

Sybil Wolfram introduces philosophical logic primarily by focussing on a number of related topics and issues in it, describing views held about them, arguing about them, and generally offering an opinion on ways of clarifying or resolving them. She shows by example how to set about considering the kinds of questions that philosophical logic addresses. Questions at the end of chapters are designed to encourage going beyond what she has written; suggested reading frequently contains other views not necessarily discussed in the text.

Written simply and clearly, employing as few technical terms as possible, *Philosophical Logic* assumes no prior knowledge of either philosophy or logic. It is designed for use as the basis for a one- or two-term undergraduate course, and will be of interest to anyone concerned with understanding the most fundamental intellectual questions.

Sybil Wolfram is University Lecturer in Philosophy at the University of Oxford

PHILOSOPHICAL LOGIC

An introduction

SYBIL WOLFRAM

ROUTLEDGE
LONDON AND NEW YORK

First published 1989
by Routledge
11 New Fetter Lane, London EC4P 4EE
29 West 35th Street, New York, NY 10001

Typeset by Columns of Reading
Printed and bound in Great Britain by
Biddles Ltd, Guildford and King's Lynn

British Library Cataloguing in Publication Data

Wolfram, Sybil
   Philosophical logic : an introduction.
   1. Philosophical logic
   I. Title
   160

   ISBN 0 415 02317 3
   ISBN 0 415 02318 1 Pbk

Library of Congress Cataloging in Publication Data

Wolfram, Sybil, 1931–
   Philosophical logic.

   Bibliography: p.
   Includes index.
   1. Logic.   I. Title.
BC71.W65   1989   160   88-23963
ISBN 0 415 02317 3
ISBN 0 415 02318 1 (pbk.)

TO STEPHEN AND CONRAD

CONTENTS

Preface   xiii

CHAPTER 1 INTRODUCTION   1
Section 1   What is philosophical logic?   1
1.1.1   Philosophical logic and formal logic   1
         Two sorts of logic – Propositional calculus and
         philosophical logic – Examples –
         Predicate calculus and philosophical logic – Examples
1.1.2   Philosophical logic and philosophy   6
         Examples
1.1.3   Philosophical logic in its own right   8

Section 2   Some preliminaries   10
1.2.1   Validity, consistency and soundness   10
         Validity and invalidity – Consistency and inconsistency –
         Soundness and unsoundness – Good and bad
         arguments
1.2.2   Sufficient and necessary conditions   15
         The terms explained – Sufficient vs necessary
         conditions – Relation of sufficient and necessary
         conditions – 'Logically' vs 'contingently' sufficient or
         necessary conditions – 'Causally' sufficient and
         necessary conditions – Inferences based on necessary
         and sufficient conditions
1.2.3   Problems about proof   21

         Notes to Chapter 1   22
         Questions and suggested reading   24

CHAPTER 2 REFERENCE AND TRUTH VALUE   26
Section 1   Typography, meaning, and what is stated   26

CONTENTS

2.1.1	Words	26
	Token and type words – Words with a meaning – Words with the same meaning – Different 'word counts' – Problems about the word 'word'	
2.1.2	Sentences	31
	Token sentences – The meaning of sentences – Sentence ambiguity and synonymy – 'Propositions'	
2.1.3	Statements	35
	The sentence–statement distinction – Counting statements – Meaningful sentences that do not make statements	

Section 2 **The problem of the King of France** 39

2.2.1	How should 'The King of France is wise' be analysed?	39
	The problem – The Theory of Descriptions – The Theory of Presupposition	
2.2.2	Reference failure and the Neglected Case	43
	Two sorts of case – The Neglected Case – Should we introduce a third truth value? – Some implications of the Neglected Case – Failure of reference – Non-radical reference failure – 'Identifying references', 'inessential', and 'referential' uses of expressions – Radical reference failure – When do meaningful declarative sentences fail to make statements? – What kinds of expressions can fail radically to refer?	

Section 3 **Vocabulary of reference** 52

2.3.1	Definite and indefinite reference	52
2.3.2	Expressions making definite references	53
2.3.3	Referring expressions	55
	Different uses of 'referring expression' – Relations of uses – Choice of use – References to particulars vs references to non-particulars	
2.3.4	Rigid and nonrigid designators	60
	Strongly rigid, not strongly rigid and nonrigid – Designators and reference – Advantages and problems	

Section 4 **Should we admit statements?** 63

2.4.1	The initial case for statements	63
	One sentence/proposition, many statements – One statement, many sentences/propositions	
2.4.2	Objections to statements	65
	Are type statements superfluous? – Type statements and criteria of identity – Type statements and referential opacity – Type statements and assertions	
2.4.3	Two comments about statements	71
	Multiplication of entities? – Truth conditions	

CONTENTS

Notes to Chapter 2   72
Questions and suggested reading   76

CHAPTER 3 NECESSARY TRUTH AND THE
           ANALYTIC–SYNTHETIC DISTINCTION   80
Section 1 **Map of distinctions and theories**   80
3.1.1   'Necessary' and 'contingent', 'analytic' and 'synthetic',
           '*a priori*' and 'empirical'   80
3.1.2   Three theories about necessary truth   82

Section 2 **Conventionalism**   85
3.2.1   The Logical Positivist picture   85
           Division of propositions – Division of truths – The
           role of ambiguity
3.2.2   Self-evidence and logical truth   88
           Self-evidence – Logical truths
3.2.3   Necessity and certainty   91
           Examples considered – Perception is unreliable

Section 3 **Scepticism**   93
3.3.1   Necessary truth and referential opacity   93
           Positivist conventionalism and reference – Quine's
           Necessity Argument – What does Quine's Necessity
           Argument show? – Necessary truths and non-analytic
           propositions – Contingent truths and analytic
           propositions – Premise 2 of Quine's Necessity Argument
           revised – 'Analytic' and 'necessarily true' – Premise 1
           of Quine's Necessity Argument revised – Positive
           results of Quine's Necessity Argument
3.3.2   Definitions of 'analytic'   102
           Relation of Necessity and Analyticity Arguments –
           Quine's Analyticity Argument – Two discarded
           definitions of 'analytic' – Three groups of definitions
           of 'analytic' – Use of 'analytic'

Section 4 **Essentialism**   110
3.4.1   Kripke's necessary truths   110
3.4.2   What is essentialism?   112
           'Essentialism': sense 1 (not analytic) – Sense 2 (not
           meaning of words) – Senses 3a (objects) and 3b
           (particulars)
3.4.3   Kripke's weak sense of 'necessarily true'   116
3.4.4   In what sense is Kripke an essentialist?   117
           Kripke's old-style justification – Kripke's new-style
           justification – Kripke's sense of 'necessarily true' and
           essentialism – necessary truth and Kripke's essentialism

CONTENTS

Section 5   **Modified conventionalism**   120
3.5.1   Modification of the relations between 'analytic' and
        'necessarily true'   120
3.5.2   Modification of 'synthetic'   122

        Notes to Chapter 3   124
        Questions and suggested reading   126

CHAPTER 4 ASPECTS OF TRUTH   129
Section 1   **Relations between *p* and *p is true***   129
4.1.1   Preliminary assumptions   129
4.1.2   Why *p* and *p is true* have the same truth value   131
4.1.3   *p* and *p is true* are not the same type statement   132
4.1.4   Propositions expressing *p* and *p is true*   134
4.1.5   *p* in *p is true* need not be a formulated statement   134
4.1.6   Relaxing assumptions 1 and 2   136

Section 2   **Ascriptions of truth and assertions**   139
4.2.1   What is an assertion?   139
4.2.2   Assertions of *p* and assertions of *p is true*   141
4.2.3   *p* and asserting *p is true* (or p)   144
4.2.4   Holding that *p is true* and asserting that *p/p is true*   146
4.2.5   Asserting and informing   148
4.2.6   Sentences and truth   149

Section 3   **Theories of truth**   150
4.3.1   What does *p is true* say about *p*?   150
4.3.2   Impediments to knowing that *p* is true   152
        A priori vs empirical knowledge that *p* is true –
        Statements and vantage points – Uncertainty and
        ascriptions of truth value
4.3.3   Comments   157
        Other theories of truth – Results

        Notes to Chapter 4   158
        Questions and suggested reading   160

CHAPTER 5 NEGATION   162
Section 1   **Affirmative and negative**   162
5.1.1   Outline of the position   162
5.1.2   Summary of the case against a distinction between
        affirmative and negative   163
5.1.3   Some propositions/statements can be expressed both
        affirmatively and negatively   164
5.1.4   The case for claiming that propositions/statements
        expressed by truly negative sentences can be
        expressed affirmatively   167

CONTENTS

Ayer's case – Widening the discussion – Defects in
Ayer's case
5.1.5   Propositions/statements with both negative and
         affirmative components   175

Section 2   Contradiction and inconsistency   177
5.2.1   Frege's account of contradictory statements   177
5.2.2   Caveats about Frege's account of contradictions   178
         Contradictory statements and propositions –
         Definitions of 'contradictory to' and 'inconsistent
         with' – Asserting and believing contradictories/
         inconsistencies
5.2.3   Inconsistency and bad arguments   183
5.2.4   'Contradictory' and 'inconsistent' as kinds of
         statements and propositions   183
5.2.5   Varieties of contradictory/inconsistent statements and
         propositions   184
5.2.6   Inconsistency and 'meaningless' sentences   186
         A problem – Why there is not a simple solution

         Notes to Chapter 5   188
         Questions and suggested reading   189

CHAPTER 6 EXISTENCE AND IDENTITY   191
Section 1   Existence   191
6.1.1   'Is "exists" a predicate?'   191
         Standard arguments against 'exist(s)' being a predicate
         – Arguments for 'exist(s)' being after all sometimes
         a predicate
6.1.2   Subject-predicate and existential form   195
         The need for a distinction – A problem – A method
         of introducing a distinction – Two conflicting
         tests for subject terms
6.1.3   Real and not real   204
         Use of 'real' – Dragons and Hamlet – 'Real' and
         'exists' – Existing at different times

Section 2   Identity   209
6.2.1   Propositions/statements of identity   209
         Numerical and qualitative identity – Particulars and
         non-particulars – Ambiguous type sentences – The
         'relation' of identity – Completing 'one and the same'
6.2.2   Sortal terms   216
         Supplying a principle of counting – Nouns which are
         too general – 'One object' – Nouns which are too
         specific – Unequivocal principles of counting – Different
         sorts of sortal term – 'a is a'

CONTENTS

Notes to Chapter 6   225
Questions and suggested reading   226

CHAPTER 7 ASPECTS OF MEANING   229
Section 1   **General terms and natural kinds**   229
7.1.1   What is a 'natural kind'?   229
7.1.2   Classifications not based on resemblance   232
   Variety of principles of classification – Examples
7.1.3   The case of biological species   236
   Intra-breeding groups – Biological species and
   'nature' – The logic of species names

Section 2   **Proper names**   243
7.2.1   Questions about proper names   243
   Proper names vs general names – Proper names as
   referring expressions
7.2.2   Features of proper names   246
   Improving the description – Proper names and
   reference – 'a' and 'b' – Proper names and dictionaries

Section 3   **Questions about meaning**   252
7.3.1   General questions about meaning   252
7.3.2   Pulling some threads together   253

Notes to Chapter 7   255
Questions and suggested reading   256

APPENDIX: Examination questions   259

Bibliography of works referred to   263

Glossary   270

Index   278

PREFACE

There are many ways of introducing a subject. I have chosen to introduce philosophical logic primarily by focussing on a number of related topics and issues in it, describing views held about them, arguing about them, and generally offering an opinion on ways of clarifying or resolving them. Proof is not a simple matter in this subject, and some readers may disagree with me. Indeed, I should not have achieved what I have set out to do if someone reading this book did not want to argue for another or a further view. Some of the questions at the end of chapters are designed to encourage going beyond what I have tried to expound; suggested reading frequently contains other views not necessarily discussed in the text. To learn a subject like philosophical logic, it is not enough, nor the most important thing, to get to know a view that is currently popular or held by a particular author. It is necessary to acquire the tools and skills with which to handle the subject matter for oneself. To this end, I have tried to write simply and clearly, employing as few technical terms as possible. However, every subject has a vocabulary, and terms commonly used in philosophical logic are explained in the text, and can be referred to in the glossary. Sometimes terms have acquired more than one meaning, and where relevant, the several different meanings are discussed.

Some of the material in some chapters of this book has been published in a different form in papers in journals or collections of articles. There are references at appropriate points in the text. Much of the material I have used has been developed in the course of teaching. Most of it has had a place in some form in one or another of the sets of lectures on philosophical logic I have given at the University of Oxford in the last twenty years, and I owe a great debt to the general ambience of Oxford, and to my pupils and members of my lecture audiences. I should also like particularly to thank my former tutor, Professor Sir Peter Strawson, for introducing me to philosophical logic in the first place, Dr B.M. Levick for reading the entire text, and members of my family who have helped test out reactions of those unacquainted with the subject.

Oxford 1988

Chapter 1

INTRODUCTION

SECTION 1   *WHAT IS PHILOSOPHICAL LOGIC?*

Logic may be said to be the study of correct and incorrect reasoning. This includes the study of what makes arguments consistent or inconsistent, valid or invalid, sound or unsound (on these terms see 1.2.1). It has two branches, known as *formal* (or *symbolic*) logic and *philosophical* logic.

1.1.1   Philosophical logic and formal logic

(i)   Two sorts of logic

One of the branches of logic, *formal logic*, codifies arguments and supplies tests of consistency and validity, starting from axioms, that is, from definitions and rules for assessing the consistency and validity of arguments.[1] At the present time there are two main systems of formal logic, usually known as the *propositional calculus* and the *predicate calculus*. The propositional calculus concerns relations of what it terms 'propositions' to each other. The predicate calculus codifies inferences which may be drawn on account of certain features of the content of 'propositions'.[2]

The other branch of logic, *philosophical logic*, which is my concern here, is very much more difficult to delimit and define. It can be said to study arguments, meaning, truth. Its subject matter is closely related to that of formal logic but its objects are different. Rather than setting out to codify valid arguments and to supply axioms and notations allowing the assessment of increasingly complex arguments, it examines the bricks and mortar from which such systems are built. Although it aims, among other things, to

1

1. INTRODUCTION

illuminate or sometimes question the formalization of arguments into systems with axioms which have been effected, it is not restricted to a study of arguments which formal logic has codified.[3]

Philosophical logic is related not only to formal logic but also to other branches of philosophy but it is convenient to begin with the relations of formal and philosophical logic. The easiest way to see the kind of relations between them is to look at some examples, first from the propositional calculus, and then from the predicate calculus.

(ii) Propositional calculus and philosophical logic

In the propositional calculus what it calls 'propositions' are symbolized by letters: p, q, r, etc.

Propositional calculus has a special interest in:

not-p (It is not raining) – *negation*
p *and* q (It is raining *and* he went home) – *conjunction*
p *or* q (It is raining *or* he went home (or both)) – *disjunction*[4]
If p *then* q (*If* it is raining, *then* he went home) – *implication*
p *if and only if* q (*If and only if* it is raining, he went home) – *equivalence*.

It lays down axioms (definitions), which cannot be questioned within the propositional calculus (they are ruled to be true):

not-p is true if p is false and false if p is true
p and q is true if and only if p is true and q is true
p or q is true if either p is true or q is true (or both are true)
If p then q is true except if it is both the case that p is true and that q is false
p if and only if q is true when p and q are either both true or both false.

The use of 'not', 'and', etc. in the propositional calculus is sufficiently close to the use of these and related terms in the natural language of English, and equivalents in other languages, for it to be possible, with the aid of notation, to symbolize many arguments in everyday thinking, and so to devise simple methods of assessing complex arguments for consistency and validity.

For instance, to take a very simple case, it can swiftly be seen that it follows (and we can validly infer) from 'If it was raining, then he went home' (If p, then q) that 'It was not raining or he went home (or both)' (not-p or q) but not that (e.g.) 'It was raining or he did not go home (or both)' (p or not-q), much less 'It was raining and he did not go home' (p and not-q) which is inconsistent with 'If it was raining, then he went home'.

In studying philosophical logic, the bricks (p, q, r) and mortar (true, false, and, or, etc.) of the propositional calculus are scrutinized.

(iii) Examples

a) *What are the 'propositions' of the propositional calculus?* It is not obvious, and indeed has been a cause of much difficulty, what *kind* of thing p, q, r stand' for when they stand for *It is raining, He went home, Here is a bank*, etc. A string of words? A sentence with a particular meaning? What someone states if he utters the sentence 'he went home', 'here is a bank' or etc.? (See 2.1.2–3, 2.4 for discussion of the difference.)

b) *Are there only two truth values?* The propositional calculus operates with two *truth values*, *true* and *false*, and thereby makes the supposition that any instance of the kind of thing that p, q, r stand for has just one of the two truth values, true and false. (This is an axiom (postulate) of the system.) In philosophical logic the question arises as to whether any one sentence with a particular meaning (or whatever p, q, r stand for in an argument) is always either true or false. (See 2.2 and 4.1 for discussion.)

c) *How well does the propositional calculus represent arguments?* The connectives (*and, or*, etc.) employed in the propositional calculus make omissions. For instance, there is no time sequence such as there often is in conjunctions in ordinary English, where there is a difference between 'He protested and was dismissed' and 'He was dismissed and protested'. The propositional calculus treats both these as true provided he was dismissed and he did protest irrespective of the order of events. 'If p then q' rates as true if very minimal conditions are satisfied, namely that p should not be true and q false. This condition is satisfied by innumerable totally disconnected sentences or statements such as 'The earth is round', 'Cats are furry', '9 is a number'. 'If the earth is round, then cats are furry' would not ordinarily be accepted as a good argument. There is a good deal to say about this case, and I shall return to it presently.

It might be said that these and other obvious discrepancies between everyday arguments and the propositional calculus arise from the fact that the axioms of the propositional calculus select only the *minimum* conditions that have to be satisfied if the conjunctions, disjunctions, etc. in terms of which we all argue are to be true. This is again a large and difficult topic.[5]

(iv)   Predicate calculus and philosophical logic

The predicate calculus is concerned with sentences containing 'predicates':

> X (a singular term or variable) is Y
> All Xs are Y
> No Xs are Y
> Some Xs are Y
> Some Xs are not Y

These were also the major preoccupation of syllogistic logic, which studied and classified conclusions which could and could not be derived from conjoining any two propositions of these forms, together containing three terms symbolized as S ('Subject'), P ('Predicate'), and M ('Middle Term'). Thus from *All Ss are M* and *All Ms are P*, it follows that *All Ss are P*, while from *No Ss are M* and *No Ms are P* or from *Some Ss are M* and *Some Ms are P*, nothing whatever follows. The codification of and generalization about syllogisms reached a sophisticated level of systematization but within what now appears a narrow range of arguments.[6]

The predicate calculus is concerned with inferences involving the *universal quantifier* (*All* xs are F (where F is the predicate)) and the *existential quantifier* (*some* (at least one) x is F). In philosophical logic there are many questions which arise from and bear on 'All', 'Some', x, y, z (*variables*), m, n, o (singular terms), F, G, H (predicates).

(v)   Examples
a)   Singular terms   Many different kinds of term are bunched

4

together as *singular terms* (terms used to refer to single things) which in the predicate calculus are commonly represented by m, n, o, or that rate as 'the sort of things that can be quantified over' (i.e. be prefaced by 'all' or 'some' or 'six', etc.), and are represented as x, y, z. The predicate calculus is happiest with proper names (John, Hitler, London) as prototype singular terms. But there are also terms other than proper names which may refer to the same things: pronouns (I, you, he, she, etc.), demonstratives ('this' and 'that'), terms like 'here' and 'now', definite descriptions ('The man round the corner') (see 2.3.2). These various terms have different features or 'logical properties', which may present problems. 'Do proper names have a meaning?', for example, is a long-standing question in philosophical logic (often receiving the answer 'no' (see 7.2)). Again, it may not be obvious what qualifies a term as being a *singular term*. For example, 'singular terms' may be restricted to terms for single objects, like persons and tomato plants, objects which can be 'quantified over' (where we can speak of some or all or six of them). In this case 'pat of butter' or 'pint of water' are singular terms, but 'butter' and 'water' are not. Some things that can be counted are *particulars* – persons, cats, tables, copies of books, or for that matter events like meals or performances of symphonies. But we can also count other sorts of things which are not particulars and speak of one species of animal, one disease, one symphony or book, such as Beethoven's *Ninth Symphony* or *David Copperfield*, one make of car, or of the number 9 (one number). Differences between particulars, items with a definite spatio-temporal location,[7] and countable items of other sorts ('non-particulars') are of interest in philosophical logic (see 6.2 and 7.1–2). The predicate calculus has no interest in them as such but only in so far as they could affect the propriety of representing terms or what they stand for as m, n, etc. or x, y, etc.

b) Subjects and predicates   The predicate calculus represents 'predicates' by F, G, H, and so on. In a sentence like 'My cat is black', 'black' or 'is black' (sometimes one form, sometimes the other) would ordinarily be said to be the *predicate*, and 'my cat' the *subject*. The 'subject' will be said to be referred to, or what the sentence is *about*, and the 'predicate' is the part of the sentence that says something about whatever is the subject.

In the study of philosophical logic it becomes evident that it is

5

very far from clear exactly what qualifies a term as a 'predicate'. Being in a particular position in a sentence seems to be one feature attributed to 'predicates' but not the only one. For instance, in 'Tigers exist', 'exist' is often said *not* to be a predicate (see 6.1.1). 'True' in 'That statement is true' has also often been said not to be a predicate (see chapter 4).

It is equally not obvious what qualifies something as the or a 'subject' of a sentence. The gloss 'what the sentence is about' might apply to anything mentioned in a sentence or just the first thing mentioned: a sentence like 'John jumped over the ditch' might with perfect propriety be said to be *about* John and/or about the ditch and/or about jumping. For someone engaged in constructing a formal system such as the predicate calculus, problems like these arise primarily at the level of translating a natural language into the calculus. And looking at philosophical logic from the angle of formal logic, it might seem that the prime task of philosophical logic is to pave the way for such translation.

c) 'All' and 'some' For reasons internal to itself, it suits the predicate calculus to treat 'all' as what is sometimes called 'lacking existential import', that is, for it to be true that all xs are F, it is not, in the predicate calculus, necessary that there should be any xs. Since there do have to be xs for 'some xs are F' to be true, it is not, in the predicate calculus, possible validly to infer that 'some pigs are greedy' from 'all pigs are greedy': the calculus treats this as an invalid inference, there being no need for there to be pigs for all of them to be greedy. This treatment of 'all', and its rationale and consequences, raise questions in philosophical logic which are not of great interest to formal logicians.

Many of the topics I shall be discussing in this book do relate in one way or another to questions that arise from or affect formal systems. However philosophical logic is not concerned just, nor even primarily, with these systems.

1.1.2 *Philosophical logic and philosophy*

In any branch of philosophy problems arise that can be said to be problems not only of that branch of philosophy but also of philosophical logic. A point arises which is not specific to the subject matter but is a point of logic, of whether this sort of argument is consistent or that valid. For example, it is a point of logic (incorporated into the propositional calculus) that 'q only if p' does not follow from 'if p then q'. There is no branch of philosophy or indeed of learning or any other area of life where someone might not erroneously infer 'only if p then q' from 'if p then q', and so, for instance, muddle '(all) smokers get lung cancer' with 'only smokers get lung cancer' but I shall select my illustrations of applications of philosophical logic from philosophy. (For a more detailed discussion of the relations between 'if p then q' and 'only if p then q', see 1.2.2.)

Examples

a) Moral philosophy and philosophical logic It was argued by G.E. Moore (1903),[8] in the course of accusing Utilitarian moral philosophers of logical error, that 'good' cannot be defined in terms of any other property. This, which I call Moore's Premise, was the premise of a further argument. He inferred from his Premise that therefore (1) 'good' cannot be defined, and (2) 'good' is a simple property. It was soon noticed that (2) does not follow from Moore's Premise because (a point of philosophical logic) an adjective need not name a property and 'good' may not name any kind of property. Investigation of 'definition' – a part of philosophical logic – makes it obvious that (1) ('good' cannot be defined) also does not follow from Moore's Premise: 'definition' of a term T does not always consist of supplying equivalent descriptions for T, of naming T's essential properties (see 7.1). It also does not follow from accepting Moore's Premise and rejecting (2) (that good is a simple property), and so concluding that 'good' is not a property at all, that e.g. '*morally* good' is not a property. It is not excluded that a *phrase* containing 'good' such as 'morally good' is after all correctly defined as (e.g.) 'conducive to the greatest happiness. . .'. Whether this is the correct account is the province of moral philosophy. Whether or not logical error is involved is a point of philosophical logic.

b) The existence of God and philosophical logic One argument for the existence of God, known as the ontological argument, was that since God is by definition perfect and existence is a perfection, so God must exist. This argument is generally attributed to St Anselm (1033–1109) in his *Proslogion II*,[9] and was frequent in Descartes'

7

writings.[10] The ontological argument was later declared fallacious on the grounds that 'exists' is not a predicate/property and therefore is not a perfection, an argument usually attributed to Kant (1781),[11] or more generally, that affirmative existential statements are never necessarily true, an argument that can be found in Hume (1748).[12] These are applications of philosophical logic to a particular question which preoccupied philosophers, as well as theologians. (See 6.1.1 for later discussions of whether 'exists' is a predicate.)

c) *The conduct of science and philosophical logic* A major concern in much philosophy, and also science and much everyday thinking, is whether a theory or belief 1. is true (or false) in virtue of the meaning of words that express it, or, on the contrary, 2. is true (or false) because of the way the world is, and requires empirical evidence (evidence of how the world is) to prove it. Locke (1690)[13] encouraged scientists to perform experiments. Among his grounds were that if a statement of the form 'Xs are Y' is to be informative about objects and events in the world, it must not be the case that 'Y' is part of the *meaning* of the term 'X'. If we include that it is malleable in the definition of 'gold', then, he explained, when we announce that 'Gold is malleable', no one has been told anything about anything in the world. The only way to increase our knowledge of what things in the world are actually like is to observe and experiment with them.

So important are questions and conclusions which are the particular province of philosophical logic to other branches of philosophy that it has a right to be considered the nuts and bolts of the rest of philosophy.

1.1.3 *Philosophical logic in its own right*

Philosophical logic has developed a life of its own and been pursued for its own sake, as one might pursue mathematics or the investigation of plants, even if that area of mathematics has no immediate or obvious application and no one else has a great interest in the plants in question. One may just be interested in the studies without considering their further applications or utility, if any. Results useful elsewhere may of course emerge but because obtaining them is not the prime object, the organization of the subject will not be geared to them.

At certain periods philosophical logic was closely integrated with formal logic, and books were written about logic which contained both formal and philosophical logic.[14] At other times, philosophical logic was not differentiated from 'epistemology' (how we know things) or from 'metaphysics'. In works by Locke or Hume about 'Human Understanding' or 'Human Nature' (or by Kant about Pure Reason)[15] there is a good deal of what would now be included as philosophical logic as well as much that comes under 'epistemology'. Locke (1690) described features of self-evident propositions or of proper names and general terms (philosophical logic),[16] as well as arguing that all knowledge requires experience (epistemology).[17] Hume (1748) drew a distinction between matters of fact and relations of ideas (philosophical logic),[18] as well as arguing that no event can be known to be a miracle (epistemology/ philosophy of religion).[19] Kant's *Critique of Pure Reason* (1781), generally classed as a work of metaphysics, opens with a distinction which became central in philosophical logic, that between what he dubbed 'analytic' (where the predicate is 'contained in' the subject) and 'synthetic' judgements (where the predicate is not contained in the subject).[20] In 1953 Ryle opposed 'informal logic', to 'formal logic' without much distinction between 'informal logic' and any other philosophical activity.[21]

But there is now a body of literature which might be termed 'pure' philosophical logic, where the primary concern is the unravelling of problems within philosophical logic rather than as a prelude to epistemological concerns or to building axiomatic systems. Among the results is that philosophical logic has standard topics, often standard questions about them, sometimes standard doctrines. Topics that have aroused interest, and often controversy, include: reference (and failures of reference), necessary truth, truth, proper names, existential statements, statements of identity, negation, 'natural kinds'. Many others could be named. Topics are not orderly, and cannot be considered branches of the subject.

9

SECTION 2 *SOME PRELIMINARIES*

1.2.1 Validity, consistency and soundness

At the opening of this Introduction, I said that logic includes the study of what makes arguments consistent or inconsistent, valid or invalid, sound or unsound. Some explanation of this vocabulary for assessing arguments is needed, especially as the relations between these concepts are complicated.

(i) Validity and invalidity

An argument is generally said to be *valid* if the conclusion follows from the premises; *invalid* if the conclusion does not follow from the premises.[22] The argument that:

It is raining and he went home, so he went home

is in this sense *valid*. The conclusion that he went home follows from the premises that it is raining and he went home.[23] The argument that:

He went home, so it is raining and he went home

is invalid. The conclusion that it is both raining and he went home does not follow from the premise 'he went home'. Ordinarily we can validly argue from 'all pigs are greedy' to 'some pigs are greedy' but not from 'some pigs are greedy' to 'all pigs are greedy': if all pigs are greedy then some must be, but that some pigs are greedy does not, as we should ordinarily say, mean that *all* of them are. However, in the predicate calculus the argument that if all pigs are greedy, then some pigs are greedy is not rated as a valid argument because 'all pigs are greedy' is translated into 'nothing is both a pig and not greedy' and may be true when there are no pigs while 'some pigs are greedy' cannot be true unless there are pigs. The invalidity of the argument arises because it is possible for the premise to be true and yet the conclusion false. For an argument to be valid, it must not be the case that the premises can be true and the conclusion false.

10

1.2.1   Box a

Valid argument: If premises are true, conclusion is true.
Invalid argument: Conclusion need not be true when
    premises are true.

(ii)   Consistency and inconsistency

For an argument to rate as *consistent* it must be the case that it is
possible for the conclusion to be true when the premises are true.

All valid arguments are consistent: if it is necessary for the
conclusion to be true if the premises are true (validity) then it must
be possible for the conclusion to be true if the premises are true
(consistency). If an argument is not consistent then it is not valid.

1.2.1   Box b

Consistent argument: if premises are true, conclusion may be
    true.
Inconsistent argument: if premises are true, conclusion must
    be false.
If an argument is valid, then it is consistent; an inconsistent
    argument is invalid.

Invalid arguments may be either consistent or inconsistent: if a
conclusion does not follow from premises then it may or may not be
consistent with them. If some pigs are greedy, it does not follow that
all are, but that all are greedy is consistent with some being greedy.
If some pigs are greedy, it does not follow that none is greedy.
Indeed this conclusion is *inconsistent* with the premise. Where a
conclusion is inconsistent with the premises in this way, it *would* be
valid to argue from the premises that the conclusion is *not* true.

Consistent arguments may be either valid or not valid: some are
one, some the other. It is consistent with 'he went home' that it
was raining and he went home, or with 'some pigs are greedy' that
all pigs are greedy, but not valid to argue from the first to the
second. It is consistent with 'it was raining and he went home' that
he went home and valid to argue from the first to the second. Both

1. INTRODUCTION

ordinarily and in the predicate calculus, it is consistent with 'all pigs are greedy' that 'some pigs are greedy'; ordinarily, but not in the predicate calculus, it is valid to argue from the first to the second (see 1.1.1 (v) c).

1.2.1 Box c

If an argument is not valid, it may be consistent or
  inconsistent.
If an argument is consistent, it may be valid or invalid.

(iii) Soundness and unsoundness

In the propositional calculus *if p then q* is true except when p is true and q is false. Whenever p is false, then *if p, then q* is true. This and other consequences (such as that p and q may be unrelated in subject matter: 'p' might represent 'pigs can fly', 'q': 'some cats like milk') of the definition of *if p then q* in the propositional calculus are sometimes called the 'paradoxes of material implication', 'material' being used to separate this special (or minimum) sense of 'implication' from its more common and fuller everyday use, where it would not generally be allowed that p implies q whenever p is false (or when they are unrelated in subject matter).

The term 'sound' can be used to distinguish valid arguments which have true premises from arguments which are valid but do not have true premises. In this terminology, a sound argument must be valid; invalid arguments cannot be sound even if they have true premises. But an argument may be valid in that it is an argument such that if the premises are true, the conclusion must be true, without also being sound: its premises may not be true. 'The earth is flat and so it is not round' is a valid but unsound argument, 'The earth is round and so it is not flat' an argument which is sound as well as valid.

12

1.2.1   Box d

Sound argument: argument which is valid and has true
   premises.
If an argument is sound, then it is valid; an invalid argument
   is unsound. If an argument is valid, it may be or may not
   be sound.

(iv)   Good and bad arguments

It is sometimes said that the truth or falsity of premises is not the
concern of logic.[24] Logic has to do with correct *reasoning* from
premises, not with establishing the truth of this or that premise. It
is however the concern of logic to distinguish the ways in which
arguments may be bad.

   In 1.2.1 (i)–(iii) I have mentioned three defects which arguments
may have: they may be inconsistent (i.e. the conclusion cannot be
true if the premises are true); they may be consistent but invalid
(i.e. the conclusion may but need not be true even if the premises
are true); they may be valid but unsound (i.e. if the premises are
true, the conclusion must be true, but the premises are false). The
terms 'inconsistent', 'invalid', 'unsound' could be used to mark off
these three different defects. We could make the terms 'mutually
exclusive', i.e. so that not more than one of them can apply to any
given argument, by ruling that only consistent arguments can be
termed 'valid' or 'invalid', only valid arguments 'sound' or
'unsound'.[25] I do not employ the terms in this way. As I am using
them, soundness requires validity, and validity requires consistency, but an argument which is not sound may be unsound
because it is invalid or inconsistent, as well as because, although
valid, it has false premises, and an argument which is invalid may
be invalid because it is inconsistent, as well as because, although
consistent, a true conclusion does not have to follow if the premises
are true.

   We may complain of an argument that it is unsound and/or
invalid and/or inconsistent. Any of these defects makes it a bad
argument. There can be other problems. Sometimes it is possible to
prove that a premise is false, so that an argument based on it must
be unsound. But sometimes we are not in a position to do more

13

than to show that a premise has not been *demonstrated* to be true, and therefore *may* be false. 'He hasn't proved his point' is a commonly heard criticism of someone's argument.

There are philosophical theories which reduce what *can* be proved to be true to very little, sometimes to nothing at all. Some of these theories allow that there can be proof of falsity, more sophisticated versions maintain that not even falsity is susceptible of proof (see 3.2.3, 3.3.2 (iv) d, 4.2.6, 4.3.2).

The question of whether certain classes of statements, for example those about the material world, can or cannot be proved to be true is the domain of epistemology. It rests on such questions as whether or when our perception of the external world is reliable. (For the purposes of this book I shall take the 'common-sense' line that perception is not always unreliable.) There are also classes of statements about which it is a matter of logic that they cannot be proved to be true or cannot be proved to be false. For example, statements of unrestricted generality,[26] that is, of the form 'All Xs anywhere anytime are Y', cannot be proved to be true by observation of Xs because it could not be possible to examine all Xs (e.g. tigers) everywhere at all times (i.e. including the future) to be sure that each is Y (e.g. fierce). Statements of this form can be known to be true only if knowledge of their truth does not require observation ('Y' being included in the definition of 'X' – see 1.1.2 c, 3.3.2 a, 4.3.2 (i)). So far as logical considerations go, if they are false, they can be proved to be false by observation: all that is required is that we should find an X (e.g. tiger) which is not Y (not fierce).

The kind of obstacle to proof by observation encountered by statements of unrestricted generality is not in general confined to proof of *truth*. In statements of a different form, such as 'Some Xs are Y', the difficulty does not affect proof of truth: we can prove by observation that some Xs are Y by finding one or two Xs that are Y. It afflicts proof of falsity. We cannot prove that *no* Xs are, were or ever will be Y by observation, any more than we can prove that all Xs are, were or will be Y, and for the same reason: there might always be more Xs which might after all turn out to be Y/not Y. If a statement of the form 'All Xs are Y' is not of a type to be proved true without observation (is not necessarily true: see 3.2.3, 4.3.2), then it cannot be proved true at all. Similarly statements of the form 'Some Xs are Y', where being an 'X' does not necessarily exclude being a 'Y', cannot be shown to be false at all.[27]

If a statement *cannot* be proved to be true, then we also cannot be sure that an argument in which it forms a premise is sound. (The case of premises which cannot be proved to be false may prevent us being sure that an argument is unsound, but is not quite parallel since the argument might be unsound on other grounds, viz. because it is invalid.) Often of course, if we take the common-sense line, the problem is not that a statement which forms the premise of an argument *cannot* be proved to be true, but simply that it has not been proved to be true, either in general or by the purveyor of the argument. If we have evidence that the premise is not true, we can rule the argument unsound. We may, however, not ourselves know whether or not the premise is true. All we know is that proof or evidence of its truth is not supplied. In this case the argument is a bad one because it has not been shown to be sound.

1.2.1   Box e

If a premise of an argument is not proved to be true, the argument has not been shown to be sound.

1.2.2   *Sufficient and necessary conditions*

Philosophers make very frequent use of the terms 'sufficient condition' and 'necessary condition'.[28]

(i)   The terms 'sufficient condition' and 'necessary condition' explained

To say that p is a *sufficient* condition of q is to say: If p then q (or: whenever p, then q). For example, to say that its raining is a sufficient condition of his going home early is to say that whenever it rains, he goes home early. This can also be expressed either as 'p is not the case without q also being the case' (it doesn't rain without his also going home early) or as 'if not q then not p' (if he isn't going home early, it isn't raining). For reasons explained below (1.2.2 (v)–(vi)), one of these modes of expression may be more appropriate than another.

To say that p is a *necessary* condition of q is to say: q only if p. For example, to say that its raining is a necessary condition of his going home early is to say that he goes home early only if it rains. This can also be expressed either as 'q is not the case unless p is the case' (he doesn't go home early unless it rains) or as 'if not p, then q' (if it doesn't rain, he doesn't go home early).

1.2.2   Box a

p is a sufficient condition of q: whenever p then q.

p is a necessary condition of q: only if p, then q.

(ii)   Sufficient vs necessary conditions

It is easy to see that p can be a sufficient condition of q without also being a necessary condition of q. Q may be the case whenever p is the case without its also being true that q is the case only if p is the case. For example, that he goes home early whenever it rains does not mean that it has to rain for him to go home early; he may go home early whenever it rains but not only when it rains (but also, for instance, on sunny days when he wants to go to the dentist).

It is equally evident that p can be a necessary condition of q without also being a sufficient condition of q. Q may be the case only when p is the case without its also being true that q is the case whenever p is the case. For example, that he goes home early only if it rains does not mean that he goes home early whenever it rains; he may go home early only if it rains without going home early whenever it rains (sometimes when it rains he stays late and catches up on the accounts).

1.2.2   Box b

p can be a sufficient but not necessary condition of q (p 'implies' q).

p can be a necessary but not sufficient condition of q (q 'implies' p).

(iii)   Sufficient *and* necessary conditions

Sometimes p is both a sufficient and a necessary condition of q. To say that p is both a sufficient *and* a necessary condition of q is to say: p if and only if q, i.e. p if q *and* p only if q. This can also be expressed: q if and only if p, i.e. q if p and q only if p. Logicians sometimes use 'iff' as a shorthand for 'if and only if' and name the relation 'equivalence' (see 1.1.1 (ii); see also 4.1.2–4). Example: It is raining if and only if (iff) he goes home early, i.e. whenever he goes home early it is raining (p if q) and only when he goes home early is it raining (p only if q). Alternative expression: He goes home early if and only if (iff) it is raining, i.e. whenever it is raining he goes home early (q if p) and only if it rains does he go home early (q only if p).

1.2.2   Box c

p can be a sufficient *and* necessary condition of q (p and q are 'equivalent').

If p is a sufficient and necessary condition of q, then q is a necessary and sufficient condition of p.

(iv)   Relation of sufficient and necessary conditions

There is an important relation between necessary and sufficient conditions, namely, that if p is a sufficient condition of q, then q is a necessary condition of p, and if p is a necessary condition of q then q is a sufficient condition of p. That this is so is easy to see from the descriptions of necessary and sufficient conditions in 1.2.2 (i)–(iii) but is worth repeating.

To say that p is a sufficient condition of q is to say that if p then q, that is, p is not the case without q also being the case. Another way of putting this is to say that p is the case only if q, in other words that q is a necessary condition of p. For example, to say that its raining is a sufficient condition of his going home early is to say that if it rains he goes home early, that is, it never rains without his going home early. Another way of putting this is to say that it is raining only when he goes home early, in other words his going home early is a necessary condition of rain: there can't be rain without his going early.

1. INTRODUCTION

To say that p is a necessary condition of q is to say that only if p, then q, that is, q is not the case unless p is the case. Another way of putting this is to say that whenever q is the case, p is the case, in other words, that q is a sufficient condition of p. For example, to say that its raining is a necessary condition for him to go home early is to say that only if it is raining does he go home early, that is, he doesn't go home early if it is not raining. Another way of putting this is to say that whenever he goes home early, it is raining, in other words, his going home early is a sufficient condition of its raining: whenever he goes home early, it is raining.

1.2.2   Box d

If p is a sufficient condition of q, then q is a necessary
   condition of p.
If p is a necessary condition of q, then q is a sufficient
   condition of p.

Some of these expressions and re-expressions look awkward for reasons to be explained.

(v)   'Logically' vs 'contingently' sufficient or necessary conditions

That p is a sufficient condition of q or a necessary condition of q is something which logicians frequently want to say as a means of saying that it is the case that whenever p then q, or alternatively that it is only when p that q.

Within this framework a distinction is commonly drawn between p being a sufficient (or necessary) condition of q as a point of *logic*, or 'necessarily', on the one hand, and p being a sufficient (or necessary) condition of q as a *matter of fact*, or 'contingently', on the other hand. (The double use of 'necessary'/'necessarily' with different meanings can cause confusion and will be discussed presently.) For example, in *A has brown eyes* is a sufficient condition of *A has eyes* (or having brown eyes is a sufficient condition of having eyes), the relation is a 'logical' or 'necessary' one. In *A drinks hemlock is a sufficient condition of A dies* (or drinking hemlock is a sufficient condition of dying), the relation is a 'factual' or 'contingent' one.

The distinction between necessary relations or truths on the one hand, and contingent ones on the other is a difficult and currently controversial topic, which is discussed at length in chapter 3 and 4.3.2 (i). For the purpose of explaining 'sufficient conditions' and 'necessary conditions', I shall draw the distinction between 'necessary' and 'contingent' by saying that a statement which is necessarily true must be true in any state of the world, 'in all possible worlds', and derives its truth from the meaning of words. It is a matter of language, and necessarily true, that to have brown eyes you have to have eyes, and thus that having brown eyes is a sufficient condition of having eyes. By contrast it is a matter of fact that if someone drinks hemlock, he dies: this is a matter of how hemlock and the human frame are constituted. And drinking hemlock is as a matter of fact, or *contingently*, a sufficient condition of someone's dying. Similarly in *He goes home early only if it is raining*, that it is raining is contingently, and not necessarily, a *necessary* condition of his going home early.

1.2.2   Box e

p may be a sufficient condition of q either *necessarily* or *as a matter of fact*.

p may be a necessary condition of q either *necessarily* or *as a matter of fact*.[29]

N.B.   'Necessary' does not have the same sense in 'necessary condition' that it has in 'necessary truth' (or 'necessarily' as used here).

Where p is a sufficient or a necessary condition of q necessarily, as a result of the meaning of words, there is, as a rule, little awkwardness in restating 'p is a sufficient condition of q' as 'q is a necessary condition of p'. *Having eyes is a necessary condition of having brown eyes* and *Having brown eyes is a sufficient condition of having eyes* are fairly clearly interchangeable, as are the respective re-expressions: *Only if A has eyes, does he have brown eyes* and *If A has brown eyes, he has eyes*.

In cases were p is a sufficient or necessary condition of q *contingently*, as a matter of fact, there is a further factor. Although the terminology of necessary and sufficient conditions, and of 'if' and 'only if' operates so that if p is a sufficient condition of q, then q is a necessary condition of p, one or other mode of expression often looks strange. *Death is a necessary condition of drinking hemlock* appears an unnatural mode of expressing *Drinking hemlock is a sufficient condition of death, His going home early is a necessary (or sufficient) condition of its raining* a curious way of making the point that rain is a sufficient (or necessary) condition of his going home early.

(vi) 'Causally' sufficient and necessary conditions

The reason for the difficulty is that in cases where a connection is contingent, there is often a *causal* connection, where one event is enough to or needed to bring about another. Dying is not *needed* to bring about the drinking of hemlock, although drinking hemlock is *enough* to make someone die. We do not suppose that someone's going home early affects whether or not there is rain, while we can readily imagine that the onset of rain might be needed or enough to make someone go home.

In saying that where p is a (contingently) sufficient condition of q, q is a (contingently) necessary condition of p, it is important *not* to incorporate the notion of bringing about or being needed to bring about in the notion of sufficient and necessary conditions.

If it is desired, as it sometimes is, to incorporate the notion of bringing about or being needed to bring about in the 'necessary and sufficient condition' or 'if and only if' vocabulary, confusion is reduced if a different word is employed, for example, 'causally'. Then we can hold (e.g.) 'Drinking hemlock is causally sufficient for death' and 'Death is not causally necessary for drinking hemlock' without denying that if p is a sufficient condition of q, q is a necessary condition of p, where sufficient conditions and necessary conditions include necessarily and contingently sufficient and necessary conditions but do not include 'causally' sufficient and necessary conditions. 'Necessary' and 'sufficient' conditions as used in this book do not include the sense 'causally sufficient/necessary'.

(vii) Inferences based on necessary and sufficient conditions

It is not uncommon to speak of p as a necessary or sufficient condition of q without specifying, or perhaps even deciding, whether the relations are necessary or contingent. Two examples which could be taken either way so far as the common meaning of the words is concerned are:

Example A

A wound is a necessary condition of a scar

We may have found that people do not get the conditions of the skin recognized as scars unless the skin was previously broken (a wound is, as a matter of fact, necessary for a scar). Alternatively we may use the term 'scar' so that conditions of the skin do not count as scars unless they were brought about by earlier wounds (a wound is necessarily a necessary condition of a scar).

Example B

D-poison is a sufficient condition of death

We may have found that ingesting certain substances, hemlock, arsenic, etc., known as 'D-poisons', results in death ((ingesting, etc.) D-poisons is, as a matter of fact, sufficient for death to follow). Alternatively we may count a substance as a 'D-poison' only if ingesting or etc. it results in death (D-poison is necessarily a sufficient condition of death).

Whichever way we construe *A wound is a necessary condition of a scar*, it will be the case that if this is so, then if he now has a scar somewhere, he once had a wound there. So, that he has a scar is sufficient to show that he once had a wound. Where p is a necessary condition of q, we can infer from q that p. If someone has no scar, we cannot tell whether or not there was once a wound: from not-q we cannot infer anything.

Whichever way we construe *D-poison is a sufficient condition of death* it will be the case that if this is so, then that someone is alive, i.e. is *not* dead, is sufficient to show that he did not ingest D-poison. Where p is a sufficient condition of q, we can infer from not-q that not-p. If someone *is* dead, we cannot from the death alone infer that he had D-poison: from q we cannot infer anything.

1.2.3   Problems about proof

In an axiomatic system like Euclidean geometry or the propositional and predicate calculus, a small number of fundamental axioms is laid down as true, and proof of any other proposition of the system consists of showing that it follows from these axioms. In an empirical subject, a subject about the world, whether a science or, let us say, history, proof and disproof rest in the last resort on the facts, on how things actually are in the world. Neither proof

21

from axioms nor proof from facts is as simple and straightforward as these descriptions suggest, but it is at least clear what *kind* of consideration is relevant to proof of a point.

Philosophical logic is neither an axiomatic system nor an empirical subject. It has no unquestionable axioms. It is not about how people *do* reason but about reasoning correctly. There is substantial difficulty about proving points in philosophical logic, and a great deal of disagreement.

The matters sketched out in this chapter are relatively uncontroversial. The topics of the chapters which follow are almost all controversial, and there is little that it would not be misleading to represent as though it were fact. In philosophical writing, it is common to proceed by attacking what someone else has written. Much of the literature is of a polemical nature. Sometimes this helps to explain why some point has not been developed or why another has acquired, at least temporarily, the status of an accepted doctrine. I shall be suggesting that in some cases seeing what an issue is may be more important than deciding in one direction or another. Quite often I hold opinions on the resolution of an issue or the correctness or incorrectness of a view. I give these, but as *opinions*.

NOTES

1. 'Axiom' as here used covers all truths laid down as initial premises (see for example 'axiom' in Flew (1979) 1983: 34). In Euclid's *Elements* (*c.*300 BC) 1908, bk I, 'axioms' as used here are distinguished into definitions (of e.g. a circle), postulates (e.g. that all right-angles are equal to one another), and 'common notions' (e.g. 'the whole is greater than the part') but sometimes (e.g. in school Euclids) only the last are called 'axioms'.

2. They are generally attributed to Frege 1879: see e.g. Kneale 1962, ch. 8, esp. sec. 4. For an early exposition of fundamentals, see Russell 1919, chs 14–15. There are many current introductions to formal logic including, for example, Newton-Smith 1985, Lemmon 1965.

3. Much of the literature is in specialized books and papers in learned journals and collections of articles. For some recent general introductions see Haack 1978, Blackburn 1980, Grayling 1982, O'Hear 1985, chs 1–3. It should be noted that the name 'logic' may be used for works containing both branches of the subject (e.g. J. S. Mill 1843, *A System of Logic*, H. W. B. Joseph (1906) 1916, *An Introduction to Logic*, W. E. Johnson 1921, *Logic*), or it may be pre-empted to one or the other. Books called 'Logic' may be devoted

entirely or largely to formal logic (e.g. W. V. O. Quine 1952, *Methods of Logic*, Lemmon 1965, *Beginning Logic*, W. Hodges 1977, *Logic*, W. H. Newton-Smith 1985, *Logic*). Oxford University BA Honours examination papers called 'Logic' are on philosophical logic.

4. 'or' is here used in its inclusive sense (one or other or both) and not its exclusive sense (either . . . or but not both).

5. See Strawson 1952, ch. 3, pt II: 78–93, Ryle 1954: 114ff, Baker and Hacker 1984: 170–9, Newton-Smith 1985: 15–28.

6. See for example Kneale 1962, ch. 2 on its development in Aristotle and e.g. Keynes 1884 for a late version.

7. See Strawson 1959: esp. 15–23, 180–6, where the ultimate distinguishing mark of particulars as a kind of individual is that there can be two which are indistinguishable except for their spatio-temporal location, e.g. two otherwise indistinguishable copies of *David Copperfield* side by side (two particulars). See 7.1.1 for a difficulty.

8. Moore 1903, ch. 1, esp. paras 5–14: 5–21.

9. See Flew (1979) 1983: 14, 254.

10. See for example Descartes (1636) 1912, pt IV; (1641) 1912, III, V; (1644) 1912, pt I, secs XIV–XV.

11. Kant (1781) 1920: A595–602/B620–631). See 6.1.1.

12. Hume (1748) 1894, sec. XII, para. 132: 163.

13. Locke (1690) 1975, e.g. bk 4, ch. 12, secs 9, 12.

14. See e.g. works cited in 1.1.1, n. 3, or Stebbing 1943.

15. Locke (1690) 1929, Hume (1739) 1911 and (1748) 1894, Kant (1781) 1929.

16. Locke (1690) 1975, bk IV, chs 7–8: 591–617; bk III, esp. chs 1–3: 402–20.

17. Locke (1690) 1975, bk I, bk II, esp. chs 1–9: 43–149.

18. Hume (1748) 1894, sec. IV, pt I, esp. paras 20–21: 25–6, sec. XII, pt III, paras 131–65: 163–5.

19. Hume (1748) 1894, sec. X, paras 86–101: 109–31.

20. Kant (1781) 1929: A7–10/B11–18, Introduction, esp. IV and V: 48–55.

21. Ryle 1954: VIII – Tanner Lectures of 1953. A recent introduction to philosophy, O'Hear 1985, that discusses philosophy under the heads: metaphysics, epistemology, logic and language, etc., includes much that is commonly regarded as philosophical logic in the chapters called metaphysics and epistemology; the section designated 'logic' is devoted to formal logic.

22. For discussions see e.g. Lemmon 1965: 1–5, Newton-Smith 1985: 1–14.

23. A proviso is discussed later: see 3.2.2; also 2.4.1, 5.2.1.

24. See for example 'valid' in Flew (1979) 1983: 363; although this is a dictionary of philosophy, with extensive entries for 'valid' and 'consistent', there is no entry for 'sound'. See e.g. 'Sound (i)' in Haack 1978: 250 for a definition of 'sound argument' similar to that given here. Lemmon 1965: 1–2 treats 'sound' and 'unsound' as

synonyms for 'valid' and 'invalid'; Newton-Smith 1985 does not use them.

25. We could introduce the finesse of distinguishing 'unsound' from 'not sound', 'invalid' from 'not valid', 'inconsistent' from 'not consistent', and treating the former of each pair as restricted in its application, while the latter is not.

26. There are also statements of restricted generality which take the form 'All Xs are Y' but restrict place and time and in which we can get to an end of 'All Xs'. Example: 'All the people now in this room are laughing' (see also 2.3.1).

27. Recent controversies relating to statements about the past or about other people's sensations are less easy to assign to the domain of epistemology or to that of philosophical logic. They concern the meaning of sentences (philosophical logic) relating to cases where proof (our knowledge – epistemology) is problematic or impossible. See 4.2.6, 4.3.2 (ii).

28. Descriptions are relatively scarce. See Haack 1978: 248, Flew (1979) 1983, Carruthers 1985: 257, 258–9 for some brief ones.

29. Carruthers 1986: 257, 258 distinguishes two 'kinds' of sufficient and necessary condition, defining them in succession; 'necessarily' is 'logically', for 'contingently'/'as a matter of fact', he has 'causally' – see below 1.2.2 (vi) on 'causally'.

QUESTIONS

When you have read this chapter, or sections in it, you may like to try your hand at these questions, and/or to keep them in mind when doing some or all of the suggested reading. Questions are framed *primarily* on specified sections, but material from other sections may help with answers. You may also like to try the examination question on this chapter in the Appendix.

1.1
1. Do you think philosophical logic should be a subject in its own right?

1.2
2. Can you explain the relations between validity, consistency, and soundness in terms of necessary and sufficient conditions?

SOME SUGGESTED READING

For guidance on a sensible order in which to do some or all this reading, consult references in text and notes. Not all the references given in this chapter are included in the list of suggested reading, and reading can be extended by following up other references in text and notes.

Blackburn, S. 1980, *Philosophical Logic*, ch. 1.

Grayling, A. C. 1982, *An Introduction to Philosophical Logic*, ch. 1.

Mill, J. S. 1843, *A System of Logic*, Introduction.

Newton-Smith, W. H. 1985, *Logic. An Introductory Course*, chs 1, 2, 4.

O'Hear, A. 1985, *What Philosophy Is*, ch. 3: 137–154.

Quine, W. V. O. 1952, *Methods of Logic*, Part I, secs 1–4, 7–9, Part II, secs 12–17.

Ryle, G. 1954, 'Formal and Informal Logic', VIII, in G. Ryle, *Dilemmas*.

Stebbing, L. S. 1943, *A Modern Elementary Logic*, ch. 1.

Strawson, P.F. 1952, *Introduction to Logical Theory*, ch. 1.

Chapter 2

REFERENCE AND TRUTH VALUE

The topic broadly called 'reference', which is the subject of this chapter, is a relatively new one that has attracted a great deal of investigation and discussion in recent decades.

SECTION 1 *TYPOGRAPHY, MEANING, AND WHAT IS STATED*

This section introduces a number of distinctions important in many parts of logic. The distinctions themselves are reasonably straightforward but terminology is not very fixed in this area, and there is much disagreement, so that it can be extremely confusing.

A way of seeing the difference between one kind of thing and another is to see how we count up things of one sort as against those of another (see 6.2.2 on counting up). A relatively simple way of grasping the basis of the counts considered in this section is to see how word processors can, could, or in some cases perhaps could not, perform them.

2.1.1 Words

(i) Token and type words

When a word processor counts the words in a piece of text, it does so by counting the sequences of characters bounded by blanks. Each character or sequence of characters without a break constitutes one word. This simple word count is of instances of words. Logicians call instances of words 'token' words.

Word processors can also find requested sequences of characters of a particular nature, such as 'can' whenever it occurs. This allows them to count how many times an identical sequence of characters occurs. Thereby they could discover how many non-identical sequences of characters there are in a piece of text. Token words which are identical in typography are termed 'type' words or 'typographically the same word'. A count of non-identical words is a count of type words.[1]

In the piece of text:

Example A

As a word processor *can* find requested sequences *of characters*, it *can* also count how many times an identical sequence *of characters* occurs.

there are twenty-three token words but since the italicized words form three pairs of identical token words, there are only twenty type words.

Logicians are concerned with spoken as well as written words, and would normally include an individual *utterance* of a word as a token word, and all spoken as well as written instances of a word such as 'of' as tokens of the same type word, viz. 'of'. (With a word processor that took down dictation or that spoke text typed into it we might well scratch our heads about adding spoken and written tokens, and prefer separate counts.)

2.1.1   Box a

'Token' word: sequence of characters (or unit of speech).

'Type' word: an identical sequence of characters (or identical unit of speech).

To count the token words in a piece of text: count the sequences of characters separated by blanks.

To count the type words in a piece of text: count the sequences of characters separated by blanks and subtract duplications of identical sequences.

(ii)   Words with a meaning

In a 'spell-check', a word processor selects sequences of characters which are not in its dictionary of permitted sequences, usually of alphabetical characters only. A suitably constructed dictionary could tell us how many token or type words should be subtracted in a given piece of text as not of a typography to constitute acceptable words in the language in which the text is written. It could then give us the count(s) of words whose typography is accepted. Words of accepted typography may be said to constitute the *meaningful* words in a language in so far as the language (e.g. English) is accurately portrayed in the dictionary. It is easy to see that one needs different dictionaries not only for different natural languages, such as English and French, but also for any 'artificial' languages.

Counting tokens of meaningful words requires the dictionary to make decisions not made in ordinary word-count programs, in particular to leave out certain sequences as not having a meaning in that language. Sequences of numbers, typically ignored in spell-check programs, would almost certainly be excluded, unless the language is designed for mathematical use; so probably would foreign words, i.e. words from a different language. Proper names, about which spell-check programs tend to be erratic, recognizing some and not others, would be more troublesome.[2]

Counting meaningful type words could be just a matter of counting how many typographically different meaningful words there are in the given piece of text. In Example A the count would be the same as the count for type words since all the token words in the text have a meaning. In the piece of text:

Example B
This toucan can catch a can. That toan can't catch a can.

there are twelve token words and eight type words. But since 'toan' is not a meaningful word, there are only eleven *meaningful* token words and seven *meaningful* type words.

2.1.1   Box b

Meaningful token word: sequence of characters which has a
  meaning.
To count meaningful token words subtract sequences not in
  the dictionary from the total number of token words.

> Meaningful type word: identical sequences of characters
> which have a meaning.
> To count meaningful type words subtract sequences without
> a meaning and duplications of meaningful identical
> sequences from the total number of token words.

(iii)   Words with the same meaning

Meaningful token words which have the same typography do not
always have the same meaning. For instance, in Example B the
first two tokens of 'can' have a different meaning: the first is a verb
equivalent to 'is able to', the second is the name of an object. When
some of a set of typographically identical token words have one
meaning and some another, the type word is said to be *ambiguous*,
i.e. to have more than one meaning. A dictionary will typically list
separate meanings of the same type word separately. Sometimes it
repeats the word (e.g. Can 1 (verb) is able to; Can 2 (noun) vessel
for liquids). Sometimes it prints the word once but lists a number
of meanings (e.g. Can: 1 (verb) is able to; 2. (noun) vessel for
liquids). If we count the entries in a dictionary the count will be
higher than a count of meaningful type words. Example B would
yield eight entries for the seven type words.

Not all cases of ambiguity are so clear cut as that of 'can' in
Example B.

Languages often contain different sequences of characters which
have the same meaning, such as 'bucket' and 'pail' in English. If
two words have the same meaning they are said to be *synonymous*.
We might wish to count how many words there are in a language
or piece of text which have different meanings: the count will
typically be lower than that of type words.

Example C
   If you have a bucket, then you have a pail

contains ten token words, all with a meaning, and seven
meaningful type words but it yields only six words which have
different meanings.

Not all cases of synonymy are as clear-cut as that of 'bucket' and
'pail' and some 'near' synonymy is systematic, e.g. 'cat' (singular),

'cats' (plural), 'see' (present tense), 'saw' (past tense).[3]

Since there are type words which are ambiguous and type words which are synonymous, a grouping of token words according to their *meaning* so that all and only token words with the same meaning count as one "word", where "word" is an invention for purposes of exposition, would not coincide with a grouping of token words into what I have been calling 'type words', that is, where all and only token words of the same typography count as one (type) word.

2.1.1   Box c

"Word": token words with the same meaning.

To count "words": count the number of token sequences of characters, subtract sequences of characters which do not have a meaning and subtract sequences of characters which duplicate the meaning of a sequence already included.

Note: "Word" is used to distinguish the unit from type words.

(iv)   Different 'word counts'

The various different counts described are useful for different purposes. The length of a text is commonly estimated by the number of token words it contains, and the simple word counts given by most word processors serve the purpose of supplying an estimate of the length of a piece of text. The length of text is now frequently and more accurately given by the number of characters. In compiling an index, glossary, or dictionary, or estimating the number of meaningful words in a language, however, it is not token words which are relevant but type words. We can readily imagine requiring every different typographical sequence (e.g. for teaching someone to read a particular language), or requiring every different meaningful typographical sequence (e.g. for compiling an English–French dictionary), or requiring a count of sequences which constitute type words with different meanings (e.g. for setting up a subject index). We may want to know how many different typographical type sequences have the same meaning (to compile a *Thesaurus* style guide for translators from foreign languages) or how many words are ambiguous (to know how many dictionary entries of typographically identical words will need more than one entry to explain their meaning).

(v)   Problems about the word 'word'

In explaining the different ways of counting up words, exposition has been rendered more difficult by the fact that the (type) word 'word' can be used for a variety of different units, in particular for token sequences of characters or for meaningful token sequences of characters, and for identical (i.e. type) sequences of characters or for identical sequences of characters which have *a* meaning (but not necessarily always the same meaning). It is evident that identity of typography may not coincide with identity of meaning, and I briefly invented "word" to refer to groups of token words with identical *meaning*. The account given in this section is very far from complete. Indeed it barely scratches the surface. When we turn to combinations of words into sentences, propositions, statements there are many further complications.

2.1.2   *Sentences*

(i)   Token sentences

A start could be made to counting token sentences in a piece of text by taking a sequence of characters and blanks bounded by a limited range of punctuation marks as one sentence. Three problems obtrude themselves at once.

(a)   Which punctuation marks terminate a sentence?   It is not obvious exactly which punctuation marks ought to be considered to mark the end of one sentence and beginning of another. In English full stops, question marks and exclamation marks clearly are markers of where one sentence ends and another starts. Commas are not. Semi-colons and colons might or might not be included.

(b)   Should we delimit sentences by punctuation marks?   For some purposes, such as commenting on style ('Your sentences are too long.' 'That is a convoluted sentence.'), punctuation marks seem

31

the right way to delimit sentences. For other purposes, such as symbolizing sentences by p, q, r in order to assess arguments (see 1.1.1 (ii)–(iii)), punctuation marks are of little service in marking one sentence off from another. Logicians commonly distinguish 'simple' sentences from complex or truth-functional ones. 'If it rains, then he goes home' is one (truth-functional) sentence but it also contains two simple sentences 'it rains' and 'he goes home', here connected by 'if . . . then'.

(c) Should sentences include only 'declarative' sentences? It is not obvious whether to include all sentence sequences as sentences or only what logicians sometimes call 'declarative' sentences, which are roughly characterized as sentences that can be used to communicate truths or 'convey information'. Questions, commands, and exclamations do not declare things and if we wish to count or discuss only 'declarative' sentences, then they need to be excluded.[4]

A decision to count as one sentence any sequence of words starting with a capital letter and ending in a full stop looks more arbitrary and less obviously useful than the analogous use of blanks to mark one word off from another. But suppose we decide to do this in order to have *a* way of counting the number of token sentences in a piece of text. We shall then be able to make the distinctions which we made with words. Our word processor can give a simple count of the number of token sentences in a text, and a more sophisticated count of sentences which are typographically different (type sentences). In theory at least, we can also have counts of token or type sentences which are meaningful, and of how many token sentences there are with different meanings.

(ii) The meaning of sentences

The decision as to whether a sentence *has* a meaning and whether two token sentences have the same meaning is more complicated than in the case of words, even if we restrict ourselves to declarative sentences and take the initial step of treating sentences which contain words that have no meaning as not meaningful. Logicians have commonly distinguished and excluded from meaningful sentences:

1) Grammatically ill-formed sentences like 'Cats blows the wind';[5]

2) Sentences which are grammatically well formed but nonsense because the wrong sort of property or activity is predicated of the subject as in 'This stone is thinking about Vienna'; and, more doubtfully,

3) Sentences which are internally inconsistent such as 'It is raining and not raining' or 'This circle is square'.

None of these can convey genuine information since none can ever express truths (so long as the words are used with their normal meaning in English). Some philosophers have wished to add sentences whose meaning precludes them from ever being *known* to express true or false statements (which are not verifiable or falsifiable) to the class of meaningless sentences.[6]

If there were a dictionary of sentences which are meaningful, it would clearly be very much longer and more liable to error than any dictionary of meaningful words. An estimate puts the number of commonly used type words in the English language at around 50,000: a language contains a large but fairly definite number of meaningful type words, the number clearly depending on the policy adopted about ambiguous and synonymous words, whether systematic variations like singular and plural or persons and tenses of verbs are treated as one or more words, what is done about the inclusion of proper names. Sentences can be constructed from words almost without limit and it is not obvious that one *could* create a dictionary of meaningful type sentences in a language like English but if one could it would run into billions of entries.

2.1.2   Box a

Separating one token sentence from another is less clear-cut than separating one token word from another.

Enquiry is often limited to 'declarative' sentences (the kind of sentences that can convey information as opposed to asking questions, etc.).

A meaningful declarative sentence is, as a first approximation, one which could express a truth (convey information).

Billions of meaningful declarative type sentences could be constructed from thousands of meaningful type words.

(iii) Sentence ambiguity and synonymy

Containing a token of an intrinsically ambiguous type word is a potent source of ambiguity in sentences but containing an ambiguous word is neither necessary nor sufficient to make a sentence ambiguous. Example B 'This toucan can catch a can' supplies an example of a sentence which contains a word, viz. 'can', which is ambiguous but where the sentence is not thereby rendered ambiguous. This is because it is quite clear which meaning each token of 'can' has.

Ambiguity of a word in a sentence is equally not necessary to make the sentence ambiguous. There are other sources of ambiguity in sentences as examples commonly given in explications of the predicate calculus make plain. 'Everyone loves a sailor' is ambiguous between: There is a sailor whom everyone loves, Everyone loves all sailors, Everyone loves one sailor each, and so on.[7]

(iv) 'Propositions'

Logicians have made a point of distinguishing typographically identical sentences from sentences with the same meaning. The word 'proposition' is used to avoid the terminological awkwardnesses we have already encountered with 'words'. It is analogous to my invented word "word". In this vocabulary, a sentence which has a meaning 'expresses a proposition', and only sentences with a meaning express propositions. Two token sentences with the *same* meaning express the same proposition, two token sentences with *different* meanings different propositions, whether or not the sentences are typographically identical. On this usage sentences from different languages can be said to express the same proposition.

Logicians have also been concerned with the token–type distinction in connection with sentences. If you and I each utter the words 'It is raining' we have two token sentences (two utterances) but only one type sentence. Given the use of 'proposition' just described we can also be said to have two token propositions (two meaningful token sentences) and one type proposition. This use of 'proposition' which allows us for instance to treat 'il pleut' (a different type sentence) as also expressing the same type proposition, would be extremely convenient were it not that 'proposition' is very liberally employed by philosophers, and does not always have this meaning.[8]

2.1.2   Box b

Ambiguity of type words can often lead to ambiguity of type sentences but the use of an intrinsically ambiguous type word (like 'can') need not lead to ambiguity of a sentence and a type sentence can be ambiguous without containing ambiguous type words (e.g. Everyone loves a sailor).

Ruling: In one usage of 'proposition', which will be employed in this book, a token sentence which has a meaning expresses a proposition, two token sentences which have the same meaning express the same type proposition, two token sentences with different meanings express different propositions.

It should be noted that 'proposition' is not always used in this way.

2.1.3   Statements

(i)   The sentence–statement distinction

The distinctions considered so far may be numerous and occasionally confusing and they have attracted their share of controversy but they are not, as philosophy goes, particularly controversial, and they have most of them long found a place in most logic books. The distinction we are about to encounter is fairly new, dating from 1950,[9] and has been extremely, perhaps at first sight surprisingly, controversial.

If we return once more to pieces of text and consider the first sentence of example B 'This toucan can catch a can', it seems evident that this type sentence can be used to make statements about different toucans on different occasions without a change in its meaning.

Example D

We are standing around in the Everglades throwing cans to toucans. Among the toucans you are throwing cans to is one who catches it. Among the toucans I am throwing cans to is another different one which also catches cans. Each of us says of our respective toucans 'This toucan can catch a can'.

Note: we have two utterances (yours and mine), each saying of a different toucan that it can catch a can.

It also seems evident that the same predicate 'can catch a can' might be ascribed to the same toucan but the toucan be referred to by an expression different in meaning from 'This toucan':

Example E

We are standing around in the Everglades. I say of my can-catching toucan 'This toucan can catch a can'. Someone hears me and passes on the message in the form of 'That toucan can catch a can'. The supervising boatman says, 'That greedy bird can catch a can'. A nearby child says, 'The toucan by the red boat can catch a can'.

Note: we have four utterances (mine, the hearer's, the boatman's, the child's), each saying of the same toucan that it can catch a can.

The expressions 'this toucan', 'that toucan', 'that greedy bird', 'the toucan by the red boat' do not have the same meaning. The four (token) sentences:

This toucan can catch a can

That toucan can catch a can

That greedy bird can catch a can

The toucan by the red boat can catch a can

are tokens of four different type sentences and each has a different meaning; using 'proposition' as described above in 2.1.2.(iv) and Box b we have four propositions.

(ii) Counting statements

We might well have occasion to wish to group together all those token sentences which say the same of the same object(s) and to distinguish them from any token sentence which does not say the same of the same object(s). This grouping together can be called a grouping together of sentences which make the same and different (type) *statements*.

Subjecting a piece of text to similar processes as we have already done with words and sentences, we shall achieve counts of how many token *statements* there are by counting token sentences and then:

a) eliminating all token sentences which do not have a meaning
b) eliminating all token sentences which are not 'declarative', i.e. are not of a kind to make statements.

In examples D and E no token sentences will be eliminated since all of them are meaningful and declarative.

Let us suppose that we are counting token sentences so that a single one starts with a capital letter and ends with a full stop. We now take the token sentences which remain (meaningful declarative sentences) and

c) 1) count as one type statement all those token sentences which say the same of the same object(s), and 2) count as different type statements all those token sentences which do not say the same of the same object(s).

Leaving aside for a moment a complication to be considered presently concerning meaningful declarative sentences which do not make statements (of which there are no examples in D or E), we now have a count of how many different type statements there are in the piece of text. Taking examples D and E together we have five token sentences which make one type statement (all those in E and mine in D) and one token sentence which makes a different type statement (yours in D).

2.1.3   Box a

To count token statements: count meaningful declarative
  token sentences (subtracting any which do not make
  statement – see 2.1.3(iii) and 2.2.2, esp. (viii) and Box d).
To count type statements: count token statements and
  subtract any duplications of tokens of the same statement.

To perform a count of type statements, the word processor would operate on different principles from those that it uses when

2 REFERENCE AND TRUTH VALUE

it counts how many *typographically* different type sentences there are in the text, or in counting how many type sentences with different *meanings* there are in the text. For a count of type *statements* it has to count how many instances there are of saying something of objects which are different either because although what is said ('can catch a can') is the same, it is said of different objects (your toucan and my toucan), or because what is said about the objects is not the same (e.g. 'This toucan can't catch a can'), or because different things are said of different objects ('This cat snores'). To perform a count of type statements the word processor needs among other things to be able to locate and bring together typographically different expressions which refer to the same object ('this toucan', 'that toucan') and to locate and separate typographically identical expressions which refer to different objects ('This toucan' (of my toucan), 'This toucan' (of your toucan)).

The task of grouping token sentences by meaning (into 'propositions' as the term 'proposition' was described in 2.1.2, so that token sentences with the same meaning express the same proposition) is already very complex, and there may be a substantial doubt whether the operation could be so done as to take into account the different meanings that individuals may give to what is typographically the same sentence in different settings within the confines of the (e.g. English) language. (Consider for example a sentence said or written sarcastically.)

The problem of grouping and distinguishing token sentences into those making the same and different type statements is very much greater because, even if theoretical difficulties which have been brought forward (and are considered in 2.4) are resolved, a detailed knowledge of facts surrounding utterances of token sentences is often required. To know which object is referred to by 'this toucan' on some occasion we need to be able to identify the particular toucan in question.

Some logicians have resisted introducing type statements. Their arguments for not distinguishing type statements and the reasons there are for distinguishing them will be considered in 2.4.

(iii)   Meaningful sentences that do not make statements

In discussing the counting of meaningful sentences, it was suggested that a word processor could set token sentences against a (very long and highly complex) dictionary of meaningful type sentences in order to eliminate token sentences which do not have a meaning. We might well suppose that just as there are token sentences which do not have a meaning, so there may be token declarative sentences which do have a meaning but do not make a statement. When the distinction between meaningful declarative sentences and statements, known as the 'sentence–statement distinction', was introduced in 1950 (see Strawson 1950), the candidates most discussed for the role of meaningful sentences which do not make statements were those meaningful subject predicate sentences where the subject expression has no actual counterpart in reality.

The favourite example was 'The King of France is wise'. This is clearly a declarative type sentence of unambiguous meaning. But like 'This toucan can catch a can' it is a sentence that could be used to make different type statements on different occasions since different persons may be King of France at different times. It differs from the sentence 'This toucan can catch a can' as it was described in Example D above in that its subject expression 'The King of France' does not (now) have anything corresponding to it, there being at present no King of France.

The suggestion that such sentences should be considered not to make true or false statements (either not to make statements at all or to make statements which are neither true nor false) proved extremely controversial and ensuing discussions raised complex issues and led to the development of a number of distinctions which will concern us in the next sections.[10]

SECTION 2 *THE PROBLEM OF THE KING OF FRANCE*

2.2.1 *How should 'The King of France is wise' be analysed?*

(i) The problem

Traditional logic books maintained that every (declarative) sentence which has a meaning is either true or false and that its denial or 'negation' has the opposite truth value. A meaningful (declarative) sentence was said to 'express a proposition' and the proposition to have a definite truth value, true or false. No such distinction as I have been outlining between sentences with the same meaning and type statements was drawn, and 'proposition' was not restricted to the meaning given in 2.1.2 (iv).[11] As used in

2.1.2, one proposition would not necessarily always have the same truth value.

2.2.1   Box a

Traditional logic books: Any meaningful declarative sentence (proposition) is true or false and its denial has the opposite truth value.

There were, and are, doubts about propositions with a meaning such that they could never be *known* to be either true or false, and some philosophers, such as the Logical Positivists, dubbed them 'metaphysical' (in a derogatory sense), and argued that they should be excluded from the realm of meaningful propositions. Examples were such propositions as 'God exists' (see e.g. Ayer (1936) 1946: 35ff, 114ff).

A difficulty was perceived about cases where the subject expression had nothing corresponding to it in reality, as with 'The King of France is wise'.

2.2.1   Box b

The (present) King of France is wise:
(1)   has a clear meaning
(2)   there is no real subject.

It hardly seems correct to say that it is true that the King of France is wise if there is no king of France. Nor does it seem true to say that a non-existent king of France is not wise. However Russell's Theory of Descriptions provided an analysis whereby 'It is not the case that the King of France is wise (or not wise)' could be said to be true and 'The King of France is wise' itself could be said to be false, thereby preserving the position that this apparently meaningful proposition is true or false, since it is false.

(ii)   The Theory of Descriptions

In his theory known as the 'Theory of Descriptions' Russell provided an analysis of subject-predicate sentences (or as he called them 'propositions') which gave a rationale for considering 'The (present) King of France is wise' as false if there is no King of France.[12]

Russell maintained that a subject-predicate proposition like 'The King of France is wise' is correctly analysed as a conjunction of three existential propositions:

(i)   There is a King of France

and

(ii)   There is not more than one King of France

and

(iii)   There is nothing which is both King of France and is not wise.

Where the subject of a proposition exists but the predicate does not apply, as for instance in 'The Queen of England is 6 ft tall', the proposition is false because (iii) is false: there is in fact something which is both Queen of England and not 6 ft tall. 'The King of France is wise' is false for a different reason, viz. that the first conjunct (i) 'There is a King of France' is false. By the tenets of the propositional calculus (see 1.1.1 (ii)), a conjunction of propositions, i.e. a proposition of the form 'p *and* q' (where 'p' and 'q' each stand for a proposition) is false if and only if any one of its conjuncts (in this case p or q) is false.

According to the Theory of Descriptions, the case of non-existent subjects of subject–predicate propositions differs from that of predicates which do not apply to subjects to which they are said to apply: a different one of the conjuncts of which the proposition is composed is false. The Theory of Descriptions resolves the problem of how such a proposition can have meaning and be true or false by an analysis of the proposition according to which it is false.

41

2.2.1 Box c

Russell's Theory of Descriptions:

The proposition 'The King of France is wise' can be
   analysed:
   (i)   There is a King of France and
   (ii) There is not more than one King of France and
   (iii) There is nothing which is both King of France and not
         wise.

When there is no King of France it is false because a
   conjunction is false when one conjunct is false, and
   conjunct (i) is false.

(iii) The Theory of Presupposition

The challenge to this position came originally in an article by
Strawson called 'On Referring' (Strawson 1950). Here Strawson
suggested, among other things, that the Theory of Descriptions is
not needed to explain how 'The King of France is wise' can be
meaningful when there is no King of France, and, further, that the
theory is mistaken to analyse 'The King of France is wise' as a
conjunction of existential statements which is false when there is no
King of France.

Strawson maintained that for a (type) sentence to be meaningful
it is sufficient that it *could* be used to make a true or false statement,
i.e. that tokens of it can make statements assessable for truth value.
This condition is satisfied by 'The King of France is wise': the type
sentence 'The King of France is wise' uttered in the reign of
Louis XIV makes a statement assessable for truth value (if we are
not too fussy about tests for wisdom). For a type sentence to have a
meaning it is not necessary for *every* token of it to make a true or
false statement. 'The King of France is wise' uttered when there is
no King of France could therefore be a token of the sentence not
making a true or false statement without jeopardizing the
meaningful status of the type sentence 'The King of France is wise'.

Strawson also maintained that a token of the sentence uttered
when there is no King of France does not make a statement which
is false but (and here there was a vacillation) makes no
statement/makes a statement which is neither true nor false.

> 2.2.1 Box d
> Strawson 1950:
> The *sentence* 'The King of France is wise' has a meaning.
>   When there is no King of France it does not make a true or
> false *statement*.

The analysis supporting this position is known as the Theory of Presupposition, and was supplied in opposition to the Theory of Descriptions. According to Strawson (1950) 'The King of France is wise' is not correctly analysed as a conjunction of: 'There is a King of France' and 'There is only one King of France' and 'There is nothing which is both King of France and not wise'. The first two conjuncts ('There is a King of France' and 'There is only one King of France') are not *stated* or *entailed* by 'The King of France is wise'. They are 'presupposed', that is, if they are not true (do not make true statements), the result is not that 'The King of France is wise' is false but that it is neither true nor false.[13]

> 2.2.1 Box e
> Strawson's Theory of Presupposition:
> *The King of France is wise* does not state or entail that there is a
>   King of France.
> It *presupposes* that there is a King of France.
> If *There is a King of France* is false, then *The King of France is
>   wise* is neither true nor false.

It is not obvious how to decide between the Theory of Descriptions and Theory of Presupposition as they stand. But the issue(s) can be clarified by the introduction of some further distinctions.

2.2.2 Reference failure and the Neglected Case

(i) Two sorts of case

In expounding his theory Strawson spoke sometimes of the sentence 'The King of France is wise' 'failing to make a statement', sometimes of it as making a statement but one which fails of truth value and is neither true nor false. (The latter formulation led to his theory being spoken of as the Truth Value Gap Theory.) These two different formulations probably arose from the fact that there were two somewhat different kinds of case in play:

1. The case of what came to be known as 'reference failure' where nothing or nobody is referred to by an expression such as 'The King of France'.
2. The case where something *is* correctly referred to but does not exist at the relevant time. Had the examples in the 1950s included 'The King of England is wise' it might well have seemed to some that there could be a *bona fide* reference to George VI by someone who did not realize that he had died and that the sovereign was now a queen.

For want of a better term I call this sort of case the 'Neglected Case': it dropped from notice (which is not to say that it did not influence discussion) and attention focussed on reference failure.

(ii)   The Neglected Case

There are many predications which can apply to persons or objects that no longer exist: innumerable past tense predications (was wise, lived for 90 years, died in 1782, etc.) and some present tense predications ('is a great loss', 'has descendants', 'is the best known of eighteenth-century British artists'). There are also many present tense predications which are not (in English) correctly made of persons or objects no longer existing, among them 'is wise' or 'is bald'.

In early discussions of presupposition we occasionally find examples of this kind of mis-predication cited as instances of statements which do not have a truth value ('He neither cares, nor doesn't care; he's dead' (Strawson 1952: 18)), and, correspondingly, there is the suggestion that the current existence of a successfully identified person or object is presupposed by (some) subject predicate statements. In this sort of case it is *statements* which presuppose other statements. However I refer to Winston Churchill, the great war leader, etc., if what I say of him is that he opened a bridge in 1988, then what I presuppose is that a particular identified person existed in 1988 (which in this instance he did not). The case of 'The King of France is wise' was almost certainly not supposed to be of this kind, but other favoured examples such as 'All John's children are asleep' or 'Jones visited the local swimming pool this morning' might or might not rate as examples of the Neglected Case.

(iii)   Should we introduce a third truth value?

One question is whether statements about identified objects that do not exist at a relevant time should be classed as false or as not having a truth value, and, if the latter, exactly which statements should be included.

There are two main options for statements to be said to fail of truth value:

Option 1.   We could say that a statement fails of truth value if the *subject* does not exist at the time when a type of predicate applying only to existent objects, is affirmed or denied of it. The rationale for this is that as there is no subject the predicate cannot be correctly affirmed or denied.

Alternatively,

Option 2.   We could say that a statement fails of truth value if *any* object/person 'about' which the statement is does not exist at a relevant time. The rationale for this is that objects/persons 'about' which the statement is cannot either stand or not stand in the relations in which they are said to stand if one of them does not exist.

Example F

In 'Jones visited the local swimming pool this morning' said of a specific morning (e.g. 1 January 1988) of an identified man and identified swimming pool, we can suppose that on 1 January 1988 Jones is dead and/or that the local swimming pool has been demolished.

On Option 1 that Jones is not alive this morning is necessary and sufficient for the statement that Jones visited the local swimming pool this morning to be said to fail of truth value. If Jones is alive this morning but the local swimming pool is demolished, then the statement rates as false. It should be noted that 'The local swimming pool was visited by Jones this morning' would have *different* truth values in the same circumstances (failing of truth value if and only if the pool is demolished, false if Jones is dead).

On Option 2 either Jones being dead or the pool being demolished or both is sufficient for the statement that Jones visited the local swimming pool this morning to be said to fail of truth value. The statement is false if and only if Jones is alive and the local swimming pool extant but Jones did not visit the pool this morning. ('The local swimming pool was visited by Jones this morning' has the same truth value in the same circumstances.)

A third alternative, *Option 3*, is to revert to the Theory of Descriptions, treating the first conjunct 'There is a man called Jones' as 'There is a man called Jones *alive at the present time*' (e.g. 1 January 1988), and adding a further conjunct 'There is a local swimming pool. . .'. We can then rule that in any of the contingencies where the statement that Jones visited the local swimming pool this morning is not true, it is false.

How are we to choose?

It seems far from evident that one of the alternatives has merits by comparison with the others such that it is the one which should be chosen.

However, it *is* important that 'failing of truth value' here operates like a *third* truth value, or, to turn things round, that there are different grounds of falsity, which could be labelled, e.g. false-sort-1 (subject not existent), false-sort-2 (some other object not existent), false-sort-3 (objects not standing in relation they are said to stand).

(iv) Some implications of the Neglected Case

One reason why such additions to or subdivisions of truth value are important is because a well-entrenched doctrine, that 'p' and 'p is true' are always 'equivalent' collapses if a third truth value is introduced or a distinction made between kinds of falsity. That this is so has been used as a reason for *not* introducing a third truth value/subdividing falsity. I shall suggest later not that we are obliged to add a third truth value or subdivide falsity but that the fact that we could do so if we chose casts doubt on the soundness of the case for considering 'p' and 'p is true' as equivalent.[14] The Neglected Case supplies an example of how it may be more important to note alternatives than to select one.

It should be observed that it is only of certain *sorts* of objects that it makes sense to say that a specific one does not exist at a specified time. Individual persons, tables or copies of books can certainly cease to exist, individual (type) books probably (if every copy is destroyed), numbers definitely not.

2.2.2   Box a

The Neglected Case: an identified object does not exist at a time when it must exist for a predicate to apply/to stand in the relations in which it is said to stand.

Statements exemplifying the Neglected Case (i.e. where some identified object does not exist at a relevant time) may be said to 'fail of truth value' or exemplify a particular sort of falsity. This is to add to truth values.

(v)   Failure of reference

With the Neglected Case out of the way, let us return to the case(s) on which discussion has centred, and where several important distinctions and lines of enquiry have emerged from much polemic. Failures of reference, that is, when an expression does not succeed in referring to anything, can be divided into two main sorts. These are often known as 'non-radical' and 'radical' failures of reference.

(vi)   Non-radical reference failure

We not infrequently misname someone or use the wrong description of something or someone that we could perfectly well identify in another way. There is then a misdescription but the speaker and often hearer knows who or what is spoken of. In the example 'The King of France is wise' (or 'is bald'), for instance, the expression 'The King of France' might in error be used to refer to the President of the French Republic: the speaker means to speak of the head of the French state, whom he mistakenly supposes to be a king, or sees a man in a procession, in fact the President, and remarks of this man that 'The King of France is looking very well today'. Or I might refer to 'statments' when I mean statements; most people reading my text would probably pick up the reference.

47

It would generally be agreed that in such cases someone has succeeded in referring to someone or something although the words themselves do not correctly characterize anything. The expression actually used does not refer to anything (or sometimes refers to the wrong thing – e.g. 'X's husband': X has a husband; however, it is not he but X's escort, Smith, of whom the speaker means to speak). However, the speaker and often hearer could supply a correct description of the thing or person (intended to be) spoken of. This is why the 'reference failure' in such cases is called 'non-radical'.

To have a case of non-radical reference failure, the name or description the speaker actually employs (e.g. 'X's husband', 'Smith') must not be one which *has* to apply for the speaker to be said to have referred to what he means to refer to, and the speaker must have in mind some other name or description which he *does* think of as having to be possessed by what he means to refer to (e.g. 'X's escort', 'the man in the green jacket') and which *does* refer.[15]

(vii) 'Identifying references', 'inessential' and 'referential' uses of expressions

In the 1960s, terms were introduced to distinguish expressions used for referring which might fail to refer in a non-radical fashion. Strawson ((1964) 1971) spoke of *identifying references* where the speaker could use a variety of different names or descriptions (e.g. 'the man over there', 'the President of the College', 'my brother-in-law') to refer to the person or object he means but selects only one for use, the one, it is often said, which he thinks will enable the hearer to identify whom or what he means.[16] Donnellan ((1966) 1977) spoke of expressions being used *inessentially* or of an 'inessential use of an expression', where if the expression fails to refer to anything, something may still be identified. He also distinguished *referential* (from *attributive*) uses of expressions. In a *referential* use of e.g. 'Smith's murderer', the speaker is speaking of Jones in the dock who, *among other things*, murdered Smith.

2.2.2   Box b

Non-radical reference failure: misdescription of that to which the speaker intended to refer.

For a reference failure to be *non-radical*, the speaker must have used the failed expression *inessentially*, i.e. he thinks of the name or description as only a *fact* about what he means to refer to. It must be an 'identifying reference'/used 'referentially', i.e. the failed expression is only one of several descriptions of the object and it is because another which the speaker can be said to have in mind applies that we can say that the reference does succeed.

Non-radical failure of reference might certainly lead one to say that a particular token sentence does not make a statement but it would not lead one to say that when the sentence was uttered no statement was made or a statement was made to which no truth value can be ascribed. For that one needs reference failure as it was originally introduced and which was later distinguished as *radical* reference failure.

(viii)   Radical reference failure

The point about *radical* reference failure is that the expression used, say, 'The King of France' or 'Smith's murderer' refers to no one (or to two people between whom the speaker cannot distinguish) *and* the speaker has no other more successful identification in mind. For this situation to obtain, he must have used the expression 'The King of France' or 'Smith's murderer' *essentially*, so that if there is no King of France or Smith was not murdered[17] (or there are two Kings of France or two murderers), the reference fails and nothing or nobody can be said to have been referred to. Donnellan, who introduced the notion of inessential and essential uses of expressions, employed the term 'attributive' use of an expression to partner 'referential' uses of expressions. Here the speaker means to refer to whoever or whatever satisfies his description (and not to something satisfying some other description).[18]

2.2.2   Box c

Radical reference failure: the expression used does not apply
   to anything and the speaker has no other means of
   identifying that to which he means to refer.

(ix)   When do meaningful declarative sentences fail to make
statements?

The case of radical reference failure is almost certainly the one
which led Strawson to wish to say that when a reference fails, no
statement is made.

On this construction of Strawson's Theory of Presupposition,
someone who says 'The King of France is wise' presupposes the
existence of the King of France in the sense that if his description
identifies no one, then what he says is neither true nor false
because it makes no statement at all (and not because, as in the
Neglected Case, an identified person does not exist at a relevant
time and the statement should perhaps be assigned a special truth
value). 'Presupposition' is a function of the expression a speaker
uses and what he presupposes is that something answers to
whatever description he uses essentially. If you and I each refer to
the same chair successfully but by the use of different descriptions
(you speak of 'that green chair in your study' and I of 'my
favourite armchair') then we make different presuppositions (you
that there is a green chair in my study and I that I have a favourite
armchair) – both might succeed or both fail or one succeed and the
other fail. Here it is only if someone's presupposition is false, that
is, an expression he uses fails radically to refer, that he can be said
to have failed to make a statement.

It is less certain that, on Strawson's theory, *all* radical reference
failure spells failure to make a statement.[19] Initially, it was only
radical reference failure on the part of the *subject expression* (often
spoken of as 'the referring expression') which was said to lead to no
statement having been made. Radical failure of reference by an
expression in the predicative part of the sentence as in 'I went for a
drive with the King of France', was agreed to lead to falsity, the
expression being 'absorbed' into the predicate. Later Strawson
(e.g. Strawson (1964) 1971: 88) used the term 'referring expression'

so that there could be a 'referring expression' in the predicate (see 2.3 for uses of 'referring expression').

Recalling the three options we considered in the Neglected Case, it seems that we have a choice as to what to say when there is a radical failure of reference. We can say:

Option 1 that if the *subject* expression of a token sentence fails radically to refer, no statement is made (since there is nothing for the statement to be about); or, instead,

Option 2 that if *any* expression in a token sentence fails radically to refer, no statement is made (since nothing definite can be said to have been stated); or, instead

Option 3 we can revert to the Theory of Descriptions and say that if any expression in a token sentence fails radically to refer, then one or another of the conjuncts into which the sentence can be analysed is false and what is said therefore false.[20]

Of these, Option 2 seems the most serviceable.

Where a reference succeeds, the same object can be referred to again, by the use of the same or a different expression: the man I identify as 'the man over there' can also be referred to in this way by you, or he can be referred to by name or role or where he is some other time. Where someone says something and every reference succeeds, the (type) statement made e.g. by 'The man over there is talking to my boss' can be made again and again, by the same and different type sentences (you can utter the same sentence; or tomorrow we can speak of him as talking to my boss yesterday). When a reference fails radically, there is no object to be referred to again. If we include token sentences containing such expressions as also 'making statements', the 'statements' have the peculiarity that the same (type) statement cannot be made again: if nothing was referred to in the first place, 'it' cannot be referred to again.

This consideration makes Option 2 seem preferable to Option 3, and also better than Option 1. It should be noted that it is not only references to persons and things but also those to times and places that can fail radically. If I use the expression 'New York, France' essentially when there is no such place, or speak of Tuesday, 11 March 1988 when there is no such day, I have failed to refer to any time or place. Attempts to associate failure to make a statement with radical reference failure on the part of the *subject* expression seem to lack rationale and be likely to lead to confusion.[21]

2.2.2   Box d

Ruling: If any expression in a token sentence fails radically to refer, then the token sentence does not make a statement.

The treatment of tokens of declarative meaningful sentences which contain an expression which fails radically to refer as failing to make a statement, likens them to tokens of meaningful declarative sentences which contain an expression capable of referring to different things on different occasions and are not asserted but, for instance, used as grammatical examples.[22] Here too no statement is made. There is no *failure* to make a statement since no one tried.

(x)   What kind of expressions can fail radically to refer?

The very short answer to this is that any expression which can name or describe anything and does not have a meaning such that it *must* always refer to that thing, can fail radically to refer.

SECTION 3   *VOCABULARY OF REFERENCE*

2.3.1   Definite and indefinite reference

Discussion of reference has generally centred on *definite* as opposed to *indefinite* reference. In 'A cat was sitting in a tree', the 'references' 'a cat' and 'a tree' are both indefinite: they are to some cat or other, some tree or other. In 'Some cats got stuck in a tree', 'some cats' and 'a tree' are again both indefinite references. A definite reference is to some specific thing. In 'The cat was sitting in the tree', 'the cat' and 'the tree' are both definite references: the intention is to refer to a specific cat and a specific tree. There can be definite references to a plurality of objects, so long as the reference is to a definite set of them.[23] It is doubtful whether in 'All cats anywhere anytime try to catch mice', 'All cats' is a definite reference. But in 'All the cats (in my house) try to catch mice', 'all the cats' and 'my house' are definite references.[24]

2.3.1 Box a

Definite reference: the reference is to a specific object or set of objects.

Indefinite reference: the reference is to one, some, or all of a kind of object.

2.3.2 Expressions making definite references

If we take grammatical divisions of expressions, then we shall probably want to include the following four kinds of expression as ones which can be used to make definite references:

a) Demonstratives: This x, That x, These xs, Those xs

It is commonly, and, in my opinion, rightly, urged that correct uses of 'this', 'that', etc. require a noun after them (this cat, that tree). 'I'll have this' understands a noun, if only 'object which I have in my hand'.

b) Proper names: John Smith, Mary Jones, England, New York, Eton College, the Churchills, etc.

It is commonly, and, in my opinion, rightly, urged that a proper name names an individual thing of a certain kind, such as a specific person, country, city, school, family. Proper names typically apply to something throughout its life span.[25]

c) Pronouns: I, you, it, they, etc.

Pronouns are generally considered to stand in for singular or plural nouns. 'I' in spoken English stands in for 'the speaker', 'you' for the person(s) addressed.[26]

d) Definite descriptions: the cat, the King of France, Smith's murderer, the man round the corner, etc.

It is convenient to include expressions containing possessives: 'my house', 'your cat', 'his neighbour'.

Definite descriptions typically pick something out through its relation to something else. 'The cat' is shorthand for 'the cat which. . .' and would normally be spelt out 'the cat just spoken of' or 'the cat that belongs to us'. This is why expressions containing possessives seem to fit into this category ('possessives' do not, of course, always mean 'possessed by' in the sense of 'owned by': 'his

53

mother' refers to a woman in a definite relation to whoever is referred to by 'him' but someone's mother is not, in most societies, his property).

The 'something else' through which a definite description picks something out has to be a definite something else and not an indefinite one. It must therefore in turn be referred to by one of the sorts of expression that can refer to definite things: the cat in *this* room, the King of *France*, the number *I* have written on *this* piece of paper, the man round the corner *from here*.

It should be noted that 'here' and 'now', 'there' and 'then' should probably be included as expressions making definite references: 'here' means 'in this place', 'now' 'at this time'. 'Objects' is often widely used by logicians, and places and times may be included. (There is a problem about places and times – and objects – which is further considered in 6.2; it consists roughly of the fact that we cannot count places, times objects or events *as such* – one object or six places makes no sense – but only through intermediary nouns. Accordingly, 'here'/'in this place' has to be further specified: 'in this room', 'spot on my arm I am touching'.)

In a definite description we 'refer' to two things: that which we are picking out, and that through which we are picking it out. It is a moot point whether we should be said to 'refer' to both or to *mention* something (Smith, France) in order to *refer* to something else (Smith's murderer', 'the King of France').[27] Whichever way we describe the matter, the (essential) 'reference' to the object through which something is identified must succeed in order for the something to be successfully referred to.[28]

2.3.2   Box a

Expressions making definite references include:
   demonstratives, proper names, pronouns, and definite
   descriptions.
Definite descriptions refer to something through its relation to
   something else, itself 'mentioned' or 'referred to' by means
   of one of these classes of expressions.

2.3.3   Referring expressions

(i)   Different uses of 'referring expression'

One of the terms commonly met in discussion of definite references is the expression 'referring expression'. This expression has developed several related but distinct uses that need to be explicitly distinguished if confusion is to be avoided. In Strawson's article 'On Referring' (1950), which brought 'referring expressions' into prominence, they were introduced by example. In Strawson's and others' work over the years, 'referring expression' came to mean any of the following:[29]

Usage 1.   A *subject* expression, or, more commonly, a certain kind of subject expression as defined, e.g. in Usages 2, 3, or 4 below;

Usage 2.   An expression which refers to (picks out or mentions) a definite *individual* (or definite set of individuals), 'individuals' including anything that can be one something or other;

Usage 3.   An expression which refers to (picks out or mentions) a *particular* or definite set of particulars. ('Particulars' include only individuals of a certain kind: as a first approximation individuals with a definite place in space and time, such as persons and material objects or events, or which must be identified through such individuals, like smiles or thoughts;[30]

Usage 4.   An expression with a meaning such that it can refer to (mention or pick out) *different* individuals on different occasions of its use without change of meaning and/or which has a meaning that does not oblige it always to refer to just one individual. (The two formations here allow for the possibility that an expression can perhaps be one which *cannot* refer to different individuals on different occasions but *can* fail to refer to anything. A way of conjoining them is to speak of an expression whose meaning does not determine to what it refers.)

2.3.3   Box a

Meanings of 'referring expression':
Usage 1.   A *subject* expression or species of subject expression.
Usage 2.   An expression which picks out/mentions a definite *individual*.
Usage 3.   An expression which picks out/mentions a definite *particular*.
Usage 4.   An expression with a meaning such that it can mention/pick out different definite individuals on different occasions of its use, i.e. whose meaning does not determine to what it refers.

Note.   The list of uses of 'referring expression' does not claim to be exhaustive.

It is easy to see that these uses of 'referring expression' are all different but related to each other.

(ii)   Relations of uses of 'referring expression'
Example G
   a)   The whale struck the ship.
   b)   The whale is a mammal.
   c)   All John's children are asleep.
   d)   9 is greater than 7.
   e)   The disease Jones caught last week is not often fatal.

According to Usage 1 (subject expression) of 'referring expression', 'the ship' in a) and '7' in d) are not candidates for 'referring expressions' since they occur in the predicate and not in the subject, nor are 'John' in c) and 'Jones' and 'last week' in e): it is not John who is the subject of c) but his children, and not Jones or last week but a particular disease that e) is about. In Usage 1 of 'referring expression', 'referring expressions' in Example G consist at most of: 'the whale' in a) and b), 'All John's children' in c), '9' in d), and 'The disease Jones caught last week' in e).

Usage 2 (expression for an individual), which is closest to 'definite reference' and the widest use, includes some expressions as 'referring expressions' which are excluded in Usage 1. In

Example G these are: 'the ship', 'Jones', and 'last week'. It also includes some expressions excluded in usage 3 ('the whale' in b), '9' and '7' in d), 'the disease' in e)), and some expressions excluded in Usage 4 ('the whale in b), '9' and '7' in d)). According to Usage 2 all the following are 'referring expressions': 'the whale' and 'the ship' in a), 'the whale' (one species) in b), 'John', 'All John's children' in c), '9' and '7' in d) and 'Jones', 'last week', 'the disease Jones caught last week' (one disease) in e).

Usage 3 (expression for a particular) excludes 'the whale' in b), '9', '7' in d), 'the disease. . .' in e) – all included in Usage 2. It includes 'the ship' in a) and 'John' in c), 'Jones' and possibly 'last week'[31] in e) (excluded in Usage 1). All expressions which are 'referring expressions' in Usage 3 are also referring expressions in Usage 2 (all particulars are individuals) and in Usage 4 (in Example G, and probably generally; it is doubtful whether a particular *can* be referred to by an expression with a meaning obliging it to refer to just that particular). However not all expressions admitted as 'referring expressions' in Usage 4 are 'referring expressions' in Usage 3: e) supplies an example of a Usage 4 referring expression which does not refer to a particular, viz. 'the disease Jones caught last week' and possibly 'last week'.

Usage 4 (expression whose meaning does not determine to what it refers/allows it to refer to different things on different occasions of its use) excludes '9' in d) and 'the whale' in b) included by Usages 1 and 2, and additionally '7', included by Usage 2. It includes 'The disease Jones caught last week', excluded by Usage 3, and 'last week', not definitely included by Usage 3. 'John' and 'Jones' are doubtful cases: some have argued that a proper name can with *one meaning* refer to at most one thing (or set of things) and some that for a proper name to have a meaning it must have been assigned to something and so always succeed in referring to that thing. If so, proper names do not count as 'referring expressions' in Usage 4 of 'referring expression' and referring expressions in Usage 3 are not all referring expressions in Usage 4, proper names supplying the exception. Not everyone agrees with this account of proper names (see 2.3.3 (iv); see 7.2 for a more general discussion of proper names).

Table 1 supplies a summary of the expressions in sentences a)–e) which are included as 'referring expressions' on the usages described.

Table 1 Expressions included as 'referring expressions' on different
usages in sentences a)–e) in Example G

Usage 1 (subject)	Usage 2 (individual)	Usage 3 (particular)	Usage 4 (meaning allows different referents)
a) the whale	the whale	the whale	the whale
—	the ship	the ship	the ship
b) the whale	the whale	—	—
c) all John's + Cs	all John's Cs	all John's Cs	all John's Cs
—	—	John	John ?John
d) 9	9	—	—
—	7	—	—
e) the disease . . .	the disease . . .	—	the disease . . .
—	Jones	Jones	?Jones
—	last week	?last week	last week

2 is the widest use; it includes all the expressions included in 1, 2, and 3. 1, 3, and 4 exclude different expressions, with the proviso that 4 includes any expression included by 3 with the possible exception of proper names. 1 is often more narrowly construed, e.g. as subject expression which refers to a particular.

(iii)   Choice of use of 'referring expression'

For the purpose of considering reference failure, Usage 4 of 'referring expression' is the most convenient. That an expression can refer to different individuals on different occasions of its use without change of meaning or has a meaning which does not oblige it to refer to just one individual (or set of individuals) on every occasion of its use is sufficient for it on occasion to refer to nothing. On Usage 4 of 'referring expression' all referring expressions can on occasion fail to refer. It is less clear that *only* such expressions may refer to nothing: apart from a problem about proper names,[32] self-contradictory expressions like 'This square circle' never refer to anything and so also cannot refer to different individuals on different occasions. They can be included as 'referring expressions' by moving to the summarizing formulation of Usage 4 where the meaning of a 'referring expression' does not determine to what it refers but the formulation must be construed as not purely negative; otherwise it will let in as 'referring expressions', e.g. indefinite references. If we make this move, and discount proper names, then on Usage 4 all and only referring expressions can fail to refer.

For other purposes, such as specifying the conditions in which two token sentences make the same type statement, Usage 2, where a referring expression is an expression referring to an individual, is the more convenient. One way of describing the circumstances in which sentences make the same type statement is to say that the referring expressions refer to the same objects and the remaining expressions have the same meaning. This is not quite accurate even when 'referring expression' is employed in Usage 2[33] but it is nearer the mark than when it is used as in Usage 4. The same individual, for instance the disease measles, can be referred to by the term 'measles' and by an expression like 'the disease Jones caught last week'. Both expressions are referring expressions on Usage 2 but on Usage 4 'measles' is excluded. For this reason, when I employ 'referring expression' I shall not infrequently use it as 'term picking out or mentioning an individual', although in general I specify the usage I am adopting by appending 'Usage 4', 'Usage 2', etc. It should be noted that on this use, Usage 2, of 'referring expression', not all referring expressions can fail to refer. '9' and '7' in d), and probably 'the whale' in b), are not expressions which can fail to secure reference.

2.3.3   Box b

Usage 2 of 'referring expression', i.e. expression which
  mentions/picks an individual, is often convenient but
  Usage 4 is for some purposes a good alternative. To avoid
  confusion 'Usage 2', 'Usage 4', etc. is appended to
  'referring expression' when the term is used.

(iv)   References to particulars vs references to non-particulars

Strawson argued[34] that references to definite particulars differ from those to definite non-particulars in several critical ways, among them that some factual statement of the form 'there is an x in place 1 at time 1' must be true if the reference is to succeed. References to a non-particular like a disease by an expression like 'the disease Jones caught last week' equally require a factual statement to be true (that Jones caught a disease last week) but individual non-particulars can also be referred to by expressions like 'measles' which, according to Strawson, are defined by their qualities so that we can know *which* non-particular, for example which disease, is meant without having to know the truth of any factual statement

(Strawson 1959: 186). The expression 'measles' therefore cannot fail to refer provided that the word has a meaning (the disease may not exist now, but that is another point: see 2.2.2). There are provisos. For instance, the expression 'measles' can be *used inessentially*: the speaker means to refer to the disease Jones caught last week. In this case 'measles' can fail to refer to the disease he means (which could be mumps instead, or no disease at all). So the point should be put that non-particulars *can* be referred to by an expression which cannot fail to secure reference, but this is not true of particulars. Those holding a theory of proper names whereby the meaning of a proper name does determine its reference would hold that a particular too can be referred to by an expression which has to refer to it, viz. its proper name.

2.3.4   Rigid and nonrigid designators

(i)   Strongly rigid, not strongly rigid, and non-rigid

In the 1970s a new set of terms was introduced into discussions of reference by Kripke.[35] These were the terms *rigid designators* and *nonrigid designators*. Kripke gave them the following meanings:

A *rigid designator* is an expression which could not designate (be used to refer to) anything but what it actually does designate, so long as it retains the same meaning. (Kripke (1971) 1977: 77–83; (1972) 1980: 48–9).

   Kripke subdivided rigid designators into:

a)   *strongly rigid designators*: these not only cannot refer to anything but what they do but also must refer to what they do refer to. Examples are '5' or '9', 'the square root of 25 or of 81'(Kripke (1971) 1977: 78); and

b)   *not strongly rigid designators*: these cannot refer to anything *else* but may fail to refer to anything at all. Examples Kripke offers include proper names like 'Kripke'.

A *nonrigid designator* is an expression which is not prevented by its meaning from referring to something other than what it always or on some particular occasion does refer to.

Examples of nonrigid designators cited by Kripke are 'The 37th President of the United States', 'the inventor of bifocals', 'the number of the planets' (Kripke (1971) 1977: 77–83).

(ii)   Designators and reference

If a 'designator' is taken to be any expression of a kind to refer to a definite individual, or set of individuals, then 'designators' can be identified with the expressions I have been speaking of as ones making definite references and with 'referring expressions' in their widest sense (Usage 2) where a referring expression mentions or picks out an individual. Kripke's distinction between rigid and nonrigid designators divides them up into different kinds. His negative category of nonrigid designators approximates to 'referring expressions' in Usage 4. His positive category, rigid designators, approximates to those 'referring expressions' in Usage 2 (terms for individuals) which are *not* 'referring expressions' in Usage 4 on either of the two formulations given of Usage 4. Strongly rigid designators are those expressions whose meaning *does* determine what they refer to. Designators which are rigid but not strongly so are expressions which cannot with the same meaning refer to different objects, although they may fail to refer to anything. In Table 1 all the expressions listed under Usage 4, except the two doubtful inclusions of proper names (John and Jones) are nonrigid designators. The expressions listed under Usage 2 but not Usage 4 are rigid designators. 9 and 7 are strongly rigid, John and Jones not strongly rigid. 'The whale' in b) is rigid but whether strongly rigid or not strongly rigid is not evident.

It should be noted that Kripke specifically excludes Donellan's *inessential* uses of expressions from consideration (Kripke (1972) 1980: 25–6). The distinctions he is drawing are all intended to concern only expressions used *essentially*, i.e. such that the expression is said to succeed in referring if and only if there is some one thing answering to the name or description actually used. That an expression 'could' or 'could not' be used to refer to something different therefore never means that it is used 'inessentially' or 'essentially'. It means that given its meaning it could or could not actually apply to different objects. Discussion of 'designators' and what they 'designate' is restricted to expressions occurring essentially.

2.3.4   Box a

Kripke 1971 and 1972:

'Designators': expressions making definite
references/referring expressions in Usage 2.

Nonrigid designator: designator which may designate (refer
to) different things without a change of meaning (cf.
referring expressions Usage 4).

Rigid designator: cannot designate different things without
change of meaning.

If *strongly* rigid: must succeed in designating and/or what is
designated must exist.

Note: Kripke confines discussion to expressions used
essentially.

(iii)   Advantages and problems

Clearly it is useful to have terms making it easy to refer to referring
expressions in Usage 4 (nonrigid designators) as well as in
Usage 2 (designators), and further to be able to speak of those
terms which have a meaning such that they can refer at most to
one thing (or set of things) (rigid designators), or cannot fail to
refer (strongly rigid designators).

This is particularly useful if there is something to be said about
rigid vs nonrigid designators or about strongly vs not strongly rigid
designators. Among the theses Kripke puts forward is that proper
names and names of certain kinds of things, often known as
'natural kinds', which include species of living things like whales,
have important features in common. Strawson's interest in the
differences between particulars and non-particulars is reflected in
his vocabulary, and similarly Kripke's interest in the resemblances
between particulars and some non-particulars (natural kinds) is
reflected in his vocabulary. But it is, of course, important that the
distinctions underlying the vocabulary are clear. Otherwise it is
difficult to use.

A distinction not too clear in the new vocabulary is that between
a designator (necessarily) succeeding in referring and the object to
which it refers (necessarily) existing. Names of numbers, and

square roots of numbers like 25 and 81, which are the only examples actually given of strongly rigid designators, are described indifferently as 'necessarily [designating] a certain number' (Kripke (1971) 1977: 78) and as designating 'a necessary existent' (Kripke (1972) 1980: 49). This creates trouble in classifying for instance 'the whale' in b) or, from another angle, 'the square root of -1', generally considered not to be a 'real' number.

SECTION 4 *SHOULD WE ADMIT STATEMENTS?*

2.4.1 *The initial case for statements*

(i) One sentence/proposition, many statements

It seems evident that there are many type sentences which with a single meaning can be used to make different type statements. In 2.1.3 (i), Example D I cited 'This toucan can catch a can' said of different toucans. I have introduced the ruling that where there is a radical failure of reference, a meaningful declarative sentence should be said to make no statement (2.2.2 (ix), Box d). But even if this were not granted and *a* statement were said to be made by any meaningful declarative sentence, it would not affect the point that different tokens of an unambiguous type sentence like 'The King of France is wise' may make different type statements and that truth value may vary accordingly. 'The King of France is wise' might be said of Louis XIV or of Louis XV. What is said may be true in the one case and false or perhaps fail of truth value (see 2.2.2 (ii)–(iv)) in the other.

It is only *some* type sentences which with a single meaning can be used to make different type statements. The sentences of which this is so are, as a first approximation, those that contain a referring expression in Usage 4 or a nonrigid designator, that is, sentences that contain[36] some expression which can refer to different individuals, including different times and places, on different occasions. There are of course type sentences that do not contain expressions of this sort and which with a single meaning always refer to the same individual(s) and can express only one type statement. Uncontroversial examples are '9 is greater than 7' or 'All cats anywhere anytime like milk'. If 'proposition' is used as in 2.1.2, i.e. so that one type proposition has one and only one meaning, then we can describe the position by saying that some type propositions can make more than one statement, some only one.

(ii) One statement, many sentences/propositions

Sometimes noticed but often less stressed by logicians is the fact that a type statement made by the use of one meaningful type sentence can also be made by another which has a different meaning.[37] In 2.1.3, Example E I cited four type sentences with different meanings, each used to say of the same toucan that it can catch a can. Provided the ruling I introduced in 2.2.2 (ix), Box d is adhered to so that radical reference failure is said to result in no statement being made, then the point that a statement can be made by means of sentences with different meanings holds of *all* statements.[38] This is because anything whatever that is successfully referred to can also be correctly referred to by some other expression, if only, as a last resort, by mentioning it and then referring to it as 'the such and such I mentioned'. The single statement made by 'All cats anywhere anytime like milk' could in suitable circumstances be re-expressed by different type sentences/ propositions such as 'All the members of my favourite species like milk', 'All cats anywhere anytime like the liquid Pippikins is drinking', 'All cats anywhere anytime have the disposition just mentioned towards milk'. Similarly the type statement made by '9 is greater than 7' can, as the world happens to be, be re-expressed by 'The number of the planets is greater than 7' or perhaps '. . .than the number we just spoke of'.[39]

Logicians have found it worth their while to make use of the term 'proposition' so that they can refer together to any set of token sentences which have the same meaning as ones which express one type proposition (even if some, like Quine, object – see 3.3.2 (iv) e). The grouping of token sentences into type statements according to what is stated, according, that is, to whether the same is said of the same objects, is different again, as we saw in 2.1.3. Among other things, the same type statement can be expressed by different type propositions and many type propositions can express more than one type statement. One might therefore consider that the introduction of 'type statements' must be a useful addition to the concepts employed in logic to describe speech and argument. After all, logic is concerned not only with meaning but also with truth value, and on the face of it, it is type statements, and not meaningful declarative sentences or 'propositions' (as used in 2.1.2) to which we ascribe truth or falsity.

2.4.1   Box a

Some unambiguous type sentences can express different type statements.

Every (genuine) type statement can be expressed by type sentences with different meanings (see 2.4.1, n.38).

Grouping of token sentences into those making the same and different type statements gives different groups from groupings of token sentences into type sentences or type propositions (cf. 2.1.2–3).

2.4.2   *Objections to statements*

Objections to the introduction of type statements include:

(i)   that they are superfluous: we can do without them;

(ii)   that no coherent criteria of identity can be found, so that we cannot say what constitutes *one* type statement nor therefore count how many there are in e.g. a piece of text;

(iii) that they are not the correct subjects of ascriptions of truth value;

(iv)   that on the use of 'type statement' described, there can be type statements which are not asserted.

These objections can seem unduly persuasive. Brief discussion is required to indicate why they are not fatal.

(i)   Are type statements superfluous?

(a)   The popular suggestion One reason for introducing type statements is that some unambiguous meaningful declarative type sentences can be used to speak of different objects on different occasions; it is convenient to say that they then express different type statements. One common objection to introducing type statements is that we do not need them for dealing with this phenomenon.

A popular suggestion is that such sentences are *contextually dependent* because they contain expressions which refer to different things in different contexts. Another name for the·expressions classed as referring expressions in Usage 4 (see 2.3.3) or as non-rigid designators (see 2.3.4) is 'contextually dependent expressions'.[40] This name is often employed when it is argued that the *context* of a token of such a sentence is what determines to what the expressions in it refer and that, while a contextually dependent sentence can have different truth values in different contexts, it always has the same truth value in the same context. Granting the meaning of such sentences to be known, then, if we also know what is often called 'the context of utterance' (although/is not intended that written tokens are excluded) of tokens of it, we can set about discovering the truth value to be assigned.[41]

To operate as an objection to introducing type statements, this suggestion, which for convenience I call 'the popular suggestion', has to supply not only an alternative, i.e. something different, but a better alternative. It does not appear to do either.

(b)   The popular suggestion criticised   In counting type statements in 2.1.3, Examples D and E, we counted together as expressing one type statement all the token sentences which said the same of the same objects. This involved not only separating different tokens of the same type sentence ('This toucan can catch a can' said by me of one toucan and 'This toucan can catch a can' said by you of another) but also putting together, as expressing the same type statement, tokens of different type sentences (in 2.1.3, Example E, among others, 'This toucan can catch a can' said by me, 'The toucan by the red boat can catch a can' said by the child). One defect of the popular suggestion is that it makes no provision for this putting together of tokens of different type sentences.[42] It attends only to separating tokens of the same type sentence.

The attraction of the popular suggestion for effecting such separations is that it seems to supply something concrete, 'the context of utterance', in place of something thought of as nebulous (type statements). But this is not really so, as we can see when we disentangle the ambiguities of the 'context of an utterance'.[43]

The 'context of an utterance' can be used to refer to the *circumstances* of the utterance of a sentence, such as who said it, to whom, when, and where. If so, the popular suggestion is a fairly concrete suggestion:[44] find out these facts and the referent of any referring expression will be known.

The suggestion remains a concrete one only so long as the 'context of utterance' does not also include, as it often does in practice, *about* whom or what the sentence was said. If this *is* included, then all that the popular suggestion says is: find out about whom or what the sentence is and the referent of any referring expression will be known.

The same emptiness afflicts the popular suggestion when it gives the 'context of utterance' another not uncommon meaning, viz. whatever are the circumstances of the utterance which will tell us who or what is referred to by a referring expression (Usage 4)/ contextually dependent expression. Then the popular suggestion says: find out what you need to, to know who or what is referred to, and the referent of any referring expression/contexually dependent expression will be known.

It is not in fact true that if we attend to who uttered a sentence, to whom, when, and where, then we shall always know to whom or what every referring expression refers. In its concrete form the popular suggestion is not correct.

Counter-example

> If we know that I said 'This toucan can catch a can' in the Everglades last Tuesday to the child by the red boat, we may or may not be on the track to discovering to which toucan 'This toucan' referred.

It is difficult to see what the less concrete forms of the popular suggestion say beyond endorsing the point that to make assessments for truth value we need to know what is referred to (we need to know what type statement is made) and reiterating that where referring expressions in Usage 4 are involved this requires knowing some facts or other (see 2.3.3).[45]

Some positive results of the discussion of the popular suggestion are summarized in 2.4.2, Box a:

2.4.2 Box a

All token sentences that say the same of the same objects
express the same type statement.

In the case of sentences containing referring expressions
(Usage 4), facts need to be known to know which token
sentences make the same type statement and which
different statements. In some cases the relevant
information can be gleaned from details of the
circumstances of the utterance of the token sentence, that is
from the 'context of utterance' in one sense of this phrase.

(ii)   Type statements and criteria of identity

There are difficulties about when two token sentences express the
same type statement[46] but they do not seem insuperable, nor
indeed graver than in the case of many other types of individuals to
which most logicians have no objection or which are involved in
alternative suggestions by critics of type statements, such as 'the
context of utterance' (see 2.4.2, n.44).

In discussing the several meanings given to 'referring expression'
in 2.3.3, I mentioned that Usage 2 (expression referring to an
individual) is the most useful for specifying the criteria of identity
for type statements, that is for explaining when two token sentences
express the *same* type statement. We can say, fairly accurately, that
two token sentences make the same type statement if the
(corresponding) referring expressions (Usage 2) in each refer to the
same individuals and the remaining (corresponding) expressions in
the sentences have the same meaning. However, because an
expression may refer to one individual (Smith's murderer, the King
of France) by means of referring to another (Smith, France), two
token sentences may make the same type statement even though
not all the corresponding referring expressions (Usage 2) refer to
the same individuals. 'The man on the beach is a spy' and 'The
man next door is a spy' may make the same statement even though
the referring expressions 'the beach' and 'next door' do not refer to
the same object. For two token sentences to make the same type
statement, it is not necessary for referring expressions (Usage 2)
which *mention* an individual in the course of *picking out* another

individual to refer to the same individuals. Only the referring expressions (Usage 2) picking out individuals need to do so. (cf. 2.3.2.)

We are able to introduce refinements like these because what is intended by 'sentences making the same type statement' is that the sentences should say the same of the same objects. If this is expressed in terms of 'referring expressions' we adjust until we reach a format equivalent to 'saying the same of the same objects'.

'Same object' or 'same individual' has a problem. Something has already been said about this (see 2.3.2), and it will be further discussed in 6.2.2 (ii)–(iii). In the meantime it is important to note that for two token sentences to be said to make the same type statement, certain restrictions are placed on what can constitute 'the same object', as a first approximation that there should be some noun, such as 'person', 'animal', 'city', 'year', such that those referring expressions in both sentences which need to refer to the same 'objects', refer to the same individual instances of that same kind of thing (cf. 6.2.2 (iii)).

2.4.2   Box b

Two token sentences make the same type statement if they say the same of the same objects, 'objects' to include any kind of individual. This condition is satisfied if and, with slight amendment, only if the (corresponding) referring expressions (Usage 2) refer to the same individuals and the remaining expressions have the same meaning.

(iii)   Type statements and referential opacity

A reason for making use of the concept of a 'type statement' is that type statements seem to be the most suitable candidates for what it is that we ascribe truth value to: other candidates, such as meaningful declarative sentences and 'propositions' (as in 2.1.2), suffer, among other things, from the problem that different tokens of the same one can have different truth values. It is therefore rather disappointing if it turns out that different tokens of one and the same type statement can also have different truth values.

This is what was claimed by Quine with respect to certain kinds of type statement, notably:

1. Statements of the form 'Necessarily such and such' or 'Not necessarily. . .', 'Possibly. . .', 'Not possibly. . .' , which are known collectively as *modal* statements;
2. Statements of the form 'He believes that such and such' or hopes, knows, fears, etc. that so and so, which are often referred to as statements about *propositional attitudes*.

Quine held that such 'contexts', or types of statement, are 'referentially opaque' (or 'suffer from referential opacity'): different ways of referring to the same objects within sentences following such terms as 'Necessarily' or 'He believes that' may lead to different truth values, even when the sentences express identical type statements.[47]

In the course of discussing our next topic, necessary truth, in chapter 3, I shall be maintaining that the argument on which Quine bases the conclusion that modal contexts are referentially opaque (i.e. that in the case of statements of the form 'Necessarily p', etc., the same type statement may have different truth values according to whether the sentence following 'Necessarily' is analytic or not (see 3.3.1 (ii), esp. n.13 and Wolfram 1975: esp. 230–7) is not sound. Given the basis of Quine's claim in modal cases, it is obvious that whatever his grounds for holding that 'He believes that. . .'[48] is referentially opaque, they are not the same as those he provides for the view that modal contexts are referentially opaque: he certainly does not claim that 'He believes that' followed by an analytic sentence is always true, much less that 'He believes that' followed by a non-analytic sentence is always false. Perhaps the grounds are better, perhaps not.[49] But, in any case, it does not look as if referential opacity is so widespread a phenomenon that it is evident that type statements must be rejected as the prime bearers of truth value.

(iv) Type statements and assertions

The relation between assertion and type statements will be further discussed in 4.2.

A not uncommon complaint about the use of 'type statement' as I have described it is that on this use we can refer to 'statements' which no one has asserted. This is because at least some type statements can be identified as the statement made by a particular type sentence. For example, we can speak of the type statement made by '9 is greater than 7'. It may be the case that there have been no tokens of the statement. No one has ever uttered or written '9 is greater than 7' before nor any other sentence making the same type statement.[50] Or it may be the case that the tokens of '9 is greater than 7' that there have been were not *asserted* but occurred, for instance, only as examples to demonstrate a point of logic or as the antecedent of a conditional statement such as 'If 9 is greater than 7, then 9 is greater than 5'.[51]

It is worth being alerted to the point that on the use of 'type statement' described it is not a necessary condition of there being a type statement, or a token statement, that the statement is asserted. But it remains to be seen whether this should be considered a disadvantage. We may like to use 'such and such a sentence makes a statement' in this way but to limit 'so and so made the statement that. . .' to cases of asserted statements. The point did not come up in 2.1.3 because we were considering a piece of text or examples where all the instances of statements were treated as asserted. All were 'uttered' (written) and no compound statements were explicitly mentioned. (See 4.2.)

2.4.2   Box c

It is not a necessary condition of there being a type statement that there should have been (previous) tokens of it nor that the tokens of it that there have been should have been cases of *assertion*.(See 2.2.2 (ix) and 4.2.)

2.4.3   *Two comments about statements*

The space devoted to type and token statements is a measure not so much of their importance as of the quantity of controversy about them. They have been treated as far more problematic than for example 'declarative sentences' (or 'contexts of utterance'), and their inclusion among concepts with which logic operates has been opposed on grounds which I have suggested seem inadequate.

(i)   Multiplication of entities?

It may look as if we have a great many entities whenever someone utters a meaningful declarative sentence which makes a statement.

We have a token sentence, and, if we admit 'propositions', a token proposition, and, if we add statements, a token statement as well. And yet all that happened was that someone said 'This toucan can catch a can'.

An analogy may make it obvious that the multiplication of 'entities' is more apparent than real. At 7 p.m. last night I ate a meal of corned beef and cabbage. We have corned beef and cabbage *and* a meal *and* supper (and cooked food and a vegetable and very likely a knife and fork): But all that happened was that I ate some corned beef and cabbage.

In introducing statements we do not introduce extra particulars into the world, but only another way of grouping such particulars as the token sentences in a piece of text.

(ii)   Truth conditions

In the last decade or two it has become common to speak of 'truth conditions', the conditions in which 'what is said' is true or not true. If the distinctions drawn in this chapter are employed, then truth conditions may need subdivision according to what they are truth conditions of.

The conditions in which an identified type statement is true or is not true may relate to what is true or not true of individual objects, however described, whether a particular toucan can catch cans for instance.

The conditions in which a meaningful declarative sentence or a proposition (as used in 2.1.2) expresses a truth or does not do so often need somewhat different description. The 'truth conditions' of the type sentence or proposition 'This toucan can catch a can' do not relate to whether some particular toucan can catch a can but rather to the circumstances in which a sentence of this meaning does or does not express a truth. The truth conditions of sentences of different meaning which can express the same truth such as 'This toucan can catch a can' and 'The toucan by the red boat can catch a can' will not be identical.[52]

NOTES

1.   In the language of 'particulars' and 'non-particulars', token words are particulars while type words are non-particulars. (See 1.1.1 (iv) a, n.7 on particulars and non-particulars.)
2.   Proper names are discussed in 7.2.

NOTES

3. Synonymy has been a very vexed subject. Some logicians, notably Quine, have denied that any two type words can ever be known to have the same meaning. See 3.3.2 (iv) e, and Quine 1960, esp. sec. 12.
4. The primacy of declarative sentences is sometimes rested on the fact that we can tack a particular style (question, command, assertion, denial, etc.) onto a sentence of declarative form. Thus 'It is raining: is it?', 'It is raining: bring it about', or 'Is it true that it is raining?', 'Make it true that it is raining', etc. (See for example Strawson (1969) 1971: 177–8.)
5. They may be more or less ill-formed (cf. e.g. Hodges 1977, sec. 3).
6. See 4.2.6, 5.2.6 for further discussion.
7. See for example Newton-Smith 1985 ch. 1.4: 8–11, ch. 5.2: 110–22 on this kind of ambiguity. Ambiguity of sentences arising from ambiguity of words is sometimes called 'lexical' or 'semantical' ambiguity as opposed to 'structural' or 'syntactical' ambiguity. See Hodges 1977, sec. 4: 23–4 for the former uses, Newton-Smith 1985, 1.4: 9–10 for the latter.
8. Sometimes 'proposition' is used for what I shall call (type) 'statement'; often it covers both of what are here distinguished as '(type) propositions' and '(type) statements'. See for example Flew (1979) 1983: 290 under 'proposition', Grayling 1982, ch. 2.
9. It was introduced in Strawson 1950. It is sometimes thought that Frege introduced the same distinction (under the terms 'sense' and 'reference') but this is open to doubt. It can look like this from Frege (1892) 1952 'Sense and Reference', and is said to be so for example by Lemmon 1966: 93–6, but 'The Thought', Frege (1919) 1967, suggests that this is not a correct reading of Frege, as was pointed out for instance in Garner 1970. 'Identity of sense' in Frege probably means not identity of meaning but *necessary* identity of reference or in what is stated. The distinction between necessary identity of reference and synonymy is discussed in 3.3.2 (iv) e.
10. Useful descriptions of the distinctions drawn in 2.1.2–3 can be found in Cartwright (1960) 1987, Lemmon 1966, Haack 1978, ch. 6.
11. See for example Joseph (1906) 1916, chs 7 and 8 (the term 'judgement' was often used at earlier periods but was gradually superseded by 'proposition'); Wittgenstein 1922: 4.02–4.06, Stebbing 1943, ch. 2, secs 1–2.
12. See B. Russell 1919, ch. XIV ('Descriptions'), and B. Russell (1905) 1956. Some other examples such as 'The author of *Waverley* was Scotch' were more prominent than 'The King of France is wise' (or as Russell more often had it, 'bald') but later discussion focussed on 'The King of France is wise'.
13. See Haack 1978, 5.3, Blackburn 1980, chs 2 and 3 on these two theories.
14. See 4.1.1–3 and 4.1 generally on this and other difficulties of the view that *p* and *p is true* are 'equivalent'.
15. I may mean to refer to someone who is *both* X's escort and a man in a green jacket or I may mean to refer to X's escort (the green jacket is

an extra) or I really mean the man in the green jacket (who I thought was escorting X). But I must have some name or description or other in mind to be said to be referring to anything definite.

16. There could of course be other reasons for selection. Logicians often write as if people spoke or wrote only to give information. However, take e.g. 'Who gave the lecture?' where the answer could correctly be 'The man over there', 'the President of the College', 'my brother-in-law', or etc. You might select 'the man over there' to assist the questioner to meet the lecturer, or he might be a competitor you wish to impress and you use 'my brother-in-law' instead.

17. A condition that can be said to obtain, *inter alia*, if 'France' or 'Smith' does not secure reference.

18. As originally introduced (Donnellan (1966) 1977), uses of an expression like 'Smith's murderer' were divided into referential (if the speaker meant Jones, who, among other things, murdered Smith) and attributive (if he meant whoever it was that murdered Smith). For consistency 'Smith' (or Jones) should also in each case be thought of as used either referentially ('the man, among other things, called Smith') or attributively ('whoever is called Smith'). Since so-called referential and attributive uses each subdivide according to whether 'Smith' is used referentially or attributively there are not two but four cases. 'Referential use' seems (essentially) identical to 'inessential' use and 'attributive' to 'essential' use of an expression.

19. If we confine 'failed presupposition' to radical reference failure which results in no statement being made, rather than extending it to all cases of radical reference failure, then we can express this doubt by saying that it is less certain whether radical reference failure is always a case of failed presupposition. Or we can identify radical reference failure and failed presupposition and say that it is not sure whether a failed presupposition always leads to no statement being made.

20. See 4.1.6 (ii) for the point that if we adopted option 3, p and p *is true* would not always have the same truth value.

21. See 6.1.2 on problems about subject terms.

22. Meaningful declarative sentences which contain no such expression and can make only one statement can be said to make a statement even if used only as examples. But if I use such a sentence as an example it is probably straining usage to say that *I* 'made a statement'. See 2.4.2 (iv) and 4.2.

23. Definite sets of objects are often called 'closed classes': a class is closed if it may be impossible for it to have any further members, e.g. 'laws enacted in 1857' cannot be added to after 1857, 'X's descendants' cease once the last one (or in recent times maybe last frozen sperm/ovum) has gone. Closed classes are contrasted to open classes whose membership can theoretically always be added to as e.g. 'All stage coaches anywhere anytime'. See also 7.1.2 (ii) C).

24. 'Singular term', mentioned in 1.1.1 (iv) a, is probably so used that it could cover not only terms of a kind to make definite references to single objects but also possibly references to 'any one such and such'; usage does not appear to be quite fixed.

25. There are many problems about proper names, further considered in 7.2.

26. Some languages have a richer vocabulary of pronouns than English. One may correctly use a different form of e.g. 'you' according to the age, status, relationship of the person(s) addressed without detracting from the point that pronouns stand in for nouns.

27. Searle 1969, sec. 4.3: 81 calls the mentioned item 'the *secondary* referent' and what is referred to by the whole expression 'the *primary* referent'. See Searle 1969, esp. ch. 2.3 and ch. 4 on these and other aspects of reference.

28. Inessential references do not have to succeed for someone to be said to have succeeded in referring to something. See above 2.2.2 (vi)–(vii).

29. These uses can be found in works of Strawson and others cited in this chapter and/or on the suggested reading list.

30. Cf 1.1.1 (iv) n.7. In Strawson 1959, pt I, Strawson argued that persons and material objects were the basic particulars.

31. 'Last week' is a doubtful case: we identify particulars through their location in time and space, and times and places themselves should probably not be included as particulars.

32. On a theory where the meaning of a proper name determines to what it refers, proper names will not count as referring expressions in Usage 4 and they also cannot fail to refer.

33. For example, it does not quite accommodate tensed verbs.

34. See Strawson 1959, esp. ch. 6, secs 1–5: 180–202.

35. Mainly in 'Identity and necessity' (Kripke (1971) 1977) and *Naming and Necessity* (Kripke (1972) 1980).

36. For ease of exposition 'contain' includes expressions understood: e.g. in 'It is raining' 'here' and 'now' are generally understood.

37. This point is not infrequently overlooked. See for example Haack 1978: 80, last sentence of para. 3.

38. If a statement is said to be made even when there is a radical reference failure, then the point holds of all statements made by sentences that do not contain expressions radically failing to refer.

39. In idiomatic English the sentence 'The number of the planets is greater than 7' can mean 'There are more than seven planets' or possibly 'Any number which is at any time the number of the planets is greater than 7'. A token of the type sentence that has either of these meanings has a different meaning from one where the subject of the sentence is a number, i.e. that number which is the (current) number of the planets. The point is taken up in 3.3.1 (iv).

40. Yet other terms are 'token-reflexive' and 'indexical', sometimes taken to include, e.g. tensed verbs. See Baker and Hacker 1984: 197–205.

41. See for example Lemmon 1966, Davidson (1967) 1985. 'The context' is sometimes also invoked as helpful in discovering the meaning of a token of an ambiguous word. And it is of course quite true that we often can tell whether for instance 'poor' in 'he's a poor violinist' is likely to mean 'indigent' or 'to be pitied' or 'not very good' from the setting, whether for example it is financial circumstances or musical

competence that is under discussion. Here what is in question is discovering the meaning of a token of an ambiguous type word – which we can also of course often be told: ' "poor" here means "indigent" '. In discussing 'contextually dependent expressions', the 'context' is supposed to tell us not the meaning of a token expression but what the token expression is used to refer to.

42. A form of provision for doing this is occasionally found. For instance, it can be read into Frege (see Frege (1919) 1952: 24–6, 37) but in the end seems to amount to supplying conditions not so much for token sentences in their context expressing the same type statement as for them doing so *necessarily*, a condition often not satisfied by sentences making the same type statement.

43. See also 2.4.1, n.41.

44. It is somewhat less concrete than it looks because there are many different possible descriptions of any one speaker or person addressed, and similarly with respect to places and times. Difficulties about saying what counts as 'one place' and 'one time' add to the problems of saying what counts as one and the same context.

45. For criticism of 'context dependent' sentences, see e.g. Baker and Hacker 1984: 197–205.

46. See for example Lemmon 1966, Haack 1978, 6.4.

47. See Quine 1953b; (1953c) 1966; (1956) 1966; 1960, secs 30–1, 41, 44.

48. At least sometimes: in Quine (1956) 1966, and 1960: 145, Quine allows a non-opaque, i.e. transparent, use of 'believe' also.

49. It is not easy to see exactly what is the basis on which Quine ascribes truth value to statements of the form 'He believes that. . .' (Wolfram 1975: 245). He appears – questionably (see 5.2.2 (iii)) – to assign falsity when 'He believes that' is followed by a sentence which could not express a truth. Otherwise it seems to be a matter of 'sincerely asserting/denying' X. See Quine 1953b: 141–2, (1956) 1966: 185, etc.; 1960, secs 30–1, 44.

50. For a contrary supposition see e.g. Haack 1978: 76.

51. See e.g. Geach 1965: 450, 453 for this objection.

52. There is an attack on the idea of 'truth conditions', partly on the grounds of not drawing this distinction in Baker and Hacker 1984: 180–190.

QUESTIONS

When you have read this chapter, or sections in it, you may like to try your hand at these questions, and/or to keep them in mind when doing some or all of the suggested reading. Questions are framed *primarily* on specified sections, but material from other sections may help with answers. You may also like to try the examination questions on this chapter in the Appendix.

2.1
1. We often speak of 'saying the same thing'. Can you explain in what ways this phrase is ambiguous?
2. What kind of difficulties have, or would have, to be overcome for word processors to be programmed to count a) type "words" (words with the same meaning), b) type propositions (token sentences with the same meaning), c) type statements (token sentences stating the same)?

2.2
3. Do you think there could be grounds for preferring the Theory of Presupposition to the Theory of Descriptions, or vice versa?
4. Explain, using your own examples, the difference between successfully referring to non-existent objects, non-radical reference failure, and radical reference failure. Does the difference seem a) clear, b) important?

2.3
5. Can you find examples in the suggested reading of the uses of 'referring expression' described in 2.3? Why do you think usage has been so varied?
6. In what ways, if any, are 'rigid designators', 'nonrigid designators', etc., an improvement on previous terms in this area?

2.4
7. We may need to know the 'context of an utterance' a) to know the meaning of a token sentence, b) to know to which things expressions in a token sentence refer. What is the difference?
8. Which do you think would be the most critical of the objections made to (type) statements? Can the objection(s), in your opinion, be answered?

SOME SUGGESTED READING

For guidance on a sensible order in which to do some or all this reading, consult references in text and notes. Not all the references given in this chapter are included in the list of suggested reading, and reading can be extended by following up other references in text and notes.

Baker, G. P. and Hacker, P. M. S. 1984, *Language, Sense and Nonsense*: 180–90, 197–205.

Blackburn, S. 1980 (Open University), *Philosophical Logic*, chs 2 and 3.

Cartwright, R. (1962) 1987, 'Propositions', in R. J. Butler (ed.) *Analytical Philosophy* (series 1), repr. in R. Cartwright, *Philosophical Essays* 1987.

Davidson, D. (1967) 1985, 'Truth and Meaning', Essay 2 in D. Davidson, *Inquiries into Truth and Interpretation* 1985: esp. 33–5.

Donnellan, K. (1966) 1977, 'Reference and Definite Descriptions', *Philosophical Review*, vol. 75 (1966), repr. in S. P. Schwartz (ed.) *Naming, Necessity, and Natural Kinds*, 1977.

Frege, G. (1892) 1952, 'On Sense and Reference', in P. Geach and M. Black (eds) *Translations from the Philosophical Writings of Gottlieb Frege* 1952.

—— (1919) 1967, 'The Thought: A Logical Inquiry', in *Mind*, vol. 65, 1956, and in P. F. Strawson (ed.) *Philosophical Logic* 1967.

Haack, S. 1978, *Philosophy of Logics*, ch. 5.3, ch. 6: 65–85.

Kripke, S. (1971) 1977 'Identity and Necessity' in M. K. Munitz (ed.) *Identity and Individuation* 1971, repr. in S. P. Schwartz (ed.) *Naming, Necessity, and Natural Kinds* 1977.

—— (1972) 1980, *Naming and Necessity*, first published in G. Harman and D. Davidson (eds), *Semantics and Natural Language* 1972. (Some excerpts in P. K. Moser (ed.) *A Priori Knowledge* 1987.)

Lemmon, E. J. 1966, 'Sentences, Statements and Propositions', in B. Williams and A. Montefiore (eds) *British Analytical Philosophy* 1966.

Russell, B. (1905) 1956, 'On Denoting', *Mind*, N.S. vol. 14 (1905) repr. in B. Russell (ed. R. C. Marsh), *Logic and Knowledge. Essays 1901–1950* 1956.

—— 1919, *Introduction to Mathematical Philosophy*, ch. XIV.

Searle, J. 1969, *Speech Acts*, chs 2.3, 4.

Strawson, P.F. (1950) 1971, 'On Referring', *Mind* 1950, vol. 59, reprinted in many places including P. F. Strawson, *Logico-Linguistic Papers* 1971.

—— (1964) 1971, 'Identifying References and Truth Values', *Theoria* 1964, xxx, reprinted in P. F. Strawson, *Logico-Linguistic Papers* 1971.

More advanced reading

Evans, G. 1982 (posth. ed. McDowell), *Varieties of Reference*.

Peacocke, C. 1983, *Sense and Content. Experience Thought, and their Relations*.

Chapter 3

NECESSARY TRUTH AND THE ANALYTIC–SYNTHETIC DISTINCTION

SECTION 1 *MAP OF DISTINCTIONS AND RECENT THEORIES*

3.1.1 'Necessary' and 'contingent', 'analytic' and 'synthetic', 'a priori' and 'empirical'

A distinction considered by many logicians to be of great importance is that between what is *necessarily* true (or necessarily false) and what is *contingently* true (or contingently false) (see 1.1.2 c), 1.2.2 (iv)). A necessary truth is true no matter what the state of the world, or, as it is sometimes put, in any possible world. An uncontroversial example would be:

Example A
Anyone who has brown eyes has eyes.

Necessary truths are contrasted to contingent truths such as

Example B
The earth is round

which are true because of the way the world is.

Two other pairs of terms mark distinctions closely related to that between necessary and contingent truths: *analytic* and *synthetic*, and *a priori* and *empirical* (or *a posteriori*). 'Analytic' means approximately 'with a meaning such that it must express a truth' in whatever circumstances it may be uttered. 'Synthetic' means, approximately, 'with a meaning such that it may or may not express a truth'. '*A priori*' and 'empirical' distinguish different kinds of knowledge. To know something *a priori* is to know it without investigation of the world. To know something empirically, or 'by empirical means', is to know it by means of investigating the world. The sentence instanced above in Example A as an example of a necessary truth, viz. 'Anyone who has brown eyes has eyes', can also be cited as analytic, since its meaning is such that it must express a truth and, further, as known *a priori* to be true: we do not need to investigate the state of the world to know that it is true. Similarly, the sentence instanced as a contingent truth in Example B, viz. 'The earth is round', can also be cited as synthetic, since its meaning is such that it may or may not express a truth, and further, as known to be true by empirical means: the earth had to be investigated to discover that it is round and not flat.

With the distinctions drawn in chapter 2 in mind, we shall be wary of concluding from Examples A and B that all three pairs of terms, 'necessarily true' and 'contingent', 'analytic' and 'synthetic', '*a priori*' and 'empirical', divide up all token sentences in just the same way. I shall indeed be suggesting that 'analytic' and 'synthetic' distinguish different kinds of type *propositions* (as 'proposition' was used in 2.1.2 (iv)) while 'necessarily true' vs 'contingent' marks a division of type *statements* (as 'statement' was described in 2.1.3 and 2.4). '*A priori*' and 'empirical' apply to knowledge, how we know or could know this to be true and that to be false, and it is convenient to defer detailed discussion of this distinction to a later chapter .(4.3.2).

It seems likely that, even if they are not exactly the same, there is a close relation between 'analytic' (meaning such that it must express a truth), 'necessarily true' (true no matter what) and '*a priori*' (knowledge acquired without investigation of the world) on the one side and between 'synthetic' (meaning such that it may or may not express a truth), contingent (truth value depends on the state of the world), and empirical (knowledge derived from investigation of the world) on the other side.[1]

This chapter looks at theories about the relations between all these categories, and makes suggestions about what they actually seem to be. But the topic is complicated because of the number of distinctions involved as well as the number of controversial theories about them, and this chapter concentrates on 'analytic' vs 'not analytic', and 'necessarily true' vs 'not necessarily true' with a brief addendum about 'synthetic' in section 5 (3.2.5). Fuller discussion

81

of contingent, '*a priori*' vs 'empirical', and also of 'necessarily not true' and 'self-contradictory', is deferred until 4.3.2 and 5.2.

3.1.1 Box a

Analytic–Synthetic: 'analytic': meaning of words necessitates truth; 'synthetic': meaning of words such that they may or may not express a truth.

Necessary–Contingent: necessarily true: true no matter what; contingent: truth value depends on how the world happens to be.

A Priori–*Empirical*: *a priori*: (known) without investigation of the world; empirical: (known) by investigation of the world.

Notes: 1. '*a priori*' and 'empirical' are sometimes transferred to truths: an *a priori* truth is one known or knowable *a priori*, an empirical truth is one known or knowable by empirical means, i.e. by investigating the world (see 4.3.2).
2. Most discussion of these distinctions has taken place on the supposition that there are only two truth values, true and false, and for this, and other reasons, the definitions are first approximations.

3.1.2 *Three theories about necessary truth*

There are three main views about the distinctions outlined in 3.1.1. These are conveniently labelled 'conventionalism', 'scepticism', and 'essentialism'. Each is considered incompatible with the other two: not more than one of them could be correct, and the proponents of each view are liberal in their criticisms of the others. Each view has had periods of popularity before this century, as well as during it. I shall make some reference to past versions of the theories but systematic discussion is predominantly directed to versions of the views put forward in the last half-century or so.

The three views – conventionalism, scepticism, and essentialism – can be distinguished in a preliminary fashion in this way.

a) *Conventionalism* holds that all necessary truths derive their truth from the 'conventions of language' (hence the name 'conventionalism'), that is, from the fact that we put a meaning on the words by which we express them which obliges them to be true, and for this reason their truth can be known without investigation of the things they are about, i.e. *a priori*.

A conventionalist theory typically sees a great divide between analytic-necessarily true-*a priori* on the one hand, and synthetic-contingent-empirical on the other. Sometimes associated with conventionalism is the view that what is analytic-necessarily true-*a priori* is *uninformative* and/or that what is informative, i.e. the synthetic-contingent-empirical, is *uncertain*. Very great importance is attributed to the distinction, in particular because many type sentences have subtle ambiguities which allow them to be construed *either* so that they express a necessary truth *or* so that they are about the world, and it is easy for anyone to be misled into supposing that a truth he embraces is both. The sentences 'A wound is a necessary condition of a scar' and 'Ingesting D-poison is a sufficient condition of death', discussed in connection with necessary and sufficient conditions in 1.2.2, supply preliminary examples.

This version of conventionalism was what Quine called a 'dogma of empiricism'. It was held by, among others, Logical Positivists and post-war Oxford linguistic philosophers, and was the predominant view among English-speaking philosophers for at least thirty years of this century (*c*.1930–*c*.1960).

b) *Scepticism* disputes the existence of a distinction between analytic/necessarily true/*a priori*, on the one hand, and synthetic/contingent/empirical on the other. One form of scepticism (exhibited by Hume in the *Treatise* (1739) 1911, Bk I, pt IV, sec. I) is to argue that the former are as uncertain as the latter. Another form, associated with Quine, is to maintain that analyticity is 'a pseudo-concept which philosophy would be better off without' (Quine (1953c) 1966) and to argue that even if 'analytic' passed muster, truths could not be distinguished into necessary and contingent. Quine's attack on the distinction between necessary and contingent derived from the new work on reference (discussed in chapter 2) which was not accommodated in the then-prevailing conventionalist picture. Quine put forward his views in some famous papers of the 1950s, as well as in *Word and Object* (1960). They became highly influential, and led to severe doubts about the adequacy of conventionalism. At the period that Quine launched his attack on conventionalism, essentialism was considered dead, and he did not discuss it. He rarely mentioned it, and when he did it was briefly and dismissively as a 'metaphysical jungle' (Quine (1953c) 1966: 174) or as 'however venerable. . .surely indefensible' (Quine 1960: 199–200).

c) *Essentialism.* An essentialist doctrine of necessary truth holds that not only are there necessary truths but there are necessary truths about things in the world. In the heyday of Positivism these truths were referred to, for the purpose of objecting to them, as 'synthetic necessary truths', a term taken from Kant's '*a priori* synthetic judgments' (Kant (1781) 1929: A9–10/B13–21). In the revival of essentialism introduced by Kripke in papers of the 1970s (see especially Kripke (1971) 1977 and (1972) 1980), discussion is more often of 'essentialism', 'essential' properties, the 'essential' nature of things. 'Essential' was a term used by Locke ((1690) 1975, e.g III.6) and by Mill (1843, I.6), in both cases in the course of disputing essentialist views.

3.1.2 Box a

a) Conventionalism: 1. Truths may be divided into necessarily true and contingent; 2. All truths which are necessary are so because of the meaning of the words that express them (by the 'conventions of language').

b) Scepticism: 1. There is no genuine distinction between analytic/necessary truth and synthetic/contingent truth; 2. There are no necessary (or contingent) truths.

c) Essentialism: 1. There are necessary truths; 2. Some necessary truths are about the world (and all possible worlds).

Note: Each of these theories is incompatible with either of the other two. But certain variants of c) included by some as essentialism are not clearly incompatible with every version of conventionalism. (See 3.4.2 for fuller discussion.)

SECTION 2 *CONVENTIONALISM*

3.2.1 The Logical Positivist picture

The picture presented by the Logical Positivists and, later, the post-war Oxford linguistic philosophers was clear-cut, neat, and relatively simple.[2] It went like this.

(i) Division of propositions

Some (declarative) sentences do not have a meaning, that is, as in the terminology of 2.1.2 (iv), do not express a proposition or at any rate do not express a *meaningful* proposition.[3] These are the sort of sentences we encountered in 2.1.2 (ii): grammatically ill-formed sentences and those which ascribe inappropriate predicates to the subject, together with a) those expressing self-contradictions, like 'It is raining and it is not raining' or, more generally, necessarily false propositions, and b) what the Logical Positivists called 'metaphysical' propositions which are propositions such that nothing could establish either truth or falsity because no amount of evidence would be sufficient.

A *meaningful* declarative token sentence, i.e. a token 'proposition' (cf. 2.1.2) is either analytic, i.e. has a meaning such that it must express a truth, or it is synthetic, i.e. such that what it expresses might be either true or false. (Meaningful) propositions (both token and type) divide into two mutually exclusive and exhaustive classes: no token (nor, so long as a single type 'proposition' has a single meaning, type) proposition belongs to both classes and every (meaningful) token (or type) proposition belongs to one or the other.

(ii) Division of truths

The division of (meaningful) propositions was presented as also one of truths. All and only truths expressed by analytic propositions were *necessary*, and all and only truths expressed by synthetic propositions were classed as *contingent*, i.e. such that whether they were truths or not depended on how the world happens to be. (On the synthetic-contingent side there was a difference between 'truths' and '(meaningful) propositions' because synthetic-contingent propositions could be false, so that synthetic-contingent *truths* were a sub-class of synthetic-contingent proposi-

85

tions. By excluding *necessarily* false 'propositions' as meaningless, analytic propositions and necessary truths were identical.)

The epithets '*a priori*' and '*a posteriori*' or 'empirical' were commonly transferred to propositions. Only, and generally all, analytic-necessary propositions were termed '*a priori*', in virtue of the fact that only they and, as many thought, all of them can be known to be true *a priori*. All synthetic-contingent propositions were termed '*a posteriori*' or 'empirical' because empirical investigation, i.e. investigation of facts in the world, of the things the proposition in question is about, is necessary, and (by the exclusion of any non-analytic propositions whose truth value cannot be discovered by empirical means as metaphysical and meaningless) sufficient to discover whether they are true or false. Only synthetic-contingent propositions were 'empirical': only in their case was empirical evidence necessary to establish truth or falsity, and, it was believed, only in their case was it sufficient.

There were some difficulties, even from within the Positivist picture, about these transfers, in particular the transfer of 'empirical' to all synthetic-contingent propositions.[4] It was well appreciated that those of general form ('All Xs anywhere anytime are Y') could not be conclusively established to be true (see 1.2.2). The problem that therefore some propositions could not be known to be true by empirical means was dealt with by positing that a proposition was meaningful, synthetic, and empirical if it could in principle be known to be false.

(iii)   The role of ambiguity

The distinction between sentences of the same *typography* (the same type sentence cf. 2.1.2) and sentences of the same *meaning* (the same type proposition cf. 2.1.2) was an important aspect of conventionalism as presented by the Positivists, as indeed also by earlier conventionalists such as Locke. It was type sentences with a given meaning, or more generally, all those token sentences which have the same meaning and therefore express the same type 'proposition' (as in 2.1.2) that were classed as analytic-necessary-*a priori* or synthetic-contingent-empirical. It was well recognized that a type sentence might be ambiguous so that some tokens of it could express an analytic proposition, others a synthetic proposition, and that, on the other hand, tokens of two different type sentences might be synonymous and express the same type proposition.

Ambiguity had a particularly significant role in positivist accounts of conventionalism. The fact that many type sentences are more or less ambiguous means that, in many cases, particular tokens have to be investigated to discover just what proposition they express and thereby whether they are analytic or synthetic or perhaps meaningless. Ambiguity of sentences was also the principal explanation given of the pernicious error, attributed to philosophers and non-philosophers, of treating some truths as *both* necessary and synthetic, that is, both such that they *have* to be true and as supplying information about the world. The conventionalist claim is that while some propositions *appear* to be both necessarily true and yet about the world, investigation always reveals that this appearance is misleading and arises from putting two different meanings on a sentence. Some favourite examples in the Positivist and Oxford linguistic period[5] were 'Nothing can be red and green all over at the same time', 'One sees with and only with one's eyes', 'Space is three dimensional'.[6]

Example C
One sees with and only with one's eyes

A typical conventionalist analysis of example C would go like this. If 'eyes' is given the meaning 'organs of sight' (meaning 1) then Example C is necessarily true but wholly uninformative. The proposition is plainly analytic. That one sees with and only with organs of sight cannot but be true and tells us nothing. If, on the other hand, 'eyes' are taken to be those organs placed in a certain way in the human face (or, e.g. of a certain structure, also perhaps found in animals) (meaning 2), then Example C is informative but by no means necessarily true. It is (only) an empirical matter that it is with and only with certain organs, known as 'eyes', that one sees. It might have been with one's shoulder as well or instead. On this construction of 'eyes' it is, as it was often put, *logically possible* that someone should see with their shoulder. To discover that people see with their 'eyes', empirical investigation of organs of the body and the activity of seeing is necessary. This is in contrast to meaning 1, where 'eyes' are defined as 'organs of sight'. On meaning 1 *whatever* anyone sees with rates as 'eyes' and it is not logically possible for them to see with anything but their eyes. If it was with their shoulder that someone saw, then their shoulder would have become their eyes. Thus we need conduct no empirical investigation to discover that Example C taken with meaning 1 is true. All we need to do is to understand the meaning of the word 'eyes' (and the rest of the sentence).

It was a common Positivist belief that *all* claims that so and so is a synthetic necessary truth arose from shifts in the meaning of words, and that analysis would invariably reveal more than one meaning as in Example C.

3.2.1 Box a

Conventionalism: all meaningful propositions are either analytic-necessarily true-*a priori* or synthetic-contingent-empirical. The same proposition cannot belong to both categories.

When a proposition appears to be both necessary and informative about the world this is always due to *ambiguity* of sentences.

3.2.2 *Self-evidence and logical truth*

(i) Self-evidence

It was a recurrent theme of conventionalism, as presented by the Positivists and post-war Oxford linguistic philosophers, that analytic-necessarily true-*a priori* propositions are uninformative and mere 'tautologies', 'tautology' being a term with a pejorative sense for 'analytic'/giving no information.

The tenets of conventionalism certainly seem to entail that analytic-necessarily true-*a priori* propositions do not give information about *any matter of fact*, about any object in the world, and when it was claimed that such propositions are 'uninformative', this was often qualified by 'about the world'.

But there was a tendency also to claim that analytic-necessarily true-*a priori* propositions are 'uninformative' in other senses of the term 'uninformative' such as 'telling us only what we know already' or 'telling us something that anyone understanding the meaning of the words spoken/written must know to be true'. There was mention of sub-classes of analytic propositions such as 'self-evident' ones or what were called 'logical truths' but the primary concern, at least in twentieth-century versions of conventionalism, was to stress the common features of all analytic propositions, not to explore differences within the category. This resulted in slightly implausible theses, such as that the whole of mathematics and formal logic is 'uninformative'.

Earlier forms of conventionalism were sometimes more sophisticated in this respect. Locke (1690) certainly drew the analytic-necessarily true-*a priori* vs synthetic-contingent-empirical distinction, although he did not name the categories,[7] but he also drew a distinction between what he called 'trifling' or 'self-evident' propositions and ones which are 'instructive'. And he included *some* analytic propositions as *instructive* along with propositions about matters of fact. The analytic propositions in question were those which are not self-evident.

A *self-evident* proposition was, and probably still would be, defined as a proposition which says no more than is included in the meaning (according to Locke, *definition*) of its terms and which is therefore such that anyone who knows the meaning of the words (in Locke, definition) thereby knows that it is true.[8] Only analytic propositions can be self-evident in this sense but there can be analytic propositions which are not self-evident. Locke cites such propositions as

Example D
   The exterior angle of a triangle is greater than either opposite
   interior angle

as, although what was later called 'analytic', instructive, in contrast to 'A triangle hath three sides', which is self-evident and trifling. 'A triangle has three sides' is a *definition* in Euclid (Euclid (*c.* 300 B.C.) 1908, bk I, Definition 19), so that if one knows the meaning of 'triangle' one must know that it is true. But Example D is a theorem (bk 1, Proposition 16), derived by a fairly complicated series of steps, from Euclid's definitions and postulates. Someone could very well know the meaning/definition of 'triangle' and all the remaining terms without knowing that it is true. The same would go for, for example, 'If a man marries his mother's brother's daughter, then his father-in-law is his uncle' or any relatively complicated analytic proposition.[9] A Positivist such as Ayer would not *dispute* this but regarded it as of minor importance, and it is easy to gain the impression that we cannot learn anything significant from e.g. mathematics because we are not learning anything about *matters of fact* or that because analytic propositions never tell us anything about the world, they never tell us anything we did not know already.

(ii) Logical truths

Another sub-class of analytic propositions to which attention is sometimes drawn is that of 'logical truths'. 'Logical truths' are those analytic propositions which depend for their truth on synonymy of tokens of the same type word/sentence, but otherwise only on the meaning of logical constants such as 'If. . . then', 'and', 'not', 'or'. Examples are commonly given from the propositional calculus: 'If p then p' or 'not (p and not p)', 'p' here representing the same type sentence, assumed to have the same meaning[10] would commonly be cited as a logical truth in contrast to, for example, 'A bachelor is an unmarried man', which is not a logical truth because its truth derives from the fact that *different* type words, viz. 'bachelor' and 'unmarried man', have the same meaning. 'If p then p' is claimed both as a logical truth and as self-evident but logical truths need not be self-evident: they can be very complicated, as examples from any formal logic book would demonstrate. 'A triangle hath three sides' or 'A bachelor is an unmarried man', on the other hand, are self-evident propositions which would not be included as logical truths.

3.2.2   Box a

'Self-evident' proposition: an analytic proposition such that knowing the meaning of the terms in it entails knowing that it is true (e.g. A triangle has three sides).

'Logical truth': an analytic-necessary proposition whose truth depends only on the synonymy of the same type words and the meaning of logical constants.

Note: 'Uninformative' in 'analytic propositions are uninformative' should be restricted to meaning 'uninformative *about the world*': they need not be 'uninformative' in other senses of 'uninformative'. (On 'informative' see also 4.2.5.)

3.2.3 Necessity and certainty

The view held, among others by the Positivists, that there could be no such things as 'synthetic necessary truths' was often accompanied by, and sometimes confused with, quite a different view, viz. that no synthetic-contingent-empirical proposition can be known for certain to be true (e.g. Ayer (1936) 1946: 93; see next paragraph). The belief that only analytic-necessary-*a priori* propositions can be known for certain to be true has been influential in epistemology as well as philosophical logic. It seems to have had two main sources, not always kept distinct.

a) Examples considered

One source of the view that certainty is confined to analytic-necessary-*a priori* truth, that, as Ayer put it in 1936, 'There are no absolutely certain empirical propositions. It is only tautologies which are certain' (Ayer (1936) 1946: 93) is the nature of the examples used by Positivist philosophers in drawing the analytic-necessarily true-*a priori* vs synthetic-contingent-empirical distinction. The difference between the two categories was almost invariably explained in terms of propositions of unrestricted generality, that is, ones of the form 'All Xs anywhere anytime are Y'.

We have already seen (1.2.1 (iv)) that propositions of the form 'All Xs anywhere anytime are Y' cannot be shown to be true by means of empirical observation because we could never get to the end of investigating 'All Xs anywhere anytime' to be sure that they are Y. However many Xs we have observed to be Y, this is never sufficient to be sure that the next X we observe will also be Y. And if the next X is not Y, then it is clearly not true that 'All Xs anywhere anytime are Y' but on the contrary false. It follows that if a proposition of the form 'All Xs anywhere anytime are Y' *is* known for certain to be true, it must be by means other than empirical observation, viz because the proposition is analytic-necessarily true-*a priori*: the meaning of Y is included in the meaning of X as 'eyes' is included in 'brown eyes' in 3.1.1 Example A (Anyone who has brown eyes has eyes).

The point that propositions of unrestricted generality cannot be known to be true by means of empirical investigation, and thus can be known for certain to be true only if they are necessarily true, does not prove that certainty is confined to necessary truths in the case of propositions of *other* forms, such as 'Some Xs are Y' or 'This X is a Y', where there is no obstacle to discovering truth by empirical means comparable to that of the 'All Xs anywhere anytime are Y' type of case. (We have seen (1.2.1 (iv)) that with 'Some Xs somewhere sometime are Y', it is *falsity* which cannot be discovered by empirical means, so that such propositions can be known to be false only if an X cannot be a Y, i.e. if they are necessarily false, like 'Some cats are dogs'[11].) If the contention that the truth or truth value of propositions of the synthetic-contingent-empirical side of the Positivist divide can never be known for certain is to be made good it must be on other grounds.

b) Perception is unreliable

There was a second source of the thesis that no contingent proposition can be known for certain to be true. This derived from the long tradition, going back at least to Descartes ((1636) 1912, pt IV; (1641) 1912) that in the case of empirical evidence, which is ultimately based on sense perception, the possibility of error is forever present.

It was often pointed out that this view gained its plausibility from the manner in which examples were described. Descartes depicts himself as mistaking the shape of towers *seen at a distance* or *sticks immersed in water* ((Descartes (1641) 1912, VI). Hume in the *Enquiry* (1748) used the example of the sun rising *tomorrow*, when he said that 'the contrary of every matter of fact is still possible' (Hume (1748) 1894, sec. IV, pt I, para. 21). That we cannot be sure that a 'proposition' is true when our evidence is relatively slight (the tower is far away, the stick in water, the sunrise in the future) does not mean that the *best* evidence (the tower right by us, the stick in our hand, the sunrise taking place now) may not be conclusive (see 4.2.6, 4.3.6, esp. (ii)).

The uncertainty of empirical evidence was also promoted on the grounds (a) that only in very limited cases, such as Descartes' 'Cogito ergo sum' (Descartes (1636) 1912, pt IV, (1641) 1912, II) or the nature of our own current perceptions, is error always impossible, and (b) that wherever one could be mistaken, one also could never be sure that one is not. This is to suggest that success can occur only if failure is impossible. It is not good grounds for identifying certainty with necessity and uncertainty with the empirical since, with the possible exception of self-evident propositions (where, provided we know the meaning of the words we must know that they are true: see above, 3.2.2), error is possible in the case of analytic-necessarily true-*a priori* propositions also.

In this connection it should be noted that earlier conventionalists like Locke considered certainty of the truth of *general* propositions to be restricted to ones which are analytic-necessarily true-*a priori* but did not extend the identification of necessity and certainty to propositions of other forms (see Locke (1690) 1975, e.g. bk 4, ch. 3)). Some later philosophers, such as Austin (1962 posth.) and Strawson (1959, ch. 1), who could be classed as conventionalists did not agree that empirical observation may not be conclusive, for example in the case of many singular statements about material objects, and some contingent statements therefore known for certain to be true.

3.2.3   Box a

We cannot fail to be certain of the truth expressed by a self-evident proposition we understand (cf. 3.2.2, Box a). We need not be certain of a truth expressed by any other sort of proposition we understand, whether analytic or synthetic: necessity is not a sufficient condition of certainty.

Conventionalists differ over whether it is possible to be certain of the truth of any contingent statement. Some, including the Logical Positivists, consider necessity to be a necessary condition of certainty, but the arguments appear inconclusive.

SECTION 3   *SCEPTICISM*

3.3.1   Necessary truth and referential opacity[12]

(i)   Positivist conventionalism and reference

It will have been noticed that while the Logical Positivists and post-war Oxford linguistic philosophers gave a central place to ambiguity in their presentation of conventionalism, their account made no mention of the kind of facts uncovered by work on reference, which we considered in chapter 2: that some expressions can with the same meaning refer to different objects and that the same object can be referred to by terms with different meanings. In the Positivist account, not only does every analytic proposition express a necessary truth, but also any necessary truth is expressed by an analytic proposition.

Quine found fault with 'analytic', and his attacks on the concept were so influential that the term gradually disappeared from the vocabulary of philosophical logic. The 'sorrows', as Quine called them, of 'analytic' are discussed in 3.3.2. This section (3.3.1) is concerned with the results Quine depicted of introducing into conventionalism the facts that the same object can be referred to by expressions of different meaning and that many expressions may with the same meaning refer to different objects. In 'Reference and Modality' (1953) and other papers, and in *Word and Object* (1960), Quine put forward in detail the view that these facts were sufficient to destroy the concept of necessary truth as depicted in conventionalism. The reasons have already been touched on in 2.4.2 (iii): whether a truth is necessary or not depends on how objects it is about are referred to and the same truth that appears necessary expressed by one unambiguous proposition ceases to seem so when expressed by another.

(ii)   Quine's Necessity Argument

For the purposes of explaining this, Quine retained the Positivist-conventionalist tenet that necessary truth depends strictly on analyticity, viz. that what is said is necessarily true if and only if it is said by an analytic proposition, and a statement of the form 'Necessarily X is Y' is true if and only if the proposition following 'Necessarily' is analytic.[13]

A few examples were sufficient to show that as soon as the new observations about reference were attended to, there was at the least a problem.

Example E
  a1.   9 is greater than 7
  a2.   Necessarily 9 is greater than 7
  b1.   The number of the planets is greater than 7
  b2.   Necessarily the number of the planets is greater than 7

In Example E, Quine's favourite example, a1 is analytic-necessarily true and a2, where what follows 'Necessarily' is analytic-necessarily true, is true. However 'the number of the planets' is an expression which as things happen to be at present refers to the number 9. (It is a 'referring expression' (Usage 4) (cf. 2.3.3) and nonrigid designator (cf. 2.3.4) (see also 2.4.1, n.39)). So what is said by b1 is the same as what is said by a1 and what is said by b2 is the same as what is said by a2. In the vocabulary of 'statements' (cf. 2.1.3, 2.4) a1 and b1 express the same type statement and so do a2 and b2. But, Quine says, b1 is synthetic-contingent, and b2 is false. So we cannot ascribe necessary truth to what is said (the same type statement) and the truth value of any particular modal (type) statement (a statement starting, or containing, 'Necessarily', 'Not necessarily', etc.) will be true if what is said is expressed in one way, false if it is expressed in another (cf. 2.4.2 (iii)).

Quine suggested that there is a similar difficulty if we take any seemingly synthetic-contingent-empirical example, such as Example B (The earth is round). If we refer to the earth by the expression 'The round earth' we shall arrive at 'The round earth is round', which Quine classed as analytic-necessarily true-*a priori*.

Example F
  a1. The round earth is round
  a2. Necessarily the round earth is round
  b1. The earth is round
  b2. Necessarily the earth is round

In Example F a1 is classed by Quine as analytic-necessarily true, but b1 which says the same is not; a2 is true but b2 is false.

I shall call the argument by which Quine sought to show that even if we could accept 'analytic' as a viable concept, there can be no truths which are necessary or contingent as such, his *Necessity Argument*. If we set it out formally it has two premises.

Necessity Argument
Premise 1: X is Y is necessarily true when and only when 'X is Y' is analytic; or, which comes to the same thing:
Premise 1A: Necessarily X is Y is true when and only when what

follows 'Necessarily', i.e. 'X is Y', is analytic.
Premise 2: All, or most, things said of objects can be expressed by both analytic and non-analytic sentences/propositions.

The conclusion Quine drew was:
Conclusion: What is said (a type statement) is not (always/ever) necessarily true or contingent *as such,*

or, which comes to the same thing:

Conclusion A: When what is said (a type statement) is a modal statement like *Necessarily X is Y*, it is not (always/ever) true or false as such.

3.3.1 Box a

Necessity Argument:
If 1. *X is Y* is necessarily true if and only if 'X is Y' is analytic
and 2. All or most things said of objects may be expressed by
    both analytic and non-analytic sentences/propositions,
then 3. *What is said* (a type statement) is not (always/ever)
    necessarily true or contingent *as such.*

(iii)   What does Quine's Necessity Argument show?

Quine's Necessity Argument is valid, that is, the conclusion follows from the premises. It is not, I shall suggest, sound: the premises are not quite correct, and when they are corrected, the conclusion Quine drew no longer follows. However, the argument does undermine conventionalism *as presented by the Positivists*, even if it does not (I shall suggest) undermine conventionalism *as such* as completely as it has often been taken to do.

(iv)   Necessary truths and non-analytic propositions[14]

Premise 1 of Quine's Necessity Argument (which identifies 'analytic' and 'necessarily true') was, as we have seen, a tenet of positivist accounts of conventionalism.

Quine argued at length that any type statement ('what is said' in Quine) expressed by an analytic proposition (with 'proposition' taken as in 2.1.2) can be re-expressed by a proposition which is not analytic. This appears correct for reasons already considered in 2.4.1. The distinctions drawn in 2.3 help us to formulate it with reasonable precision.

In Example E, '9' is an expression which, with its normal meaning, must refer to a single number and, unlike perhaps 'the square root of −1', the number to which it refers cannot fail to exist. '9', in Kripke's terminology, is a strongly rigid designator. The same is true of '7'. And the proposition '9 is greater than 7' expresses a single type statement, which is necessarily true. However, as we saw in 2.4.1, *any* object can be referred to by an expression which does not have to refer to it. Since there are in fact currently nine planets, the number 9 can be referred to by, for example, the expression 'The number of the planets' (taken to mean 'that number which is the current number of the planets'). The proposition 'The number of the planets is greater than 7'[15] expresses the same type statement as '9 is greater than 7'. But it is clearly not analytic. 'The number of the planets' is a referring expression (Usage 4), and a nonrigid designator: it does not *have* to refer to the number 9 in *all* circumstances since at some other time or in some other solar system the expression could without change of meaning refer to a different number. The proposition 'The number of the planets is greater than 7' therefore need not always make the same type statement, and, in some circumstances (for example, if said in a solar system with five planets), might make a (type) statement which is false.

These considerations, which are set out clearly and convincingly by Quine (1953b: 143–4, 1960: 195–9) are sufficient to show that the Positivist account of the relation between analytic propositions and necessary truths has the consequence, unfortunate to them, that there are no necessary truths: if, as appears to be the case, any type statement expressed by an analytic proposition can also be expressed by a proposition which is not analytic, then there are no type statements which can be expressed *only* by analytic propositions, and hence no category of 'truths that are analytic'.

(v) Contingent truths and analytic propositions

Quine did not present an equally cogent argument for the claim he also made, viz. that any type statement can be expressed by an analytic proposition, and hence, on the Positivist identification of 'analytic' and 'necessarily true', that any type statement can be so expressed as to rate as necessarily true. The argument for the claim that all type statements can be expressed by analytic propositions is not set out in detail. Examples like Example F are very much less convincing support for this claim than Example E is for the claim that all statements can be expressed by non-analytic propositions. And, on consideration, there seems no reason to suppose that this claim is true.

'The round earth is round' in Example F is not a plausible candidate for a proposition which is analytic. One way of putting this point is to say that, although if we make certain choices it cannot express a *false* statement, the expression 'the round earth' could fail to refer in a radical fashion, so that the proposition can fail to make any statement, or that to which it refers could fail to exist at the time when the predicate is applied, so that the statement it makes is not true (but fails of truth value) (cf. 2.2.2). In other words, even if we make choices about when to assign falsity which do not allow 'The round earth is round' to rate as false, this will not allow us to class it as 'analytic' in the sense of being a proposition which must in all circumstances express a *truth*.

A more general way of putting the point that not all statements can be expressed by analytic propositions is that it is not true of all objects that they can be referred to by a strongly rigid designator, i.e. by an expression which satisfies both the condition that it *has* to refer to just one object and the condition that the object to which it refers *has* to exist. It certainly seems a necessary condition of a proposition rating as analytic, as the Positivists conceived of 'analytic propositions', that all the referring expressions (Usage 2) which it contains are strongly rigid.

(vi)   Premise 2 of Quine's Necessity Argument revised
The implication for Quine's Necessity Argument is that Premise 2 should be weakened to:

Premise 2': All type statements expressed by analytic propositions can also be expressed by non-analytic propositions.

(It should omit 'All type statements expressed by non-analytic propositions can also be expressed by analytic propositions', for this does not seem to be true.)

The corresponding conclusion Quine could correctly draw is that, given the Positivist tenet, Premise 1, there are no type statements which are necessarily true, and no type statements of the form 'Necessarily. . .' which are true, as such. With the correction of Premise 2 to Premise 2', he is not entitled to draw the conclusion that 'Necessarily. . .' may not be *false* as such nor that there are no type statements which are *not* necessarily true.

3.3.1   Box b

Necessity Argument: premise 2 revised to 2':

If 1. *X is Y* is necessarily true if and only if 'X is Y' is analytic,

and 2'. All (type) statements expressed by analytic propositions can also be expressed by non-analytic propositions

then 3'. There are no (type) statements which are necessarily true as such.

(vii)   'Analytic' and 'necessarily true'

Premise 1 of Quine's Necessity Argument posits that a truth is necessary if and only if it is expressed by an analytic proposition. Coupled with the fact that *any* truth can be expressed by a proposition which is not analytic, retention of Premise 1 is incompatible with maintaining that there are truths which are necessary as such. Clearly conventionalism as presented by the Positivists is not satisfactory. We cannot both identify 'analytic' and 'necessarily true' (as they did) and maintain (as they also did) that there are truths which are necessary as such. Even without considering the problems of the concept of 'analytic' we can put aside the neat and simple Positivist picture described in 3.2.1.

It is by no means equally evident that conventionalism is to be put aside. Among the facts that seem to emerge from Quine's depiction of his Necessity Argument is that 'necessarily true' is intended to apply to one kind of thing, 'what is said', as Quine expresses it (type statements in the vocabulary of 2.1.3), while 'analytic', 'non-analytic', 'synthetic' distinguish between 'how [they] are said' (type sentences or type propositions). Given that some type statements can be expressed by both analytic and non-analytic propositions, there is no prospect of defining a necessarily true statement to be one which *is* expressed by an analytic proposition and retaining the view that some type statements are as such necessarily true. However, the distinctions Quine makes in the course of his Necessity Argument open the way to a revised account of the relation between 'analytic' and 'necessarily true'.

Quine offers no argument, implicit or explicit, which suggests that 'necessarily true' has to be defined *as* 'analytic' or for assigning truth and falsity to 'Necessarily X is Y' according simply to the analyticity or otherwise of 'X is Y'. In order to attack conventionalism as then accepted, he had no need to: this just was how the relation of 'analytic' and 'necessarily true' was represented. But it does not follow that this particular relation of 'analytic' and 'necessarily true' has to be retained in order to retain a view which rates as 'conventionalist', i.e. in which necessary truths are true because of the meaning of sentences which express them and not because of the way the world has to be. 'Necessary truth' will still *depend on* the analyticity of sentences if instead of positing that a (type) statement rates as necessarily true if and only if it *is* expressed by an analytic proposition, we rule that a (type) statement is necessarily true if and only if it *can* be expressed by an analytic proposition, i.e. by a sentence with a meaning such that it must express a truth whatever the circumstances of its utterance.

3.3.1 Box c

Ruling: A necessary truth is a type statement which *can* be
  expressed by an analytic proposition.

(viii) Premise 1 of Quine's Necessity Argument revised

If this ruling replaces Premise 1 of Quine's Necessity Argument, we arrive at a version from which it can no longer be deduced that no type statements are necessarily true. The fact that any type statement expressed by an analytic proposition can also be expressed by a proposition which is not analytic does not prevent statements expressed by analytic propositions from rating as necessarily true. Since Quine does not succeed in establishing that statements such as that 'The earth is round' (at this or that time) can be expressed by propositions which will rate as analytic, the class of necessary truths remains, in the ruling of 3.3.1 Box c, a particular class of truths, viz. those which *can* be expressed by analytic propositions.

3.3.1   Box d

Necessity Argument: Premises 1 and 2 revised

If 1'. *X is Y* is necessarily true if and only if *X is Y can* be
   expressed by an analytic proposition
and 2'. All (type) statements expressed by analytic
   propositions can be re-expressed by non-analytic
   propositions,
then 3''. If some (type) statements can be expressed by
   analytic propositions, there are necessary truths (all of
   which can also be expressed by non-analytic
   propositions)[16]

(ix)   Positive results of Quine's Necessity Argument

Two results of our discussion of Quine's Necessity Argument are that:

a)   'Analytic', 'non-analytic', and 'synthetic' are terms by which meaningful token declarative sentences may be distinguished into different kinds of type *propositions* (as in 2.1.2). The terms 'necessarily true', 'not necessarily true', 'contingent', on the other hand, are terms for grouping meaningful token declarative sentences into those expressing different kinds of type *statements* (cf. 2.1.3, 2.4); and
b)   The classing of meaningful token declarative sentences into 'analytic', etc. and 'necessarily true', etc. will not coincide: all analytic propositions express necessary truths but not all necessary truths are always expressed by analytic propositions. For example, tokens of the sentence 'The number of the planets is greater than 7' are not analytic even if the proposition expressed is 'That number which is the current number of the planets is greater than 7'. But tokens of this proposition may express the same type statement as

the analytic proposition '9 is greater than 7' and by the ruling of 3.3.1. Box c (a necessary truth is a type statement which can be expressed by an analytic proposition) this is a type statement which is necessarily true.

3.3.1 Box e

'Analytic' is an epithet of certain propositions (cf. 2.1.2) while 'necessarily true' is an epithet of certain type statements.

A necessarily true (type) statement is one which *can* be expressed by (but not only by) an analytic proposition. Cf. 3.3.1 Box c.

3.3.2 Definitions of 'analytic'

(i) Relation of Necessity and Analyticity Arguments

At least as influential as Quine's Necessity Argument in discrediting conventionalism was the attack he made on the concept of 'analytic', which I here call his 'Analyticity Argument'.

Quine's attack on necessary truth was two pronged. On the one hand he tried to show that analyticity, in terms of which conventionalists defined necessary truth, is not a satisfactory concept (his Analyticity Argument). On the other, he argued that even if 'analytic' is acceptable, necessity is not a feature of truths (true type statements) as such (his Necessity Argument).

We have seen that Quine's Necessity Argument, although showing that the Positivist identification of 'analytic' and 'necessarily true' was an oversimplification, does not prove his contention that no class of necessary truths can be distinguished in terms of analyticity. His case against the possibility of distinguishing statements which are necessarily true from ones which are not therefore rests on his claim that analyticity is not an acceptable concept.

3.3.2 Box a

Quine: Analytic is not a satisfactory concept (Analyticity Argument).

Even if analytic were a satisfactory concept, necessity could not be a feature of 'truths', i.e. true (type) statements (Necessity Argument).

(Essentialism (necessary truth without analyticity) is indefensible.)

(ii) Quine's Analyticity Argument

In the course of Positivist discussions of the 'analytic-synthetic' distinction, definitions of the term 'analytic' (and 'synthetic') had proliferated. Quine's attack on 'analytic', put forward in 'Two Dogmas of Empiricism' (Quine (1953a) 1987), which I call his Analyticity Argument, consisted of taking one proposed definition of 'analytic' after another, and finding fault with each. One was circular, a second vague, another made it impossible to prove that any proposition is analytic, or resulted in the class of analytic propositions having no members, or made the distinction between analytic and synthetic one of degree instead of kind, and so on.

The sheer number of definitions examined and points that Quine makes in 'Two Dogmas of Empiricism' certainly made it appear that there must be something seriously amiss with 'analytic'. Many logicians ceased to use the term. Yet the attack was necessarily inconclusive. Demonstration of the deficiencies of any set of definitions of 'analytic' cannot, however large the set, actually prove that there cannot be a satisfactory definition. Apart from the fact that an alleged deficiency may prove not to be one, it is always possible that the set examined is not exhaustive, and that there is after all a definition, inside or outside the set, which escapes the criticisms made (if, on the other hand, difficult to demonstrate that any definition escapes all criticism). This section (3.3.2), examines the main definitions and explications of 'analytic' considered by Quine together with his reasons for rejecting them. This also serves as an introduction to the ways in which this historically very important concept has been seen by philosophers. (It should be noted that in 'Two Dogmas of Empiricism' Quine applied the term

103

?
sentence

'analytic' to 'statements' but without elucidating 'statement', which sometimes renders accurate exposition difficult.)

3.3.2   Box b

Analyticity Argument: definitions of 'analytic' have all been unsatisfactory.

(iii)   Two discarded definitions of 'analytic'

Quine put two definitions of 'analytic' on one side as clearly unsatisfactory.

a)   Contradictory self-contradictory   The first was the popular gloss of analytic 'statements' as those which *cannot be denied without self-contradiction.* Quine's criticism of this account was that it said too little. Indeed, he claimed that this was totally uninformative because self-contradictoriness 'in the quite broad sense needed for this definition of analyticity [i.e. probably 'necessarily not true'] stands in exactly the same need of clarification as does the notion of analyticity itself. The two notions are the two sides of a single dubious coin' (Quine (1953a) 1987: 42). Maybe so. But one way of explaining that Example 1 'Anyone who has brown eyes has eyes' is analytic, viz. has a meaning such that it must express a truth (given the normal meaning of the terms and/or the meaning of the terms in a token of the sentence) is to point out that one cannot make sense of the notion that someone could have brown eyes without having eyes.

b)   Predicate contained in subject   The second definition Quine put on one side was Kant's account of an analytic 'statement' as one *attributing to its subject no more than is already conceptually contained in the subject.* It was Kant who had introduced the words 'analytic' and 'synthetic' and given them this sense (Kant (1781) 1929, A6–10/ B10–18 – see 3.2.1, n.7) but in a section devoted to 'judgments' of subject-predicate form. Interpretation of and extrapolation from his account of 'analytic' and 'synthetic' had always been a matter of conjecture.[17] According to Quine, as to others, Kant's definition suffered not only from limitation to subject-predicate statements but also because the concept of 'containment' is unclear: 'the notion' Quine complained 'is left at a metaphorical level' (Quine (1953a) 1987: 43).

It is worth noting that Locke, probably one of Kant's sources, had used the subject 'containing' the predicate to mean 'includes in its definition', and he spoke of propositions attributing to the subject no more than is already contained in it as all self-evident but he did not treat the description as one which defined even (all) self-evident propositions, much less as defining what were later (for example, by the Logical Positivists) called 'analytic' propositions. It is not absolutely clear that 'analytic' as introduced by Kant was intended to delimit the class of propositions later called 'analytic'. However, we can say that if it was, then it does not seem to be a description which would include all propositions later called 'analytic', viz. all those whose meaning obliges them to express truths.

The description has a further defect, less often noticed. As it stands, it includes, or at least does not clearly exclude, subject-predicate propositions which are not analytic as the term was later employed. This is because the class of propositions attributing to the subject no more than is already contained in it could be taken to include propositions with a subject term whose meaning allows it to fail to secure reference (like 'This can-catching toucan can catch cans') or to refer to something which may not exist at a relevant time (like 'The round earth is round'). Propositions of these sorts were not discussed by Kant – or Locke – so that we cannot tell whether they would have included them as 'analytic'.[18] It is possible that *Quine*'s inclusion of propositions like 'The round earth is round' as analytic in his Necessity Argument (see above 3.3.1 (ii)) rested on a use of 'analytic' extended in this way. But since 'analytic' is certainly intended to be confined to propositions whose meaning obliges them to express a truth, we can say with confidence that this is not a correct use of 'analytic' as understood at the period Quine was writing.

(iv)   Three groups of definitions of 'analytic'

Quine discussed other accounts of 'analytic' in more detail, grouping them into three main sorts: definitions of 'analytic' so that it applies to 'statements' no one would deny, definitions of 'analytic' so that it applies to what is 'true come what may' and definitions of 'analytic' in terms of meaning ('true in virtue of meaning', etc.).

These accounts and Quine's complaints are briefly reviewed in c), d), and e).

c) *'Analytic' as what no one would say was false (or not true)*[19] This account differs from that in a). An 'analytic statement' is not here one which no one could *correctly* deny, but one which no one would *actually* deny. Since anyone might *say* anything at any time, this test of analyticity would mean that no 'statement' could ever be known (by observation) to be analytic: someone might yet deny it. 'It' here was probably intended to be, perhaps among other things, a type sentence. Evidently anyone could utter the *words* 'It is not the case that everyone with brown eyes has eyes', without necessarily denying what is *generally* meant by 'Anyone who has brown eyes has eyes'. Probably too, although this is sometimes questioned, people can assert contradictions and inconsistencies (see 5.2 (iii)).

If 'analytic' were defined as 'what no one would say is false (or not true'), we should not ever be able to be sure that any 'statement' (token declarative sentence) is 'analytic'. However, the definition clearly does not capture what 'analytic' is supposed to mean, viz. with a meaning obliging it to express a truth – so that anyone denying an analytic proposition is mistaken.

d) *'Analytic' as 'true come what may'* Among the best known of Quine's attacks on 'analytic' was his attack on it construed as 'true come what may' (Quine (1953a) 1987, sec. 6: 63). 'True come what may' is more appropriate for defining 'necessarily true' than 'analytic'. Still, it was not uncommonly said that an analytic proposition is one which expresses a truth come what may.

Quine's claim Quine argued that no statement is 'immune to revision' and that there is no statement which might not be preserved in the face of a 'recalcitrant experience', or of all such experiences ('recalcitrant experiences' are ones going contrary to previous experience) (Quine (1953a) 1987, sec. 6: 63–6).

His grounds for this came from the thesis accompanying positivist accounts of 'analytic' and 'synthetic', viz. the uncertainty of empirical/all truths. The Positivists tended to concentrate on the point that one cannot be certain of the *truth* of any statement by empirical means. Quine added the corollary that in that case no statement can be known for certain to be *false*. This follows because if we cannot be certain of the truth of 'X is Y', then we also cannot be certain of the falsity of 'It is not the case that X is Y', and if 'It is not the case that X is Y' cannot be known to be true, then 'X is Y' cannot be known to be false. Quine suggested that any statement can be held to be true whatever happens by discounting apparent contrary evidence, and, on the other hand, that no 'statement' is immune to revision, i.e. any 'statement' might be decided to be false in some circumstance.

This could be taken to have two slightly different consequences, both of which have been attributed to Quine. One is that there are no analytic or synthetic 'statements' as here defined, since there are no statements satisfying the conditions for a statement to be analytic or to be synthetic. The other is that the distinction between 'analytic' and 'synthetic' is not one of kind but only one of degree: the difference between e.g. Example A (Anyone who has brown eyes has eyes) classed as 'analytic' and Example B (The earth is round) classed as 'synthetic' consists only in how likely we are to give them up in the event of a 'recalcitrant experience' – one contrary to our usual or previous experience.

Objections to Quine's claim   A great deal could be and was said about this objection to the analytic-synthetic distinction. Three points deserve mention.

1. It seems evident that the Positivist thesis that we can never be certain of the truth of any statement by empirical means is not consistent with distinguishing what is synthetic-contingent-empirical from the *metaphysical* propositions they regarded as meaningless (see 3.2.1).
2. If we do not accept the Positivist uncertainty thesis (see 3.2.3), then there will be synthetic-contingent-empirical statements/propositions (like 'the earth is round at such and such time') which can be known for certain to be true and which, therefore, cannot *any longer* be shown not to be true by recalcitrant experiences. It is a mistake to try to identify analytic-necessarily true-*a priori* propositions as ones which cannot be shown not to be true since this is a feature shared by *established* propositions/statements of the other category. We might say

107

that they are ones which would be true no matter how the world were ('in all possible worlds'): the world could have been such that the earth was not round but oval, square, or flat, but it could not ever be such that one could have brown eyes without having eyes. This difference could be explained by saying that in the latter case, unlike that of the earth's being round, the meaning of the words precludes the possibility of the or a world being such that the proposition does not express a truth.

3.   A way of discovering or explaining what a sentence means or what it states is to discover/explain the circumstances in which what it expresses is true or false. This encourages the view that we can discover/explain that a sentence expresses an analytic proposition by discovering/explaining that it always expresses a truth, and expresses a non-analytic proposition if there is or could be or could have been a circumstance in which it might not express or might not have expressed a truth. It is not clear that this is the only way in which the meaning of sentences, and hence whether they express analytic propositions, can be discovered/explained. Knowledge of the meaning of the individual words in a sentence might be another method, and the one which enables us to be sure that e.g. 'Anyone who has brown eyes has eyes' has a meaning obliging it to express a truth in any circumstance.

e)   Definitions of 'analytic' in terms of meaning   'Analytic' was not uncommonly explicated as 'true in virtue of meaning', or 'true by definition'. Quine's main criticism of such definitions was that they all rested more or less directly on the concept of 'synonymy', i.e. identity of meaning. This, he said, is in 'no less need of clarification than analytic itself' (Quine (1953a) 1987, sec. 1: 45). He went further, and maintained that synonymy is itself defined in terms of 'analytic'. Hence all accounts of 'analytic' along these lines were circular.

This alleged circularity rested on a definition of 'synonymy' as 'necessary identity of reference', and is fairly clearly not a correct account of identity of meaning. Quine claims that to say that 'X' and 'Y' are synonymous is to say that 'X is Y' or 'X=Y' is analytic/necessarily true, or, in other words, that to say that 'X' and 'Y' have the same meaning is to say that they necessarily refer to the same object (Quine (1953a) 1987, sec. 3: 49–53).

It is easy to see that however identity of meaning is to be explained, this cannot be a correct account. We have already seen in detail that two tokens of the same type word or two type words may have the same meaning without necessarily referring to the same object. There are words which with one meaning can refer to only one object. For example, '9' with the same meaning always refers to the same number, and tokens of the word ('9', 'nine') or of any word with the same meaning, such as 'neuf' in French, will always refer to the same object. These are the terms Kripke calls (strongly) rigid designators (see 2.3.4). But innumerable words are not rigid designators and do not have a meaning such that they always refer to the same object. Many are not of a kind to refer to objects at all, for example 'and' or 'hello'. Of those which are of a kind to refer to objects, many do not have a meaning such that they necessarily refer to just one object (e.g. all referring expressions (Usage 4)/nonrigid designators). Tokens of such type words or expressions do not all have necessarily to refer to the same object even if they have the same meaning. Two tokens of 'he' or of an expression like 'that man' may be identical in meaning. They cannot necessarily refer to the same object since, as we saw in chapter 2, each may refer to something different or to nothing at all. Hence, 'necessarily referring to the same object' is not the, or even a, defining characteristic of identity of meaning as 'identity of meaning' is ordinarily thought of.

It is a little more plausible to suggest that if two token or two type words necessarily refer to the same object then they have the same meaning, i.e. that Quine correctly described a sufficient condition of synonymy even if he did not give the right account of what is necessary for two words to have the same meaning. But even this is not clearly true. It is by no means evident that '9' and '3 × 3' and 'the square root of 81' have an identical *meaning*, even though all these expressions necessarily refer to the same number.

(v) Use of 'analytic'

As I have employed 'analytic', I have made use of the notion of 'necessary' to the extent that I have spoken of a (type) proposition as analytic if and only if it has a meaning such that it must, i.e. necessarily does, express a truth. I have also suggested that this condition is satisfied only by sentences with certain features. A sentence cannot be analytic if, for example, it contains an expression whose meaning allows different tokens of it to refer to different objects (like 'he' or 'that man'), i.e. if it contains a referring expression (Usage 4)/nonrigid designator. It is not evident that this is in any way vicious.

3.3.2   Box c

Quine's arguments against 'analytic' do not appear decisive against defining an analytic proposition as a proposition (in the sense of 'proposition' given in 2.1.2 (iv)) with a meaning such that it must express a truth in any circumstance.

SECTION 4   *ESSENTIALISM*

3.4.1   *Kripke's necessary truths*

Since the 1970s the notion of necessary truth has regained its respectability, mainly as a result of two influential papers by Kripke: 'Identity and Necessity' ((1971) 1977) and *Naming and Necessity* ((1972) 1980). Kripke revived not only the view that there are after all necessary truths but, further, the view that there are necessary truths about *things*.

The principal candidates he put forward as necessary truths about things were certain statements of identity.[20] 'Identity statements between *proper names*', he wrote, 'have to be necessary if they are going to be true at all' (Kripke (1971) 1977: 140; my italics). Examples included not only statements of the form 'X is X' (like 'Kripke is Kripke') but also ones of the form 'X is Y' (like 'Hesperus is Phosphorus'). Necessary identity statements also included what Kripke sometimes called 'theoretical identifications':

> I think that in both cases, the case of names and the case of theoretical identifications [e.g. heat is the motion of molecules, water is H_2O] the identity statements are necessary and not contingent. That is to say they are necessary if *true*: of course, false identity statements are not necessary. (Kripke (1971) 1977: 77; Kripke's italics)

Kripke further proposed that things like 'This lectern' might have 'essential properties'. One such passage opens:

> Another example that one might give relates to the problem of essentialism. Here is a lectern. A question which has often been raised in philosophy is: What are its essential properties? What properties, aside from trivial ones like self-identity, are such that this object has to have them if it exists at all, are such that if an object did not have it would not be this object? For example being made of wood and not of ice, might be an essential property of this lectern. (Kripke (1971) 1977: ibid.; 86–7)

The views Kripke put forward were widely considered to have been *essentialist* views or, in positivist idiom, to make the claim that there are 'synthetic necessary propositions' (Schwartz 1977: 25), and as a result of his work, discussion of necessary truth shifted in focus.

The problems Quine had raised about necessary truth in his Necessity Argument receded into the background. Kripke tended to avoid 'analytic'.[21] But he did offer an account early in *Naming and Necessity*:

> [L]et's just make it a matter of stipulation that an analytic statement is, in some sense, true in virtue of its meaning and true in all possible worlds by virtue of its meaning. Then something which is analytically true will be both necessary and *a priori*. (Kripke (1972) 1980: 39)

3.4.1   Box a

Kripke: (1970s) There are necessary truths. Some necessary truths are about things. Statements of identity 'between proper names' and 'theoretical identifications' are, if true, necessarily true. 'Things' may have other essential properties besides self-identity.

One reason for which Kripke's views about necessary truth are regarded as essentialist in nature is probably because he extended necessary truths beyond ones expressed by analytic propositions. However, there are also reasons for doubt on this score. It is not

3 NECESSARY TRUTH & THE ANALYTIC-SYNTHETIC DISTINCTION

clear exactly what constitutes an 'essentialist' view of necessary truth. Kripke somewhat alters the earlier meaning of 'necessarily true', interpreting it, in his own word, 'weakly' (Kripke (1971) 1977: 68). Additionally one justification for his claims about which statements are necessarily true could be construed as 'conventionalist' in nature.

3.4.2   What is essentialism?

A necessary preliminary to discovering whether Kripke's views are 'essentialist' (or indeed exactly what they are), and important in its own right, is to see what is or may be meant by 'essentialism'. In literature on the subject, 'essentialism' has acquired several somewhat different meanings.

(i)   Essentialism: sense 1 (not analytic)

One sense which can be given to 'essentialism' is that it is the view that there are necessary truths which do not owe their truth to the analyticity of sentences/propositions.

If 'essentialism' is used in this way, then its precise content depends on how 'analytic' itself is used. For example, on Kant's original definition of an analytic judgment as one where the predicate is contained in the subject (see 3.3.2 (iii) b), '7 + 5 = 12' would not count as 'analytic': the sentence '7 + 5 = 12' is not of subject-predicate form, and in at least one sense of 'contained in' '12' is not 'contained in' '7 + 5' (one could know the meaning of '7', '+' and '5' without knowing the meaning of '12', a term one might not have met, and which is not any part of the definition of '7 + 5'). With a re-definition of 'analytic' so that any sentence which must express a truth in all circumstances rates as 'analytic' (see 3.3.2 (v)), '7 + 5 = 12' would be included as 'analytic'.

Kant might be considered an essentialist purely on the grounds that he included the truth that 7 + 5 = 12 as necessary while not including the proposition '7 + 5 = 12' as 'analytic', and indeed calling it, on the contrary, 'synthetic'. But this proposition is 'analytic' in senses of 'analytic' such as 'having a meaning such that it must express a truth', widely employed by others, such as the Positivists. Therefore Kant might be considered after all not to be an 'essentialist' or at least not on the grounds of including the truth that 7 + 5 = 12 as necessary since, in one sense of 'analytic', the proposition expressing this truth rates as 'analytic', so that this example is not one of a necessary truth that does not owe its truth to the analyticity of sentences.

(ii) Essentialism: sense 2 (not meaning of words)

A second, perhaps more plausible sense of the term 'essentialism' is that it is the doctrine whereby there are necessary truths which do not owe their truth to the meaning of words but to the way the world is (or has to be). Mill, who considered essentialism to be a 'fundamental error' and 'an unmeaning figment', seems to have had this sense in mind when he credited Locke with having 'extirpated the parent error' by convincing 'philosophers that the supposed essences of classes were *merely the signification of their names*' (Mill 1843, 1.6.2; my italics).

This sense of 'essentialism' does not make it vary according to the exact sense put on 'analytic'. With 'analytic' taken as 'having a meaning such that it must express a truth', any view which makes necessary truth depend on the analyticity of sentences will be excluded from being an essentialist doctrine. If necessity is taken 'weakly' (so that certain truths are included as necessary which would not be included in the 'strong' sense of 'necessarily true'), then a doctrine which does not rest necessary truth on the analyticity of sentences in this last sense (with a meaning such that they must express a truth) might nevertheless make it depend on the meaning of words, and therefore rate as not essentialist in sense 2, although *as* essentialist in sense 1 of essentialism.

As we shall see (3.4.2–3), Kripke widens the sense of 'necessarily true' to include statements which would not be included in its earlier sense of 'true no matter what', and he offers at least one justification for the inclusion of, for example, true identity statements as necessarily true which makes their truth follow from the meaning of sentences that are not analytic. His views might therefore be ones that should be included as essentialist in sense 1 of the term but not in sense 2.

(iii) Essentialism: sense 3

A third sense that has been given to 'essentialism' is that it is the view that there are necessary truths about *objects* or *things* which are independent of the way that the objects or things are designated.[22] Quine speaks of Aristotelian essentialism as 'the doctrine that some of the attributes of a thing (quite independently of the language in which the thing is referred to, if at all) may be essential to the thing' (Quine (1953c) 1966: 173–4). 'Essentialism' in sense 3 covers at least two different views.

A. Essentialism: Sense 3a (objects) One construction which can be put on the claim that there are necessary truths about *objects* or *things*, independently of how they are designated, is simply that, contrary to Quine's necessity argument, there are *type statements* which are necessarily true independently of the sentence used to express them (i.e. even though there are sentences which can express them whose meaning does not guarantee their truth). If it is agreed that the type statements in question are those which *can* be expressed by analytic propositions (see 3.3.1 Box c), then someone may be an essentialist in this sense (sense 3a) while not being one in either sense 1 or sense 2 – but on the contrary a conventionalist i.e. holding that all necessary truths (necessarily true type statements) owe their truth to the analyticity of sentences with given meanings or to the meaning of words.

The words 'object' and 'thing' are notoriously vague, and essentialism in sense 3a is easily confused with a different view, here distinguished as essentialism Sense 3b.

B. Essentialism: Sense 3b (particulars) Essentialism in sense 3b claims that there are necessary truths about *particulars*, particulars being the paradigm 'things' and qualifying most readily as things in the world. There is more than one version of this claim. The Positivists, for example, allowed that there are necessary truths 'about' open classes of particulars: they considered that propositions of unrestricted generality about particulars (all Xs anywhere anytime are Y, where Xs might be, for example, 'toucans' and Y, for instance 'birds') could be analytic,[23] or in other words that propositions/statements of this form could be classed as necessarily true without concurring with essentialism in sense 1 or 2. However, we might for convenience call these propositions/statements about *kinds* of things and restrict essentialism sense 3b to the view that there necessary truths about *individual* particulars. In this case someone could very easily be an essentialist in sense 3a without being one in sense 3b: it can readily be held that there are necessary truths about things but not about individual particulars.

114

Kripke's claim to be an essentialist might then be due to his claim that there are necessary truths about things that are particulars in the sense of there being, for example, statements asserting the identity of definite particulars (Kripke is Kripke, Hesperus is Phosphorus) which are necessarily true.

Kripke lays no stress on the distinction between particulars and non-particulars (see above 2.3.4) except in so far as his strongly rigid designators (which must secure reference to something which must exist – see 2.3.4) appear to designate only non-particulars like the number 9. Designators which are rigid without being strongly rigid (cannot refer to something different from what they in fact refer to but may fail to refer to anything or what they refer to not exist) include the proper names of particulars, like Kripke, and of non-particulars like 'heat' or 'gold' (see 2.3.4). The important point about particulars in this connection (see above 2.3.3, esp. (iv)) is that they are objects of a kind which must in the last analysis be identified by an expression of the form 'The such and such (person, toucan, table, etc.) in such a place at such a time', and expressions of this sort never *necessarily* secure reference: it is always a contingent and not a necessary matter whether there is/was/will be something answering to a description of this sort. Or to put this another way, it is true of any particular that it might not have existed. Consequently, to hold that there are necessary truths about definite particulars is to hold a view which seems very likely to be combined with adherence to essentialism in sense 2, i.e. with holding that there are necessary truths whose truth is not a result of the meaning of words.

3.4.2 Box a

'Essentialism' has several senses:

Sense 1 (not analytic): There are necessary truths which do not owe their truth to the analyticity of sentences.

Sense 2 (not meaning of words): There are necessary truths which do not owe their truth to the meaning of words.

Sense 3: There are necessary truths about *things*:

Sense 3a) (objects) Type statements may be necessarily true;

Sense 3b) (particulars) Statements making assertions about individual particulars may be necessarily true.

115

The question of whether Kripke should be classed as an essentialist in sense 2 as well as in sense 3b is complicated by the fact that he re-defines 'necessarily true', and any consideration of his views about 'necessary truth' must take account, among other things, of the fact that 'necessary truth' is given a new sense.

3.4.3 Kripke's weak sense of 'necessarily true'

Kripke's re-definition of 'necessarily true', which appears early in his work, is this:

> Let us interpret necessity here weakly. We can count statements as necessary if *whenever the objects mentioned therein exist*, the statement would be true. (Kripke (1971) 1977: 68; my italics).

On this definition a statement can rate as 'necessarily true' even if there are circumstances in which it might *not* be true, as when 'the objects mentioned therein' do not exist. And statements which would not rate as 'necessarily true' in the old sense of 'true no matter what' are included as 'necessarily true'. In some passages there is a further weakening of the notion of 'necessary truth': identity statements are said to be necessary *if true* (see quotations from Kripke above, 3.4.1).

But the initial weakening already explains the inclusion of statements 'between proper names'. Proper names, as opposed to names, are often thought of as the names of particulars (or sometimes closed classes of particulars like families) (see 7.2 on proper names). Kripke does not hold that statements about the existence of particulars are necessarily true, any more than conventionalists like Locke or the Positivists, and in claiming that 'Kripke is Kripke' is a necessary truth, he does not claim that (a particular man named) Kripke necessarily exists. 'Kripke' is a rigid designator: the 'meaning' of a proper name is such that the same proper name cannot apply with the same meaning to different things. But it is not a *strongly* rigid designator: its meaning does not oblige it to refer to just one thing (person) or to something which necessarily exists. The truth which is necessary, according to Kripke, is that *if* the object or person called 'Kripke' exists, then it is necessarily true that Kripke is Kripke.

3.4.3 Box a

Kripke weakens 'necessarily true' so that not only statements true in all circumstances are called 'necessarily true' but also those which are true provided 'the objects therein exist'.

It is worth noticing in passing that certain apparently startling claims which Kripke makes, for instance that the truth of some necessary truths may be known only by empirical means, and not *a priori*, are clearly correct given his sense of 'necessarily true'. On the other hand, the change in the meaning of 'necessarily true' makes it unclear how Kripke takes 'contingent', and therefore difficult to evaluate suggestions such as that there are 'contingent *a priori*' truths.

3.4.4. In what sense is Kripke an essentialist?

The question of the sense in which Kripke is an essentialist is complicated not only by the fact that he re-defines 'necessarily true' (with the result that it is not obvious what his position is with respect to 'necessarily true' in its old sense) but also by the fact that he appears to have two rather different justifications of his view that the statements, especially statements of identity, he considers 'necessarily true', in his sense of 'necessarily true' are necessarily true.

(i) Kripke's old-style justification

One justification is that every true statement of identity owes its truth to the self-evident truth that 'What is, is' or 'Everything is what it is and not another thing'. Thus Kripke says:

> So, as Bishop Butler said, 'everything is what it is and not another thing.' Therefore 'Heat is the motion of molecules' will be necessary, not contingent. . . (Kripke (1971) 1977: 97)

Locke, an opponent of the essentialism of his day, had held 'What is, is' up for ridicule (Locke (1690) 1975, bk IV, chs 7 and 8). Whether this is what statements of identity sometimes or always say will be considered further in 6.2 and 7.2.2.

(ii)   Kripke's new-style justification

The other justification is not made explicit but fits in with much that Kripke says and provides a coherent and fairly successful defence of his position, among other things, against Quine's Necessity Argument.

It will be recalled that Kripke introduces one class of his necessary identity statements as 'between proper names'. It may also have been noticed that his views appear to take no account of Quine's Necessity Argument, which made the point that anything referred to by an expression necessarily referring to it can also be referred to by a different expression which does not necessarily refer to it (see 3.3.1). An obvious corollary is that what is said by an 'identity statement between proper names' can be re-expressed so that the same objects are referred to by expressions which are not proper names. Since it is 'identity statements between proper names' which are supposed to be necessary, the truths they express (which Kripke claims to be necessary truths about things) will rate as after all not necessary, when the same objects are referred to without the use of proper names. On the face of it, this is, at the least, a complication for Kripke's claim that identity statements are necessary even in his weak sense.

Kripke was of course familiar with Quine's Necessity Argument. No serious philosopher was ignorant of it. He also quoted it:

What is Quine's famous example? If we consider the number 9, does it have the property of necessary oddness? Has that number got to be odd in all possible worlds? Certainly it's true in all possible worlds, let's say, it couldn't have been otherwise that *nine* is odd. Of course, 9 could also equally well be picked out as the *number of the planets*. It is *not* necessary, not true in all possible worlds, that the number of the planets is odd. For example if there had been eight planets, the number of the planets would not have been odd. And so it's thought; Was it necessary or contingent that Nixon won the election? (It might seem contingent. . .) . . . . But if we designate Nixon as 'the man who won the election in 1968', then it will be a necessary truth, of course, that the man who won the election in 1968, won the election in 1968. (Kripke (1972) 1980: 40. See also Kripke (1971) 1977: 79–80)

A possible explanation of Kripke's apparent neglect of Quine's Necessity Argument is that he believed that he had tacitly supplied an answer to it, along the lines of treating a statement as necessary if it *can* be expressed in a particular way. In 3.3.1 I suggested that a type statement can be considered to be necessarily true if and only if it can be expressed by an analytic proposition (with a meaning such that it must express a truth in all circumstances). In Kripke's writings, the relevant sentences take a different form which accords with his different sense of 'necessarily true'.

Kripke appears to treat expressions of type statements by means of sentences containing no designators other than *rigid* ones as the test of necessary truth or otherwise. Type statements expressed by such sentences are necessarily true if they are true so long as the objects mentioned therein exist. All identity statements about particulars, as well as non-particulars, may be expressed with the same rigid designator (the name of the object) on either side of 'is'. Thus, for example, 'Kripke is the author of *Naming and Necessity*' may be rendered 'Kripke is Kripke'. In this way all true identity statements rate as necessary, in Kripke's sense of 'necessary'.

On this account, the justification for treating 'Kripke is Kripke' as a sentence/proposition which expresses a necessarily true type statement seems to be that the sentence/proposition 'Kripke is Kripke' must express a truth provided that 'the objects mentioned therein exists, that is, 'Kripke' has a referent and the referent exists, i.e. is alive.

(iii)   Kripke's sense of 'necessarily true' and essentialism

If we accept Kripke's re-definition of a 'necessary truth', then his claims are essentialist in senses 3a and 3b: he presents necessary truths, in his sense, as about things, including particulars. His views are also essentialist in sense 1: his necessary truths extend beyond truths which can be expressed by analytic propositions to truths which can be expressed by sentences like 'Kripke is Kripke' (whose meaning obliges them to express truths not in *all* circumstances but only if 'the objects mentioned therein exist'). It is not clear that Kripke rates as an essentialist in sense 2 of the term, for it appears as if his reason for classing for example identity statements between proper names as in his sense necessarily true is that the meaning of the words is of a particular sort, viz. such that they must express a truth provided all the objects mentioned therein exist.

119

(iv)   Necessary truth and Kripke's essentialism

There is no obvious answer to the question of whether Kripke is an essentialist with respect to necessary truths in the *old* sense, i.e. true no matter what, since this is not a question he considers. However, there are no arguments supplied for including statements about individual particulars as necessary truths in the 'true no matter what' sense; and it seems to be precisely to include statements not necessarily true in the old sense (statements of identity about *particulars*) *as* necessarily true that Kripke widens the sense of 'necessarily true'. We may perhaps infer that Kripke did not consider essentialism in sense 3b (particulars) to be true of necessary truths in the earlier sense of 'necessarily true'. We cannot reasonably guess whether or not he believes the old sort of necessary truth to rest on analytic sentences or the meaning of words, i.e. whether he thinks essentialism in sense 1 (not analytic) or 2 (not meaning of words) is correct in their case.

3.4.4   Box a

Kripke's doctrine is essentialist concerning *his* sense of
'necessarily true' (see 3.4.3 Box a) in senses 1 (not
analytic), 3a (objects) and 3b (particulars), but probably
not in sense 2 (not meaning of words).
It is not possible to establish whether Kripke is an essentialist
or not in any sense of 'essentialism' with regard to the *old*
sense of necessarily true, i.e. true no matter what.

SECTION 5   *MODIFIED CONVENTIONALISM*

3.5.1   *Modification of the relations between 'analytic' and 'necessarily true'*

We have seen that the conventionalism advanced by the Positivists is not tenable as it stands. The new work on reference showed that *any* type statement can be expressed by a non-analytic proposition. To retain a class of necessary truths defined in terms of analytic propositions it is therefore necessary to distinguish them as those type statements not which *are* but which *can be* expressed by an analytic proposition (a sentence with a meaning obliging it always to express a truth). Since, contrary to a premise of Quine's Necessity Argument, not all statements, but only those customarily thought of as necessarily true, can be expressed by an analytic proposition, this modification of the relations of necessarily true type statements and analytic propositions supplies a clear and acceptable way of distinguishing meaningful declarative token sentences into those that express necessarily true type statements and those that do not (see 3.3.1). Thus, a word processor which could sort token declarative sentences into meaningless and meaningful, and into propositions, i.e. into those having the same and different meanings (cf. 2.1), should also be able to class them into those with a meaning such that they must express a truth in all circumstances (analytic propositions) and those which may not express truths (non-analytic propositions). The former (analytic propositions) would all express necessary truths, and so would any token sentence which could be found to express the same type statement as any proposition identified as analytic by the word processor.

This account of necessary truth is conventionalist in the sense that all necessary truths owe their truth to the meaning of words/analyticity of sentences, and that none of them says anything about 'things in the world'. Because 'essentialism', traditionally opposed to conventionalism, is sometimes defined in a fashion making it compatible with conventionalism in these senses (see essentialism Sense 3a (objects): 3.4.2), this doctrine, which I call 'modified conventionalism', cannot be considered non-essentialist in *every* sense of the term 'essentialism'.

I have suggested that Kripke's views, generally regarded as essentialist, may possibly be classifiable as *not* essentialist in sense 2 (not meaning of words) but that he includes a somewhat different range of true type statements as necessarily true than has been usual. This is effected by a deliberate 'weakening' of the meaning of 'necessarily true' so that possible non-existence of the objects that a statement is about does not of itself exclude them from the 'necessarily true' class. The principal newcomers are statements of identity about particulars.[24] The mechanism for distinguishing necessary truths in the new sense is by whether sentences expressing them which contain only *rigid* designators have a meaning obliging them to express a truth provided that the objects mentioned exist.

It remains an open question what useful purpose is served by changing the meaning of 'necessarily true' in this way, and for the purposes of this book I shall retain the traditional sense of 'necessarily true' whereby it means 'true no matter what' and requires expressibility by a sentence with a meaning obliging it to express a truth in all circumstances, which I term an 'analytic' proposition.

3.5.1 Box a

It is convenient to retain the old sense of 'necessarily true', i.e. true no matter what, and to use 'analytic' in the sense 'with a meaning such that it must express a truth'.

Old conventionalism: analytic = necessarily true.

Modified conventionalism: All analytic propositions express necessary truths. A necessarily true type statement is one which *can be* expressed by an analytic proposition. (All necessary truths can also be expressed by non-analytic propositions.)

It should be noted that essentialism Sense 3a (objects) is not incompatible with modified conventionalism.

3.5.2 *Modification of 'synthetic'*

The modification of the relations between 'analytic' and 'necessarily true' has the consequence that necessarily true statements may be expressed by propositions which are not analytic, and the question arises as to whether or not these non-analytic propositions should be termed 'synthetic'.

In the heyday of Positivist conventionalism, when it was believed that all meaningful 'propositions' were either analytic-necessarily true-*a priori* or synthetic-contingent-empirical, 'synthetic propositions' were treated both as

1. those meaningful propositions which are not analytic, *and* as
2. contingent propositions/statements.[25]

A proposition like 'That number which is the (current) number of the planets is greater than 7' is not analytic (its meaning does not oblige it to express a truth) but it expresses necessary and not contingent statements. If the number in question is 9, so that the statement expressed is the same type statement that is expressed by '9 is greater than 7', it expresses a necessary truth. Were the number 5, it would express a necessarily false statement. If a proposition of this sort is classed as 'synthetic', then the traditional link between 'contingent' and 'synthetic' disappears: we can then have 'synthetic' propositions which express necessary and not contingent statements. The alternative is to class such propositions as *not* synthetic because they do not express contingent statements. In this case there are meaningful propositions which are neither analytic nor synthetic, and the neat Positivist division of all (meaningful) propositions into 'analytic' and 'synthetic' breaks down. These terms remain mutually exclusive (no sentence can, with a single meaning, be both analytic and synthetic) but they are not *exhaustive* of the class of (meaningful) propositions.

Since we have the term 'non-analytic' at our disposal, it seems sensible to use it to refer to (meaningful) propositions which are not analytic and to reserve 'synthetic' for the sub-class of propositions whose meaning is such that they express (or express only) contingent statements, i.e. statements whose truth value depends on how the world happens to be. The pristine simplicity of Positivist conventionalism cannot in any case be preserved since it neglected the complications introduced by studies of reference, and, among the advances brought about by this work, is that propositions may be susceptible of more sophisticated classification than into just 'analytic' and 'synthetic'.

3.5.2   Box a

In old conventionalism 'synthetic' meant *both* meaningful
proposition which is not analytic *and* expressing a
contingent statement. Since there are non-analytic
propositions which express not contingent but necessary
statements, both meanings cannot be preserved.

Ruling: 'Synthetic' will be restricted to propositions expressing
contingent statements. The term 'non-analytic' covers *both*
synthetic propositions *and* propositions which are not
analytic for other reasons (e.g. because they may express
either a necessarily true or a necessarily false statement).

NOTES

1. See Sloman 1965 for description of these senses of the terms –
    unfortunately all applied to the same kind of item which he calls
    'proposition'.
2. See for example Ayer (1936) 1946, ch 4, Waismann 1965 (posth.),
    ch. 3.
3. The problem discussed in 2.2 as to whether one should say that no
    statement is made or one is made which is not true or false when
    there is radical reference failure was replicated over whether a
    meaningless token sentence should be said to express no proposition
    or a proposition which is not meaningful. The former is the more
    consistent choice. (See 5.2.6 for further discussion.)
4. This and other difficulties are discussed later: see 3.3.2 (iv) d), 3.5.2,
    4.3.2. Here and throughout 'Positivist' refers to the Logical Positivists
    (see Glossary).
5. Locke often used 'All gold is malleable'. See Locke (1690) 1975, e.g.
    3.6.35, 4.6.9–10.
6. See e.g. Pears 1953, Brotman 1956.
7. The terms 'analytic' and 'synthetic' were coined by Kant (1781)
    1929: Introduction IV, A6–10/B 10–18: see 3.2.3 (iii) b). Leibniz
    distinguished 'truths of reason' and 'truths of fact' (Leibniz (1720)
    1898, secs 31–7, (1765) 1981: 49–51, 361–76, etc.), Hume 'relations of
    ideas' and 'matters of fact' (Hume (1748) 1894, sec. IV, esp.
    paras 20–2). 'Analytic' and 'synthetic' did not become common terms
    in English until the mid-nineteenth century: Kant's *Critique* was not
    translated into English until 1838. In the first edition of Mill 1843,
    Mill did not use the terms: he added them in a note to the 5th edition
    of 1862 (see Wolfram 1978: 30–4).
8. See Wolfram 1978: 42–4.

9. See Locke (1690) 1975, bk 4, chs 7 and 8. This account of Locke's views is elaborated in Wolfram 1978 and 1980. In these papers I claim, among other things, that Locke identified 'self-evident' (and not 'analytic') with 'trifling', and has been misinterpreted in particular by assuming that he meant 'telling us about the world' by 'instructive'.

10. It was not initially appreciated that these conditions might be satisfied without the propositions being analytic at all. In Strawson (1957) 1971, Strawson gave the example of 'If he is sick, then he is sick' – where so far as meaning is concerned 'he' could refer either to the same or different people, in the latter case clearly not expressing a necessary truth.

11. 'Cats are not always dogs' might be preferred as a necessary truth which can be known to be true by empirical as well as *a priori* means – see below 4.3.2 (i).

12. See Wolfram 1975: 230–46 for a more detailed version of the argument in 3.3.1.

13. In the literature that followed, it was not always noticed that Quine's ascriptions of truth and falsity to statements of the form 'Necessarily . . .' (a mode of expression he preferred to that of speaking of ascriptions of necessary truth to non-'modal' statements) depended on nothing more mysterious than whether or not the proposition following 'necessarily' was analytic. Quine was quite explicit on the point: 'The general idea of strict modalities is based on the putative notion of *analyticity* as follows: a statement of the form "Necessarily. . ." is true if and only if the component statement which "necessarily" governs is analytic' (Quine 1953b: 143; Quine's italics. See also Quine 1960: 195–6). His ascriptions of 'true' and 'false' in particular cases are entirely consistent with such statements, i.e. Quine ascribes 'true' to 'necessarily' followed by what he considers an analytic sentence, 'false' when it is followed by a sentence which is not analytic.

14. 'Non-analytic' is used in preference to 'synthetic' because an effect of Quine's Necessity Argument is to display an ambiguity of 'synthetic' considered in 3.5.2.

15. Taken to mean 'That number which is the current number of the planets is greater than 7'; cf. 2.4.1 (ii), n.39.

16. It should be noted that the substitution of Premise 1' for Premise 1 would not lead to a conclusion satisfactory for conventionalism if combined with Quine's original Premise 2: if all type statements could be expressed by *analytic* propositions, as Quine suggests but does not successfully demonstrate, then the introduction of Premise 1' would lead to all truths rating as necessarily true. With the replacement of the original Premise 2 by 2' this untoward conclusion does not result.

17. See Wolfram 1978: 38–43 for discussion of this point.

18. Locke may well have been aware of a problem in this direction: his examples conspicuously never take the form '*This* X is an X', i.e. he probably excluded such propositions. See Wolfram 1978: 41–2.

19. This group appears at greater length in Quine 1960, sec. 14: 66.
20. Kripke uses the word 'statement' but its exact sense is not quite certain.
21. In 'Identity and necessity' he confined himself to 'a prioricity and necessity' Kripke (1971) 1977: 84. In *Naming and Necessity*, he said: 'Another term used in philosophy is "analytic". Here it won't be too important to get any clearer about this in this talk' (Kripke (1972) 1980: 39). Or again: 'I have not attempted to deal with the delicate problems regarding analyticity in these lectures. . .' (Kripke (1972) 1980: 122, n.63).
22. See e.g. Cartwright (1968) 1987, or Quine (1953c) 1966: 173–4.
23. It will be recalled that 'All Xs anywhere anytime' was construed without 'existential import': i.e. did not claim that there are Xs, being taken as 'Nothing is/was/will be X and not Y' or 'If anything is X, it is Y' (1.1.1 (iv) c).
24. And possibly about 'natural kinds'. See 7.1.
25. This view can still be found for example in Swinburne (1975) 1987: 177. See also 4.3.2 on 'contingent'.

QUESTIONS

When you have read this chapter, or sections in it, you may like to try your hand at these questions, and/or to keep them in mind when doing some or all of the suggested reading. Questions are framed *primarily* on specified sections, but material from other sections may help with answers. You may also like to try the examination questions on this chapter in the Appendix.

3.1
1. Is it plausible to suggest that 'analytic' really applies to propositions but 'necessarily true' to statements?
2. Can you explain the kinds of issue at stake between conventionalism, scepticism, and essentialism?

3.2
3. Why do conventionalists attach so much importance to the division between analytic, etc. and synthetic, etc.? Do you think there is an important distinction here?
4. Should 'self-evidence' be distinguished from 'logical truth'?

3.3
5. How can necessary truth be salvaged from the difficulty that necessary truths can be expressed by non-analytic propositions?

6. Do you think that any of Quine's 'reservations' about 'analytic' justified its expulsion from logic?

3.4

7. Does Kripke's alteration of the meaning of 'necessarily true' serve a useful purpose?
8. In what ways are Kripke's doctrines incompatible with a) conventionalism, b) scepticism?

3.5

9. What can we now make of the 'analytic–synthetic distinction'?
10. Can you draw a map of the relations between 'analytic', 'necessarily true', 'synthetic', and 'contingent'? Is one of the terms (e.g. 'analytic') the primary one, by means of which the rest are defined?

SOME SUGGESTED READING

For guidance on a sensible order in which to do some or all this reading, consult references in text and notes. Not all the references given in this chapter are included in the list of suggested reading, and reading can be extended by following up other references in text and notes.

Ayer, A. J. (1936) 1946, *Language, Truth and Logic*, London: Gollancz, ch. 4: 71–86.
Cartwright, R. (1968) 1987, 'Some Remarks on Essentialism', *Journal of Philosophy* LXV (1968), repr. in R. Cartwright, *Philosophical Papers* 1987.
Grayling, A. C. 1982, *An Introduction to Philosophical Logic*, ch. 3.
Hume, D. (1748) 1894, *An Enquiry Concerning Human Understanding*, sec. IV, pt I.
Kant, I. (1781) 1929, *Critique of Pure Reason*, Introduction, esp. IV and V (A6–10/B10–18).
Kripke, S. (1971) 1977, 'Identity and Necessity', in M. K. Munitz (ed.) *Identity and Individuation* 1971, repr. in S. P. Schwartz (ed.) *Naming, Necessity and Natural Kinds* 1977.
—— (1972) 1980, *Naming and Necessity*, first published in G. Harman and D. Davidson (eds) *Semantics and Natural Lan-*

guage 1972 (some excerpts in P. K. Moser (ed.) *A Priori Knowledge* 1987).

Leibniz, G. W. (1720 in German, posth.) 1898, *The Monadology*, secs 31–7.

—— (1765 in French, posth.) 1981, *New Essays Concerning Human Understanding*: 49–51, 361–76.

Locke, J. (1690) 1975, *An Essay Concerning Human Understanding*, bk 4, chs 7 and 8.

Mill, J. S. 1843 et seq., *A System of Logic*, bk 1, ch. 6.

Quine, W. V. O. (1953a) 1987, 'Two Dogmas of Empiricism' in W. V. O. Quine, *From a Logical Point of View* 1953, reprinted in many places including P. K. Moser (ed.) *A Priori Knowledge* 1987.

—— 1953b, 'Reference and Modality' in W. V. O. Quine, *From a Logical Point of View* 1953.

—— 1960, *Word and Object*, esp. secs 14 and 41.

Sloman, A. 1965, ' "Necessary", "A Priori", and "Analytic" ', *Analysis*, vol. 26 (1965).

Swinburne, R. J. (1975) 1987, 'Analyticity, Necessity and Apriority', *Mind*, vol. 84 (1975), repr. in P. K. Moser (ed.) *A Priori Knowledge* 1987.

Waismann, F. (1965) (posth.), *The Principles of Linguistic Philosophy*, ch. 3.

Wolfram, S. 1975, 'Quine, Statements and "Necessarily True" ', *Philosophical Quarterly*, vol. 25 (1975).

—— 1978, 'On the Mistake of Identifying Locke's Trifling-instructive Distinction with the Analytic–synthetic Distinction', *The Locke Newsletter*, no. 9 (1978).

—— 1980, 'Locke's Trifling-Instructive Distinction – a Reply', *The Locke Newsletter*, no. 11 (1980).

Chapter 4

ASPECTS OF TRUTH

Most of us, most of the time, do not have too much trouble operating the notions of truth and falsity. Some of the distinctions made by logicians, discussed in other chapters, may well not be formulated by many of us in our day-to-day thinking, but the question of truth as against not truth, we encounter all the time. This is not to say that we always think that we know whether or not something is true. But the idea that something is or is not true is an everyday notion most of us handle without undue difficulty. Logicians however have found the concept extremely troublesome. This chapter discusses a few of the problems that have been raised.

SECTION 1   *RELATIONS BETWEEN* P *AND* P IS TRUE

It is commonly held that a statement and the statement that that statement is true, represented by 'p' and 'p is true', have, and must have, the same truth value, so that they are 'equivalent' (see 1.1.1 (ii) on equivalence).[1] This has resulted in problems such as why, in that case, we should ever say 'p is true' instead of saying just 'p'. This section examines the 'equivalence' of 'p' and 'p is true'.

4.1.1   *Preliminary assumptions*

For purposes of exposition, I shall begin by assuming that the correct subjects of the predications 'is true' and 'is false' are type statements, and further that p in 'p' and 'p is true' represents the *same* type statement.[2] These assumptions, which will be discussed later (see 4.1.6), involve leaving on one side, on the one hand, mispredications of 'is true', mispredications being predications of 'is true' to anything that is not a type statement, and, on the other hand, radical reference failure on the part of 'p' in 'p is true'. For the present we are making the following assumptions.

Assumption 1: 'Is true' is not mispredicated.

If any sentence predicates 'is true' or 'is false' of something which is *not* a type statement, it cannot make a true statement.[3]

Example A
 That chair is true
 That question is false

The sentences in Example A cannot express true statements (even if the subject expressions secure reference). The meaning of the subject and predicate words precludes the predicate from applying to the subject, with the result that the sentences cannot express a truth. We are assuming that what is represented as 'p is true' does not have this defect: 'p' is a type statement.

Assumption 2: 'p' in 'p is true' makes a successful reference.

If a token sentence of the form '. . .is true' or '. . .is false' has an expression referring to a type statement as its subject term, but there is no such statement and reference fails radically, then it does not make a true or false statement. (On Option 2 in 2.2.2 (ix) and by the ruling introduced in 2.2.2 Box d, it makes no statement.)

Example B
 The policeman's statement is true
 when 'the policeman's statement' radically fails to refer, makes no statement.

We are assuming that what is expressed as 'p is true' does not have this defect: 'p' successfully refers to a type statement. If 'p' in 'p is true' successfully identifies a type statement, then 'p is true' will make a statement, which is itself assessable for truth value.

We need a further supposition to reach the position that *p* and *p is true* always have the same truth value:

Assumption 3: There are only two truth values, true and false.

If there are only two truth values, true and false, then a statement of the form *p is true*, where *p* represents a successfully identified statement will be true if *p* is true and false if *p* is false. In other words, a statement ascribing truth to another statement, *p*, always has the same truth value as that statement, viz. *p*.

4.1.1 Box a

If *p* in *p is true* is a successfully identified type statement, and we operate with only two truth values, true and false, then *p* and *p is true* always have the same truth value.

4.1.2 Why p *and* p is true *have the same truth value*

It is important to see that the identity of truth value of a statement (*p*) and the statement that that statement is true (*p is true*) arises from nothing more profound than the fact that we normally operate with only two truth values, true and false.

However many truth values are in use, the truth value of statements ascribing truth value (*p is true*/*p is false*/*p fails of truth value* (see 2.2.2, esp. Box a)) must *depend on* the truth value of the statements to which they ascribe truth value i.e. on the truth value of *p*. With only two truth values, true and false, we have a simple picture.

Table 1 To show the truth values of ascriptions of truth value to p, with two truth values

p	*p is true*	*p is false*
T	T	F
F	F	T

In this table (and Table 2), T represents 'is true', F represents 'is false'. The truth values of any statement p are depicted in the left-hand column and resultant truth values of the statements *p is true* and *p is false* are shown horizontally for each value of p.

The dependence of the truth value of *p is true* and *p is false* on the truth value of *p* need not give rise to *p* and *p is true* always having the same truth value in the way that they do in Table 1. If a third truth value, let us say 'failing of truth value', is introduced (see 2.2.2 (iii)–(iv)), the relations of the truth values of *p is true*, etc. to the truth values of p are more complicated than if we operate with two truth values. In particular, *p is true* and *p* will not always have the same truth value: their truth values differ if *p* fails of truth value, for *p is true* is then false. The chart of relations between the truth value of *p* and the truth value of ascriptions of truth value for this case is shown in Table 2.

Table 2   To show the truth values of ascriptions of truth value to *p*, with three truth values

p	*p is true*	*p is false*	*p F'*
T	T	F	F
F	F	T	F
F'	F	F	T

See Table 1 for notation. In this table F' represents 'fails of truth value'.

4.1.2   Box a

If we operate with more than two truth values, *p* and *p is true* do not always have the same truth value.

4.1.3   p *and* p is true *are not the same type statement*

The identity of truth value between an (identified) type statement (*p*) and the statement that that statement is true (*p is true*) which occurs when we assume only two truth values, true and false, is not infrequently supposed to show that *p* and *p is true* are 'equivalent' in a sense of 'equivalent' stronger than that they always have the same truth value.[4] In particular, it has been held that they state the same or have to state the same (or that sentences expressing them mean the same or have to express the same statement or statements of the same truth value (see 4.1.4)). So it should be noted that:

1.   *Identity of truth value is not sufficient to delimit one type statement*
It is obvious that two (token) statements having the same truth value is not a sufficient condition of their being one and the same type statement: there are, as we are supposing, only two truth values (or at most, three) while there is an indefinite number of type statements.

2. *Necessary identity of truth value is not sufficient to delimit one type statement*

a) That two (token/type) statements *have* to have the same truth value is also not a sufficient condition of their being the same statement: every necessarily true statement has to have the same truth value as every other, viz. true, but there are many different necessary truths. These are considered to be different (type) statements because they are about different objects (e.g. *9 is greater than 7* is not the same statement as *8 is greater than 7*), or say something different about the same objects (e.g. *9 is greater than 7* is not the same statement as *9 is greater than 6*), or both (e.g. *9 is greater than 7* is not the same statement as *Anyone who has brown eyes has eyes*).

b) That two propositions (as 'propositions' were described in 2.1.2 (iv)) have a meaning obliging them to express statements of the same truth value is equally not a sufficient condition of them expressing the same statement: all analytic propositions have a meaning obliging them to express statements of the same truth value, viz. true, but they do not all express the same statement (see examples above in 2a).

4.1.3   Box a

Given the three assumptions in 4.1.1, the statements *p* and *p is true* are 'equivalent' in the sense of having to have the same truth value. It does not follow that they are 'equivalent' in the sense of being the same statement.

Despite their close relations, given the three assumptions we are making, *p* and *p is true* cannot *be* the same type statement, since, as it has been pointed out,[5] *p is true* is about the statement that p, whereas *p* itself will not (normally) be about *p* (itself) but about some other subject (a nearby toucan for example) and what is said in *p* is not that p is true but that its subject has some property or other (can catch a can, for example). (For *p* to be about p, i.e. itself, it would have to be a puzzle-style case, sometimes formulated as 'This statement is. . .'; to suppose *p* also to predicate the same as *p is true*, *p* would have to take the form 'This statement is true'. Such cases might well be excluded as being no statements at all.)

4.1.3   Box b

p and *p is true* cannot be the same type statement since the
subject of *p* is not normally *p* nor the predicate normally 'is
true'.

4.1.4   *Propositions expressing* p *and* p is true

Still assuming that *p* represents the same type statement in both *p*
and *p is true* and that there are only two truth values, we can easily
see that the sentences/propositions/expressions representing *p* in
the two cases (i.e. in *p* and *p is true*) need not have the same
meaning nor meanings obliging them to express the same
statement or statements of the same truth value.

Example C
   I say 'My cat is on the mat' (*p*). You say (referring to the same
   cat and mat) '(The statement that) your cat is on the mat is
   true', or perhaps 'Your statement is true' (*p is true*).

In Example C, the truth value of *p is true* depends on the truth
value of *p* in a regular fashion: if and only if *p* (my statement) is
true is *p is true* (the statement that my statement is true) true, but
'My cat is on the mat' and '(The statement that) your cat is on the
mat is true' are not sentences which are identical in meaning nor
sentences which have a meaning such that they have to make
either the same statement or statements with the same truth value.
'Your statement' may be used to refer to the statement made by
'My cat is on the mat', but is obviously not identical in meaning to
'My cat is on the mat', and it does not *have* to refer to the statement
made by my token sentence 'My cat is on the mat' (nor to a
statement of the same truth value).[6]

4.1.5   p *in* p is true *need not be a 'formulated' statement*

It is a convention of, at least, English that in order to assert
something, it is normally necessary to utter/write a sentence which
expresses a statement. Similarly to ask a question or give a
command it is normally necessary to utter or write a sentence

which expresses a question or command.[7] 'Normally' is inserted because it could be said that sometimes we assert something or ask a question or give commands by smiles, frowns, nods, winks, etc. A token sentence which expresses a statement *p* is sometimes called a *formulated* statement or a *formulation* of *p*. Although a statement must be formulated to be *asserted* (i.e. there must be a token sentence expressing it which is uttered/written), no statement *p* has to be formulated in order to be successfully *referred* to. A (type) statement can be identified in other ways, for example, as 'your statement', that is, as the statement made by a particular token sentence, the token sentence in question being identified as the one uttered by a particular person at a particular time, or, for instance, as the statement made by the third token sentence on page 10 of a particular book.

Many tokens of the same or different type sentences/propositions can express the same type statement *p* (see 2.1.3 and 2.4.1 (ii)), and each of these tokens can be referred to in a variety of different ways ('The policeman's statement', 'your statement', 'his statement', etc.). We might certainly wish to say that there must *be* a formulation of any successfully identified statement (i.e. a type sentence/proposition which can be used to express that statement), but there can be references to definite individual statements in which the statements are not identified through a formulation of them. (Such references can be inessential, i.e. what the speaker really means to refer to is a particular formulated statement, the statement that a particular toucan can catch cans, for example. But they can also be essential: the speaker means to refer to that statement which X made – see 2.2.2 (vi)–(vii).)

From the formulation of Assumption 2 (see above 4.1.1: that 'p' in 'p is true' makes a successful reference) it might look as if successful reference to statements had to be to a definite individual statement. But the supposition of successful reference does not really involve this. Ascriptions of truth value to statements are not confined to predicating 'is true' or 'is false' of *individual* statements. (Assumption 2 could be re-phrased: 'p' in 'p is true' does not fail to secure reference.) Since we can speak of one type statement, we can also quantify over statements and speak of 'some statements', 'all statements', 'six statements', and make such statements as that 'Some of the statements he made are true', 'All statements made by analytic propositions are true', 'One statement in each numbered set of statements on this examination paper is true (mark it)'. In such cases it would not always be possible to represent the subject expression by a formulated statement or set of formulated statements, even although it remains the case that the truth value of '. . . is true' depends on the truth value of statements it is about. (At least one statement he made must be true for 'Some of the statements he made are true' to be true, etc.) 'The statements he made' form a closed class each of whose members could be formulated, and what is said about them, viz. that some are true, could be re-expressed as 'Some of the following statements are true' followed by sentences expressing the statements he made. But where open classes are in question this is not possible: for example, we cannot formulate *all* the statements made by analytic sentences as a means of referring to some or all of them.[8]

4.1.5   Box a

In order for something to be *asserted*, it must be 'formulated', i.e. expressed by a sentence which expresses the statement in question.

A statement may be *referred to* without being formulated, e.g. as 'the policeman's statement'.

There must *be* a formulation of an individual statement, i.e. some sentence which expresses it. But references to statements include ones to some or all of a group. In some of these cases there may not be a way of formulating the statements referred to.

4.1.6   Relaxing Assumptions 1 and 2

Still retaining the suppositions that truth value is correctly ascribed to type statements and that there are only two truth values, true and false, let us now relax the other two assumptions we have been making.

(a)   Relaxing Assumption 1 (that 'is true' is not mispredicated)

In agreeing that p and p *is true* always have the same truth value, we have assumed that p always represents a type statement (treated as the correct subject of predications of truth value).

However, we must take account of the fact that since only certain sorts of things (assumed to be type statements) *could* have truth value, it is possible to mispredicate 'is true' or 'is false' by predicating them of something which could not have a truth value, that is, to which it does not make sense to ascribe either 'is true' or 'is false'. In this case, on the face of it, the statements making the ascriptions of truth or falsity have a truth value, viz. false, while that to which truth value is ascribed does not have a truth value. If '*p*' were allowed to represent anything to which truth value might be ascribed, including chairs and questions, then the case of mispredication could be described by saying that *p* has no truth value while *p is true* is false. Thus, it is clearly not correct to say that in *any* statement predicating 'is true' of *anything*, that of which 'is true' is predicated has the same truth value that it has itself. In other words, when we relax assumption 1 it is no longer true that *p* and *p is true* always have the same truth value. We can infer that identity of truth value between the two holds only if both *p* and *p is true* are type statements (or whatever it is to which it is correct to ascribe truth value).

It might be argued that mispredications of 'is true' do not really form an exception to the rule that a statement predicating 'is true' has the same truth value as its subject. The argument would be that sentences like 'That chair is true' or 'That question is false' do not have a meaning and so express no proposition or no meaningful proposition, and hence express no statement. Since if 'is true' is mispredicated no statement results, this is not after all a case of *p* and *p is true* having different truth values since neither has a truth value.

There are two difficulties about this argument. First, it is not clear that sentences like 'That chair is true' and 'That question is false' should be said to lack meaning, as opposed to being treated (as above) as sentences/propositions with a meaning such that if they make a statement, it is a false one (or possibly fails of truth value because an object referred to does not exist at a relevant time). This is further discussed in 5.2.6. Secondly, the same statements that may be said to be made by 'That question is false' could be made by means of sentences which clearly have a meaning. 'What the policeman said is false' is a sentence with a perfectly respectable meaning, which could express a truth. However, its subject expression 'What the policeman said' might on some occasion secure reference to a question, so that the statement it makes must be false. The statement ascribing truth is false but that to which truth is ascribed is not false but of no truth value whatever. We might perhaps say it necessarily has no truth value.

(b)   Relaxing Assumption 2 (that 'p' in 'p is true' makes a successful reference)

In Example B we supposed that in 'The policeman's statement is true' 'The policeman's statement' fails to refer in a radical way. (The expression is used essentially and there was no policeman or the identified policeman made no statement.) In this case, by the ruling in 2.2.2 (ix) Box d, 'The policeman's statement is true' fails to make a statement and there is no such thing as 'the policeman's statement'. This possibility creates no difficulty for the view that a type *statement p* and a statement ascribing truth to that statement (*p is true*) always have the same truth value. In this case, described in this way, we have no type statement *p* and also no type statement *p is true*. We do have a token sentence of the form 'The statement p is true', and need to note that not all token sentences of the form 'The statement p is true' express statements of the same truth value as the statement they are about (since sometimes they fail to make a statement and are about nothing). We also need to note that if, instead of adopting the ruling in 2.2.2 (ix) Box d (whereby a proposition containing an expression which fails radically to refer is said to make no statement), we reverted to the Theory of Descriptions, and treated propositions containing an expression that radically fails to refer as making false statements, then the case of radical reference failure in a proposition ascribing 'is true' to a statement would provide a further exception to the rule that the subject of ascriptions of 'is true' always has the same truth value as the ascribing statement. Describing the subject here as '*p*', this would be a case where *p* is non-existent while *p is true* has the truth value false.[9]

4.1.6   Box a See also 4.1.2 Box a.

Mispredications of 'is true' or radical reference failure of its subject term may result in cases where *p* and *p is true* do not have the same truth value since *p is true* may rate as false while *p* is not false, but of no truth value or non-existent.

SECTION 2 *ASCRIPTIONS OF TRUTH AND ASSERTIONS*

4.2.1 What is an assertion?

It is a convention, at least of English, that if a 'declarative' sentence (one of a grammar/meaning to express a statement) is uttered or written, then, with certain signalled exceptions, what it says is being asserted. The utterance/writing of sentences that are not of a grammar/meaning to express a statement does not rate as asserting, or trying to assert, anything.[10]

Example D
  X says/writes a)   All cats anywhere anytime like milk
           b)   That toucan can catch a can
           c)   Who did it?

In Example D, X would be supposed to be making (or trying to make) the statements expressed by sentences a) and b), or, in other words, to be *asserting* that which they state. He would not be said to be *asserting* c), and he could be said to have failed to assert anything if 'that toucan' radically failed to refer (see 2.2.2 (viii)–(ix)).

There are a number of exceptions to the rule that uttering/writing a declarative sentence like a) or b) constitutes asserting (or trying to assert) what they state. Exceptions include:

Case 1.   Cases where the sentence expressing the statement is prefaced by such phrases as 'It is not the case that', 'I do not believe that', 'I wonder whether', 'Do you think that'.
Case 2.   Cases where the sentence expressing the statement is part of:

i) a truth functional sentence/statement as in 'If a, then. . .', or 'If. . ., then b' or 'Either a or. . .'.[11]

ii) a sentence/statement of the form 'X said/believed/denied, etc. that. . .' as in 'He denied that a' or 'He claimed that b'.

Case 3.   Cases where the sentence expressing the statement is presented for assessment of truth value. Common examples are multiple-choice examination papers, and forms, where the applicable descriptions/true statements have to be marked or inapplicable/false ones crossed out.

Case 4.   Cases where sentences which could or do make statements are presented as examples (for instance to be translated into Latin, or to demonstrate a stylistic, grammatical, or logical point).

Case 5.   Cases where sentences of a type to make statements occur in the course of stories.

A statement (p) and an assertion (of that statement p) differ in that to assert something it is necessary not only to say or write a sentence expressing p but also to do so in the *assertive style*. There could be a convention whereby someone is considered to have asserted p only if he prefaces a sentence expressing p in a certain way. Logicians have invented the sign ⊢, called the 'assertion sign',[12] to perform this task. In spoken English it could be done by, for example, the use of a particular pitch or special syllables before the utterance of any sentence intended to assert something. 'It is the case that' or 'It is true that' could almost but not quite supply these syllables. In Cases 3, 4, 5 of non-asserted statements 'It is true that' and 'It is the case that' do not correctly preface statements. However in Case 2, and probably 1, it would be quite correct to say 'It is true that' or 'It is the case that' before sentences not intended to assert something (as in 'If it is true that a, then. . .', 'He believed it to be true that b', 'I do not believe that it is the case that. . .'). In practice, the device used is to mark off cases of *not* asserting a sentence of a kind to make a statement in some fashion ('I am telling you a story', 'These are examples:') and to treat declarative sentences that are *not* marked off as being in the assertive style, so that uttering/writing them without a marking-off device constitutes asserting them.

In discussing how a word processor could count the token and type sentences, propositions and statements in a piece of text in 2.1.2–3, we made the simplifying assumption that one token sentence is a series of words bounded by full stops, and that a single token proposition or statement is similarly bounded. Retaining this assumption, we can say, as a first approximation, that for a word processor to count token and type *assertions* it must count token and type statements and then subtract those which do not occur in the *assertive* style. Due to the simplifying assumption that one token sentence makes only one token statement (even if statements can be distinguished within it), there will be no tokens of statements which are excluded from being assertions through being instances of Case 1 or 2. But there may be tokens of statements which are not assertions because they are instances of Case 3, 4, or 5. A type assertion on this usage consists of all the tokens of a type statement which are in the assertive style.

4.2.1   Box a

To count token assertions: count meaningful declarative
  token sentences (subtracting any which do not make
  statements – see 2.1.3 Box a), and then subtract any which
  are not in the assertive style as in Cases 3–5.
To count type assertions: count token assertions and delete
  any duplications of the same type statement asserted more
  than once.

If we ask what needs to be added to/done with, etc. a statement for it to be an assertion, the answer seems to be that a sentence expressing it must be uttered or written in the assertive style. If we then ask what it is to utter/write a sentence expressing a statement in the assertive style (what the introduction of a sign like the assertion sign ⊢, or equivalent device, does), the short answer seems to be something like: to put a statement forward *as true*.

4.2.2   *Assertions of* p *and assertions of* p *is* true

In 4.1 we discussed the view, which will be called *Thesis 1*, that a *statement p* and the *statement* that *p is true* are equivalent. We saw that if and only if *p* is assumed to be a statement which is successfully identified in *p is true* and we operate with two truth values, then the statement that p and the statement that p *is true* are 'equivalent' in the sense that they always have the same truth value, although they are not 'equivalent' in other, stronger senses sometimes given to 'equivalent', such as that they are the same statement or that sentences expressing them have the same meaning.

The suggestion that p and p *is true* are 'equivalent' does not always take the form of maintaining (or of maintaining only) that the *type statements* p and p *is true* are equivalent. Among the other theses that have been put forward are that in ascribing 'is true' to p we say no more than or nothing different from what we do if we *assert* p, and that ascribing truth to p could always be replaced by asserting p.[13] This has led, among other things, to the belief that some explanation is required of why we should ever use the form 'p is true'.

The notion of 'ascribing' truth to p is ambiguous. It can be used simply to indicate the nature of the sentence/statement under consideration, one in which p is the subject and 'is true' is predicated. But it can also mean, on the one hand, *asserting* that p is true and, on the other, 'holding'/thinking or believing that p is true. In this section we are considering what I shall call Thesis 2.

Thesis 2 is that in *asserting p is true* we say no more or nothing different from what we do if we assert p, and that asserting p *is true* could always be replaced by asserting p.

There are three related respects in which Thesis 2 seems incorrect:

Reason 1.　Since p and p *is true* are not the same *statement* they also cannot rate as the same *assertion*. If I say in the assertive style 'My cat is on the mat' and you say in the assertive style 'Your statement is true', that which we assert (our assertions) are not the same (see above 4.1.3–4).

Reason 2.　It is only on certain assumptions (that 'p' in 'p is true' successfully refers to a type statement and that we are operating with two truth values) that the assertions we make are 'equivalent' even in the sense of 'having the same truth value'. We have noted exceptions. With three truth values, the statements p and p *is true* may have different truth values. If 'is true' is mispredicated in p *is true*, p is not the kind of thing which could be asserted. If 'p' in 'p is true' radically fails to secure reference there is no p to be asserted. (See above, esp. 4.1.2, 4.1.6.)

Reason 3. We can *assert* only formulated statements, whereas we can *refer* to statements by other means, as, for example, 'the statement made by X at such and such time', 'all the statements X made that night', 'all the statements made by analytic sentences' (see above 4.1.5). There are cases where we could not as a matter of fact formulate a statement to which we can correctly refer because we do not know 'what it is' (i.e. any formulation of it), and there are cases where we could not in principle formulate the statement(s) of which we can predicate 'is/are true' because they are an open class of statements as in 'All the statements expressed by analytic sentences are true' or 'No statement of the form "All Xs are Y" can be known to be true'. In some cases it is not true to say that we could assert *p* instead of asserting *p is true*.[14]

If there were not a convention that a statement must be formulated to be asserted, if we could, for example, write '⊢ the statement X made' or if saying in the assertive style 'Your statement' constituted asserting the statement which you asserted (*p*), there would be more truth in the claim that we could always assert *p* instead of *p is true*, although reasons 1 and 2 would still hold, viz. that *p* and *p is true* are not the same statement and have the same truth value only if we make certain unobligatory assumptions.

Thesis 2 is sometimes put forward as if it supplied grounds for claiming that the notion of *asserting* is in some way *prior to* that of ascribing truth to statements. If, as I have suggested (see 4.2.1), to 'assert' *p* involves putting *p* forward *as true*, we should expect a close relation between asserting *p* (i.e. putting *p* forward as true) and asserting *p is true* (i.e. asserting about *p* that it is true), but we could hardly suggest that ascribing truth is therefore secondary to asserting, since the notion of 'asserting' consists of putting something forward as *true*.

4.2.2   Box a

Thesis 2 (that asserting *p is true* could always be replaced by
asserting *p*) is not correct: *p* and *p is true* are not the same
statement (see 4.1.3); sometimes *p* can be referred to in *p is
true* but not formulated: *p* cannot then be asserted.

Since 'asserting *p*' involves 'putting *p* forward as true'
'asserting' cannot be considered prior to ascribing truth.

4.2.3   p *and asserting* p is true *(or* p*)*

Sometimes confused with, or at least not clearly distinguished
from, Thesis 1 (that *p* and *p is true* are 'equivalent') and Thesis 2
(that asserting *p is true* could always be replaced by asserting *p*), is
the view that to say of a statement that it is true is not to *add*
anything to *p*, nor to say anything *about p*.

Thesis 3: To say of *p* that it is true adds nothing to/says nothing
about *p*.

If we think of *p*, or a set of statements *p*, *q*, *r* as *presented* as
opposed to *asserted*, for example (as in 4.2.1: Case 3) put on the
blackboard or in an examination paper for assessment by means of
formulated tokens, then it seems obvious enough that to say of
statements that they are true is to add something to them and to
say something about them, or, in other words, that Thesis 3 is not
correct.

The difference between presenting a statement and saying of it
that it is true or not true is easy to see. Above I *presented* Thesis 3,
while at the end of the last paragraph I asserted about it that it is
not true. If you asserted that, on the contrary, it is true, you and I
would have said different things *about* Thesis 3. Each of us adds
something to Thesis 3 as presented above. What we add is an
ascription of truth value.

If we think of a set of statements, put on the blackboard or in an
examination paper, for assessment of their truth value, and we
suppose that some are true and others not true, then we can
express the point by saying that the set of true statements is a
subset of the set of statements. Students in the classroom or

examinees are asked to assess all the statements, and each ascribes truth to some statements (probably those statements he/she believes to be true). Some ascriptions of truth will themselves be true, others may be false. Here the teacher/examiner presents a set of statements for assessment of truth value, the student/examinee assesses them as true or false and the teacher/examiner assesses the assessments as true or false. A more sophisticated form of such an exercise, suitable perhaps for students/examinees in logic, would be to present a set of token sentences for assessment, including among them sentences which are not declarative or not meaningful or which are ambiguous or may make more than one statement or make statements which fail of truth value, and to request appropriate assessments. In an exercise where true/false answers only are requested, the exercise is ill-set if the sentences included have features like these; and for this reason the student/examinee could be asked to *write out* the true sentences/statements in the set, instead of stating which are true. The written-out sentences/ statements, unlike the set presented for assessment, rate as *asserted*, i.e. put forward as true. The more sophisticated exercise requires more sophisticated treatment, in the sense that more epithets than true/not true (false) are in play, the non-true category being subdivided. The categories could of course be subdivided in other ways, for example, it could be requested that true statements are divided into the necessarily true and the not necessarily true.

The list of Cases in 4.2.1 of when uttering/writing a declarative sentence does not constitute asserting it, supply other common instances where statements are *presented* and where it is correspondingly easy to see that we add something to and say something about p, when we say of p that it is true. For instance, in Case 2 where p is part of a truth-functional sentence/statement such as 'if p then q' or one of the form 'X said/believes, etc. that p', to say about p that it is true is clearly to state something not already stated. If p represents the statement that it is raining (in some particular place at some particular time), in, for example, 'If it is raining, he will go home' or 'She believes that it is raining', there can be no doubt that to say of p that it is true is to say something not already said: p has not been put forward as true, so to assert p is to assert something not already asserted. Likewise, if someone told a story enquires whether the set of statements it contains ('Angus was a toucan who lived in the Everglades. . .

(etc.)') is true, he is told something *about* the statements when he is told that this is a *true* story, or, alternatively, no, not a true story.

The temptation to think that to say of p that it is true adds nothing to/says nothing about p arises from the fact that it is easy to slip into thinking of p as the *assertion* that p (i.e. p put forward as true) so that to assert that p *is true* seems to add comparatively little and the assertion of p nothing at all. If p is considered as a statement which is presented (or, let us say, mentioned) then it becomes plain that ascribing truth value, whether explicitly by saying of p that it is true or tacitly by asserting p, i.e. putting it forward as true, is distinct from and additional to a statement that p.

4.2.3   Box a

Thesis 3 (that to say of p that it is true adds nothing to/says nothing about p) is not correct. This is easily seen by considering p as *presented* (instead of asserted (i.e. put forward as true)) and noting that true statements are a subset of statements.

4.2.4   Holding that p *is true and asserting that* p/p *is true*[15]

In rejecting Thesis 3 (to say of p that it is true adds nothing to/says nothing about p), presenting a set of statements p, q, r was contrasted to selecting the true statements by distinguishing presenting statements from asserting them or asserting about them that they are true. The aspect of 'asserting p' stressed in this contrast is that asserting p involves putting p forward *as true*. However, 'asserting' has another aspect, namely that it normally involves *saying* or *writing* something, or, in other words, performing an action (often called a speech episode). Viewed as an action, asserting has such features as that someone does it at a specifiable time, usually publicly in the sense that something is said/written to hearers or readers, and asserting, like other actions, usually has a purpose.

We could draw the distinction between presenting p and ascribing truth to p by considering, instead of the difference between presenting p and asserting that p is true, the difference between

146

presenting p and *holding* that p is true, i.e. believing it to be true. It is equally evident that something is added to presenting or considering a statement (such as Thesis 3) when I believe it to be true or you believe it not to be true, and that what is added (or part of what is added) is an ascription of truth value. The variant of Thesis 3 (*Thesis 3a*: to hold/believe about p that it is true adds nothing to p) is no more correct than Thesis 3 as considered above.

The concept of 'holding' or 'believing' that p is true is more complex, and more nebulous, than that of asserting that p is true. From our point of view what is important is that 'holding' or 'believing' that p is true is not an action. Believing that p is true may last a long time, and be simultaneous with innumerable other beliefs held by the same person. It need involve no specific acts, may be quite private, and is not the sort of thing that can be said to have a purpose. Asserting that p involves saying or writing a token sentence expressing p, and we can count up episodes of asserting by counting relevant token declarative sentences (those in the assertive style). We could count how many people believe that p is true at this or that time but not how many beliefs that p is true there are.

The differences between asserting that p is true and holding that p is true make it wholly unsurprising, and we all know it to be the case that someone can hold that p is true without ever (much less throughout the duration of his belief) asserting that p is true. Equally it is possible to assert that p is true while not believing that p is true. If we ask why someone believes that p is true, we expect an answer in terms of the evidence he has that p is true, or perhaps the causes that have led him to believe that p is true. If we ask why someone asserted that p is true, the appropriate answer is normally in terms of his *purposes*. The purposes may but need not be 'making someone acquainted with his belief that p is true'.

4.2.4   Box a

In holding or asserting that p is true, a truth value is ascribed to p, but holding that p is true and saying/writing that p is true (or asserting p/p *is true*) differ, as a first approximation because asserting p/p *is true* is an action and normally has a purpose while holding that p is true is not.

4.2.5   Asserting and informing

Logicians not infrequently speak as if the purpose of asserting *p* is and must be to give the *information* that p (to a hearer or reader).

It is of course quite correct that anything that is asserted, i.e. any token or type statement, 'informs' in the sense that, unlike a question or command, it *states* something, so that if a token assertion that *p* or that *p is true* is made *to* someone, then it states to someone that *p* or *p is true*. However to suggest that the *purpose* of asserting something is to state something is, as it stands, to suggest that we make token assertions for the sake of making token or type assertions.

There are, as we have seen (3.2.2), other senses of 'giving information'. 'Giving information' can mean giving *genuine* information, i.e. stating what is *true*. (Declarative sentences are not infrequently excluded as 'meaningless' if they cannot state anything true. Cf. 2.1.2 (ii), 5.2.6.) 'Giving information' can mean, as well or instead, stating something not already known to (or believed by) the hearer/reader. (Analytic sentences are sometimes spoken of as 'uninformative' on the grounds that anyone must already know that which they state. Cf. 3.2.2.) It is not true in either of these senses of 'giving information' that the purpose of asserting that *p* is true must be to give information. Someone can assert that *p* is true in order to *mis*inform someone (lead him to believe something that is not true) or for a multitude of purposes that involve giving misinformation (to secure someone's vote, to keep out of prison, to gain a favour, and so on). In some situations, such as examinations, assertions do not have the purpose of giving *new* information. It is not the purpose of, for example, an examinee's assertions to give information in the sense of telling the examiner something he/she does not already know. The purpose of these assertions is rather to display the examinee's knowledge of certain truths.

What are the most common purposes for which people actually make assertions, i.e. utter/write meaningful declarative sentences in the assertive style, seems a matter for empirical study. But we may have some prior doubts about the suggestion that giving information, in the sense of asserting something true and new to the hearer/reader, is often a sufficient account of why someone in fact asserted something or justifies (i.e. supplies a good reason) for asserting or having asserted something. A minimum addition in most cases seems to be that the speaker/writer supposed this true, new information to be something the hearer/reader would want or ought to have at this moment or at this juncture in a text.[16]

4.2.5 Box a

Asserting something 'gives information' in the sense of *stating* something but it is a mistake to suppose that all acts of assertion are performed in order to give true and/or new information or that many can be described as performed only for this purpose.

4.2.6 *Sentences and truth*

Logicians are by no means agreed that it is type statements, rather than, for example token or type sentences or propositions (as introduced in 2.1.2) which are the correct subjects of predications of 'is true'.

Among favoured contenders as the correct subjects of the predicate 'is true' are declarative type sentences/propositions. This is most common where what is chiefly under discussion is a particular theory about the meaning of sentences, namely that the meaning of a sentence is to be explained in terms of its 'truth conditions', that is, the circumstances in which it could be said to say something true or false.

'Truth conditions' of sentences/propositions are most often considered in relation to sentences of particular sorts of meaning. A much discussed case is that of sentences/propositions in the past tense ('That toucan caught a can last week'). Further common examples include sentences which have the feature of being used to attribute sensations to people other than the speaker ('You have a pain') or to speak about events specified as occurring at a distance from the speaker. Sentences/propositions in the past tense, which are sufficient to illustrate the problem, have the feature of expressing type statements about matters which, at the *time* that this sort of sentence/proposition is correctly employed to express them, lie in the past. The activity attributed to the particular toucan referred to by 'That toucan caught a can last week' is attributed to it as having occurred the week before the utterance of the sentence. There is a problem about the kind of evidence that is relevant to determining (or failing to determine) the truth or falsity of a statement that a sentence/proposition of this kind expresses, because the statement, as made by such a sentence/proposition, concerns what happened in the past, and evidence about the past is or may be inconclusive. This in turn raises problems about the nature of the 'truth conditions' of sentences/propositions concerning the past, i.e. about the circumstances, if any, in which sentences/propositions of this sort can be said to express statements of a determinate truth value.[17]

For the purposes of such discussions it is not necessary, nor does it seem helpful, to suppose that 'is true' is predicated of the type sentences/propositions in question ('That toucan caught a can last week') instead of to (as I have been assuming, and argued for in chapter 2) individual type statements such sentences/propositions are used to present or assert (as when X utters the sentence 'That toucan caught a can last week' at a particular time about a particular toucan). What is under discussion is a problem about understanding or explaining the *meaning* of sentences/propositions of a particular sort, in the light of the fact that such sentences/propositions are used to assert (or present) statements at a point in time when it is, or may be, impossible any longer to ascertain their truth or falsity: we may not at the time of the utterance of the sentence be able to discover whether or not a particular toucan caught a can at the time it was said to have done so, viz. the previous week. This arises if whether or not the toucan caught a can was not ascertained at the time. The problem is compounded if the very sceptical view is taken that we cannot *ever* now be sure what happened in the past since even if we think we witnessed it, we may be mistaken. (See also 4.3.2(ii)–(iii).)

SECTION 3 *THEORIES OF TRUTH*

Some theories that are called 'theories of truth' are concerned with elucidating what it is that is ascribed to something by saying about it that it is true. The question is a notoriously difficult one.

4.3.1 *What does* p is true *say about* p?

One reason why it is difficult to see what is said *about* a statement when it is said to be true is that what has to be the case for each different subject of the predication 'is true' (i.e., as I am claiming, each different type statement) to be true is different, and it is difficult to see what, if anything, there is in common between all true statements that makes them true. By analogy with other predicates such as 'is red' or 'is male' we might say that just as what red things have in common is their colour or what creatures that are male have in common is their sex, so what true statements have in common is their truth value. But this seems to say so little as to be almost empty of content.

One way of looking at some of the theories called theories of truth is that they try to supply a little more content to this correct but not very illuminating account of what it is that is said about a statement when it is said to be true. Among these theories are:

a) The correspondence theory which says that to describe a statement as true is to say that it corresponds with or accords with the facts; and

b) The coherence theory which says that to describe a statement as true is to say that it coheres with other statements that are true.[18]

Frequently urged against the correspondence theory is that it says nothing. It treats a statement's being true as its being related in a certain way to the world but the posited relation has no substance: 'facts' are what true statements state, so to say that a true statement accords with facts is just to say that a true statement accords with what it states. A common complaint about the coherence theory is that it is not obvious how we can tell whether one statement 'coheres' with another. It treats a statement's being true as its being related in a certain way to other statements of the same kind but without clarifying the supposed relation.

It is not difficult to read more into either theory. For example, the correspondence theory could be interpreted to be saying that there is one and only one way to discover the truth of any statement and that is to see whether what it states is the way things actually are, presumably, since it speaks of facts, the way things actually are in the world. We have seen that some statements, such as that 9 is greater than 7, or that anyone who has brown eyes has eyes, can be discovered to be true without seeing how things actually are in the world. So the correspondence theory, construed in this more substantial way, does not seem to give a correct account of what is needed to discover the truth of *all* statements but at most only of some.

The coherence theory could also be interpreted as telling us how to discover the truth or falsity of statements. It might be taken to say that the way to discover whether a statement is true is to see whether its truth is compatible with the truth of other statements known or perhaps ruled to be true. If not, it is not true. If, however, the statement coheres with the rest in the stronger sense that its truth (apart from being consistent with the truth of the others) follows from the truth of certain of them, then it is true. As a method of discovering whether statements are true this seems most appropriate to the statements of deductive systems which have axioms, i.e. statements treated as initial truths, as in mathematics or formal logic.

It might therefore seem that the correspondence theory tells us how to discover the truth or falsity of a statement about the world and the coherence theory about the way it can be discovered whether statements that form part of axiomatic systems are true or not. We might feel we have been told something in being told that what is said about a statement when it is said to be true is that what it states accords with a fact *or* follows from axioms (or results from the meaning of words).

On this view, the trouble with the correspondence and coherence theories, which are generally presented as alternatives, is that each asserts something about all truths whereas in fact what each says is true about only one of the two sorts of truth, earlier distinguished as necessary and non-necessary (see 3.1–3). And a trouble about the predicate 'is true' that emerges is that it is not immediately evident what these two sorts of truths have in common.

4.3.2 *Impediments to knowing that* p *is true*

The question of what is said about a statement when it is said to be true is apt to get involved with questions about knowing that a statement is or is not true. What kind of statements can or cannot be known to be true, by what means and from what vantage point might be selected as the most central preoccupation of philosophy. Here we are concerned with only a few aspects. Among them is that the kind of justification there can be for ascribing 'is true' to a statement is different according to whether the statement is necessarily or contingently true.

(i)   *A priori* vs empirical knowledge that *p* is true

The epithets '*a priori*' and 'empirical' have sometimes been transferred to necessarily true and contingent statements respectively in the belief that this division of statements corresponds to a difference in the means by which their truth value can be known (3.2.1). The relations between them are close, if not so close as this transfer suggested.

It seems fairly clear that we could not establish or know the truth of any but necessarily true statements by *a priori* means: it seems that any statement *p* which can be known to be true *a priori* (in particular by seeing that the meaning of a proposition expressing *p* obliges it to express a truth, i.e. it is analytic (cf. 3.3.1)) is by that very fact a necessary truth (expressible by an analytic proposition: cf. 3.3.1). So long as we retain the definition of a necessary truth according to which a necessarily true statement is one expressible by an analytic proposition, the truth of all necessary truths can normally be known by *a priori* means. (This is not so if Kripke's 'weakened' sense of 'necessarily true' is adopted. In the weakened sense Kripke gives to 'necessarily true' ('true provided that the objects mentioned therein exist' (see 3.4.3)) the truth of a necessary truth may depend on the truth of statements of the forms 'X exists/there are Xs', which cannot be known to be true by *a priori* means.) Exceptions to the rule that the truth of all necessary truths (in the stronger sense of the notion) can be known have been adduced from axiomatic systems.

That all (or nearly all) and only necessary truths can be known to be true *a priori* seems an acceptable claim, although it should be noted that 'can be known' is capable of slightly different constructions (. . . known by a sufficiently skilled mathematician, by anyone, etc.). However, it does not follow, and does not seem to be the case, that it may not be possible to establish the truth of a necessary truth by empirical *as well as a priori* means. Many necessary truths have a *form* such that empirical evidence could never conclusively show them to be true, notably the form 'All Xs anywhere anytime are/were/will be Y' (see 1.2.1 (iv)). But if a necessary truth can be found that is not of such a form there seems no reason why its truth should not be known by empirical means.

One could perhaps offer 'Cats are not always dogs' as a statement which can be known to be true by observation of a cat or two as well as *a priori*.[19]

For a statement to rate as contingent it must not be necessarily true or necessarily false (or necessarily such that it fails of truth value).[20] No statement which could be expressed by an analytic proposition or by a proposition whose meaning obliges it to express a false statement can rate as contingent, that is, as having a truth value which depends on how the world is. Consequently no contingent statement can be known to be true (or false) *a priori*. For a statement to be included as contingent it is normally required in addition to its not necessarily being true, not necessarily being false, not necessarily failing of truth value, that it should not be impossible, in some state of the world, to establish what its truth value is by empirical means. Statements whose truth value could not be known whatever the state of the world are usually put in a separate category ('metaphysical' in Positivist usage; the term 'vacuous' is sometimes used). It does not follow that the truth value of every contingent statement can be known. If a contingent statement of the form 'All Xs anywhere anytime are Y' is true, as the world actually is, then its truth value cannot be established by empirical means since no amount of empirical evidence would be sufficient. The truth value of statements of this form can be known only if the world is such that they are false. Conversely, the truth value of statements of the form 'Some Xs somewhere sometime are Y' can be known only if the world is such that they are true. If contingent statements are defined in the way suggested here, there are inevitably impediments to knowing the truth value of some of them.

4.3.2   Box a

Necessarily true statements: only these can be known to be true *a priori*. It is less clear that all can be known to be true. There is no reason, except, in many cases, their form, why their truth should not be known by empirical means.

Contingent statements (defined as non-necessary *and* such
that there could be a state of the world in which their truth
value could be known): none can be known to be true *a
priori*. They can be known to be true/false only by empirical
means. Some contingent statements have a form such that
if they are true it is not possible to know it.

(ii) Statements and vantage points

It does not follow from the fact that a statement can be known to
be true, whether *a priori* or by empirical means, that it is known to
be true to everyone all the time.

As we are employing the notion of a type statement, viz. so that
we have the same type statement when and only when the same is
said of the same object(s), it may well be that the truth value of a
statement of the contingent class can be established only at some
particular time(s), in some particular place(s), or by some
particular person(s). For example, the truth value of the type
statement we could formulate, a little awkwardly, as 'Toucan *a*
catches/has caught/will catch a can in week *b*'[21] can (arguably: see
4.2.6) be established in and only in week *b* by and only by someone
in the proximity of, or with instruments trained on, toucan *a*. The
truth value of some statements about particular persons (such as
'X has a pain at time 1') can be established by and only by X at
time 1. And so on. If we allow that a contingent statement can be
known to be true by 'establishing' its truth, and only by this
means, then there will be many contingent statements whose truth
value, since it has not been established by anyone, cannot, at least
at the present, be known by anyone. There will be others which
have been established to be true by someone and therefore can be
known to be true at least by that person, and, if we are reasonably
liberal about what constitutes 'knowing', by others through the
information of that person. But we are all aware of pitfalls:
observations can be less than perfect, things are forgotten, people
give misinformation, not everyone hears, etc., so some of us may
not know, or not know for sure, the truth value even of statements
whose truth value is 'established' in the sense described.

It is important to note that such groupings as 'statements about
the future', 'statements about the past', 'statements about other

people's sensations' are not groupings of type statements. There can be tokens of any type statement that specifies a time t at which an object is so and so which occur before the time specified in the type statement, i.e. before t: these are 'statements about the future'. Similarly there can be tokens of a type statement about a person X's sensations which are not produced by X: these are 'statements about other people's sensations'. Problems about establishing the truth value of 'statements' about the future, past, or other people's sensations are therefore not necessarily problems about establishing the truth value of particular type statements but only problems about doing so at certain times or for one person as against another.

4.3.2   Box b

The truth value of many contingent type statements that can
be known to be true can be established only in particular
places, at particular times, sometimes by particular people.
They cannot be established at other places or other times
or by other people and hence may in fact not be known or
knowable.

(iii)   Uncertainty and ascriptions of truth value

It is sometimes suggested that the correspondence theory can be construed as treating contingent statements as statements whose truth value can be established by observation and thereby known to be true or not to be true, while the coherence theory denies that this is often or ever possible and hence proposes that, since we can never (or rarely) know the truth value of a contingent statement, the position is rather that we choose (within rather nebulous limits) which statements to hold 'true' and which to cast off as 'false'.

Recognition that this is not what we think we mean when we say of a (contingent) statement that it is true or is false has sometimes led to the suggestion that we should desist from futile attempts to justify predicating truth value to statements and should substitute justifying the assertion of statements. A difficulty about this suggestion (arising from the fact that assertions are acts performed for many purposes) was mentioned above (4.2.5, n.16). I have also suggested that 'asserting' cannot be delimited from other utterances except by treating an assertion as putting a statement forward as *true*.

4.3.3 Comments

(i) Other theories of truth

Not all the theories known as theories of truth are concerned with what it is that is ascribed to statements when they are said to be true.

(a) The redundancy theory of truth The 'redundancy theory' of truth claims that nothing is ascribed to a statement by saying of it that it is true. The views called the 'redundancy theory' generally consist of what I called Thesis 1 (that p and p is true are 'equivalent') and/or Thesis 2 (that asserting that p is true could always be replaced by asserting p) and/or Thesis 3 (that to say of p that it is true adds nothing to/ says nothing about p). I have devoted much of this chapter to suggesting (4.1. and 4.2.2–3) that these theses are not correct and that even if e.g. Thesis 2 were correct this could not warrant the conclusion that 'true' is a dispensable notion (4.2.2).

(b) The semantic theory of truth What is known as the semantic theory of truth (whereby 'snow is white' is true if and only if snow is white, and so on for other sentences) is generally discussing how to explain the meaning of sentences, and usually takes the form of trying to relate sentences in a particular language with their 'truth conditions'. A little has been said about it in 4.2.6.(See also 7.3.)[22] I have suggested (2.4, 4.1.4–5) that although meaning is predicable of sentences/propositions, 'is true' is not.[23] It follows that what is known as the 'semantic theory' of truth is not likely to be helpful in explaining the notion of truth: its prospects seem confined to illuminating meaning.

Neither of these theories considers that 'is true' says something about statements, the former because it denies that 'is true' says anything, the latter because it ascribes it not to statements but to sentences/propositions. It is possible that the concentration on them in recent years has retarded progress in 'theories of truth'.

(ii) Results

In this chapter I have made a variety of claims about 'is true', in particular that it is type statements of which we predicate 'is true', and that such predications say something *about* type statements (although I have been unable to say exactly what). I have also tried to show that the notion of 'asserting', not infrequently treated as making predications of 'is true' otiose and/or the notion of truth dispensable, on the contrary cannot perform quite the same tasks and, in any case, cannot be delimited without making use of the notion of truth.

NOTES

1. The classic statement of this position, known along with associated ones (see 4.2) as the 'redundancy theory' of truth, is in Ramsey (1927) 1931: 142–3, although it could also be attributed to Johnson 1921, Pt I, 4.2: 51–3. An early influential statement of it can be found in Ayer (1936) 1946, ch. 5: 87–90, a recent version in Devitt and Sterelny 1987, ch. 9. For descriptions of some aspects see Haack 1978: 128–34, Grayling 1982: 152–7, O'Hear 1985: 94–7.
2. A rule of the propositional calculus is that the same letter p may only be used again to represent the *same* (as I am supposing here) type statement. See 1.1.1 (iii) on the point that there is difficulty as to what kind of things p, q, r represent in the propositional calculus.
3. It should be noted that the case differs from predicating 'is true' of a necessarily false statement or 'is false' of a necessarily true one. In these cases, the opposite predication, 'is false' and 'is true' respectively, yields a truth. Where there is 'mispredication' neither *p is true* nor *p is false* can be true.
4. See e.g. 'equivalent' in Flew (1979) 1983 on some senses of 'equivalent'.
5. See Strawson (1964a) 1971, and for counterargument Jones 1968.
6. Ramsey ((1927) 1931: 142) spoke of 'p is true' 'meaning' no more than *p*: ' "It is true that Caesar was murdered" means no more than that "Caesar was murdered" '
7. See Davidson (1979) 1985 for a discussion of the relation.
8. See Dummett (1959) 1978: 4, Devitt and Sterelny 1987, ch. 9.1–2: 159–65.
9. If the policeman said 'The King of France is wise', which on the Theory of Descriptions is a false statement, there would be no failure of reference in 'p is true', which would also be false. But this is not the only reason for which 'the policeman's statement' could radically fail to secure reference: the policeman might have said nothing or asked a question or there be no policeman.

NOTES

10. It is not always clear whether utterances of 'declarative' sentences whose meaning might be said to prevent them either from expressing a statement (e.g. 'That square circle is well drawn') or from expressing a true statement (e.g. 'That chair is true', 'It is raining and not raining') rate as 'assertions'. But this is left on one side for the moment (see 5.2.2 (iii)).

11. In 'Since p, therefore q', as opposed to 'If p, then q', p and q are asserted.

12. This goes back to Frege 1879.

13. This is the form in which the redundancy theory was put forward by Johnson 1921, I: 52–3.

14. It should be noted that it does not follow that (as Strawson maintained in papers of the 1960s: see esp. Strawson (1964a) 1971) in referring to a statement or statements and saying of it/them that it/they is/are true we always explicitly or tacitly, essentially or inessentially, refer to or mention a previous case of someone asserting *p* or to a 'speech episode' of any other kind (a spoken token of *p*, but not necessarily in the assertive style). Nor does it follow that (as Strawson maintained in papers in the 1950s (see Strawson (1949) 1954; (1950) 1964) that the *occasion* (cause) of our using the form 'p is true' rather than 'p' is always a previous asserting of *p*.

15. See Wolfram 1985 for elaboration of views in 4.2.4–5.

16. The notion of 'assertibility conditions of p', i.e. when it is justifiable to assert *p*, generally rests on the supposition that good reasons for believing *p* to be true and good reasons for asserting *p* can be more closely identified than this account suggests is the case. (See Dummett (1959) 1978: esp. 17–18, and e.g. Grayling 1982: 177–80, 289–91; O'Hear 1985: 194–7.)

17. See Dummett (1959) 1978, Grayling 1982, ch. 8: esp. 253–62, Devitt and Sterelny 1987, ch. 11 on this issue.

18. See Haack 1978: 87–97, Grayling 1982: 132–41, 143–51 for discussions of these views.

19. It should be noted that what is then known is that the statement is true – not that it is *necessarily* so. With Kripke's weaker sense of 'necessarily true', examples of necessary truths which can be known to be true by empirical means abound (see 3.4.3).

20. This necessary condition is not infrequently treated as a sufficient condition. See e.g. Swinburne (1975) 1987: 184.

21. Such formulations are sometimes known as 'eternal sentences'.

22. See Tarski (1944) 1949, Haack 1978: 99–127, Grayling 1982, ch. 6: 157–70 and ch. 8, O'Hear 1985: 95–7, 191–200 for descriptions.

23. For criticism of the view that 'true' applies to sentences, see Baker and Hacker 1984: 180–90.

QUESTIONS

When you have read this chapter, or sections in it, you may like to try your hand at these questions, and/or to keep them in mind when doing some or all of the suggested reading. Questions are framed *primarily* on specified sections, but material from other sections may help with answers. You may also like to try the examination questions on this chapter in the Appendix.

4.1
1. Can you explain the reasons there are for saying that p and p *is true* are *not* equivalent?
2. Is it important that while we can refer to statements without formulating them, we cannot assert an unformulated statement?

4.2
3. In what circumstances is saying or writing a declarative sentence not an assertion?
4. In what ways, if any, do reasons for believing that p is true differ from reasons for asserting p?

4.3
5. What is your opinion of the Correspondence Theory and Coherence Theory as 'theories of truth'?

(with ch. 3)
6. What is the connection between *a priori* vs empirical knowledge, and necessary vs contingent truths?

SOME SUGGESTED READING

For guidance on a sensible order in which to do some or all this reading, consult references in text and notes. Not all the references given in this chapter are included in the list of suggested reading, and reading can be extended by following up other references in text and notes.

Aristotle (4th century BC) (1908) 1928, *Metaphysica*, trans. L. D. Ross (vol. 8 of *The Works of Aristotle*) 1011b.

Ayer, A. J. (1936) 1946, *Language, Truth and Logic*, ch. 5: esp. 87–90.

Baker, G. P. and Hacker, P. M. S. 1984, *Language, Sense and Nonsense*: 180–90.

Davidson, D. (1969) 1985, 'True to the Facts', *Journal of Philosophy*, vol. 66; reprinted as Essay 3 in D. Davidson 1985, *Inquiries into Truth and Interpretation*.

Devitt, M. and Sterelny, K. 1987, *Language and Reality. An Introduction to the Philosophy of Language*, ch. 9.

Dummett, M. (1959) 1978, 'Truth', *Proceedings of the Aristotelian Society*, vol. 59 (1958–9); repr. in P. F. Strawson (ed.) *Philosophical Logic* 1967, and in M. Dummett, *Truth and Other Enigmas* 1978.

Grayling, A. C. 1982, *An Introduction to Philosophical Logic*, chs 5, 6, 8, 9.

Haack, S. 1978, *Philosophy of Logics*, ch. 7.

Johnson, W. E. 1921, *Logic* I, 4.2: 51–3.

O'Hear, A. 1985, *What Philosophy Is*: 88–97, 190–200.

Ramsey, F. (1927) 1931, 'Facts and Propositions', in *Aristotelian Society*, Supplementary Volume 7; repr. in F. Ramsey, *The Foundations of Mathematics* 1931: 142–3.

Strawson, P. F. (1964a) 1971, 'A Problem about Truth', in G. Pitcher 1964, *Truth*; repr. in P. F. Strawson, *Logico-Linguistic Papers* 1971.

Tarski, A. (1944) 1949, 'The Semantic Conception of Truth', *Philosophy and Phenomenological Research* 4 (1944); repr. in H. Feigl and W. Sellars, *Readings in Philosophical Analysis* 1949.

Wolfram, S. 1985, 'Facts and Theories: Saying and Believing', in J. Overing (ed.) *Reason and Morality*.

Chapter 5

NEGATION

SECTION 1 *AFFIRMATIVE AND NEGATIVE*

5.1.1 Outline of the position

For many centuries logicians distinguished what they called two 'qualities' of propositions/statements: affirmative and negative. The distinction was important in syllogistic logic: the rules governing the validity and invalidity of syllogisms included some that rested on it, for example that nothing follows from two negative premises, that a negative conclusion requires a negative premise, that an affirmative conclusion can follow only if both premises are affirmative.[1] And at first sight the distinction seems straightforward enough. An affirmative proposition/statement says that something *is* the case ('affirms' it). A negative proposition/statement says that something is *not* the case ('denies' it). However, in 'Negation', translated into English in 1952, Frege propounded the view that the distinction between affirmative and negative propositions/statements is not needed in logic, and further that no clear-cut or useful distinction can be drawn between them. He was, he wrote, in

> favour of dropping the distinction between negative and
> affirmative judgments or thoughts until such time as we have a
> criterion enabling us to distinguish with certainty in any given
> case between a negative and an affirmative judgment. When we
> have such a criterion we shall also see what benefit may be
> expected from this distinction. For the present I doubt whether
> this will be achieved. (Frege (1919) 1952: 125–6)

162

Others, notably Ayer, in an article called 'Negation' ((1952) 1954), also disputed the possibility of distinguishing affirmative and negative propositions/statements, and the absence of any genuine distinction between them has been fairly generally accepted since that time.

It is not denied that one statement may be inconsistent with, or more strongly, the contradictory of another. Two statements are inconsistent with each other if they cannot both be true, or more specifically if the truth of one would entail the falsity (non-truth) of the other. Some statements which are inconsistent with each other, such as 'X is red (all over at t1)' and 'X is blue (all over at t1)', where 'X' refers to the same object and 't1' to the same time, can both be false. The object referred to as 'X' might be neither red nor blue, but, say, green at the specified time. Statements in this relationship are termed *contraries*. In other cases two statements not only cannot both be true but also cannot both be false (not true). If two statements are such that they must be of opposite truth values, or more specifically such that if one is true the other must be false (not true) *and* if one is false (not true), the other must be true, they are said to be *contradictories*, and each is said to be the 'negation' of the other: 'X is blue (all over at t1)' and 'It is not the case that X is blue (all over at t1)', where 'X' refers to the same object and 't1' to the same time.[2] The notions of inconsistency and contradiction are regarded as very fundamental but the statements between which these relations hold are conceived of as on a footing with each other, notwithstanding the affirmative appearance of 'X is blue' and negative appearance of such sentences as 'X is not blue' or 'It is not the case that X is blue' (see e.g. Quine 1952: 1–2).

The topic of negation has been relatively little discussed in recent years, and since there has been considered not to be a separate category of negative propositions/statements their features have naturally received little attention, with the result that complexities, such as those that arise from the new work on reference discussed in chapter 2, have been neglected.

5.1.2 Summary of the case against a distinction between affirmative and negative

The claim is that while we can distinguish affirmative and negative sentences according to whether they do not or do contain negative words like 'not', 'no', 'nobody', 'nothing', 'nowhere', or what are recognized as negative prefixes or suffixes, such as 'non-','un-', or '-less', this does not itself supply and also cannot yield a difference in meaning or in what is stated such that a distinction could be drawn between affirmative and negative meanings (propositions as in 2.1.2) or statements.

The principal difficulties that have been adduced in, or objections to, drawing a distinction between affirmative and negative propositions/statements are conveniently divided into three:

A. Some propositions/statements can be expressed by both affirmative and negative sentences.
B. All propositions/statements can be expressed by both affirmative and negative sentences.
C. Some propositions/statements cannot be classified as affirmative or negative because they have both negative and affirmative components.

5.1.2   Box a

Rulings:

A sentence is *affirmative* if it contains no negative particles, i.e. words or parts of words (explicitly or tacitly (via the definition of an included term)).

A sentence is *negative* if it contains one or more negative particles (explicitly or tacitly).

It is held that the distinction between affirmative and negative sentences does not supply nor yield a criterion enabling us to distinguish propositions/statements into affirmative and negative.

5.1.3   Some propositions/statements can be expressed both affirmatively and negatively

The claim that some propositions/statements can be expressed by either an affirmative or a negative sentence is clearly correct and obliges us to agree that some affirmative and negative sentences have the same meaning as each other and may express the same statements.

The most obvious example of negative and affirmative sentences which have the same meaning and/or may express the same statement is where there is 'double negation', that is, where two negative particles in the same sentence cancel each other out.

Example A
    'It is not the case that X is not blue (all over at t1)' would generally be considered identical in meaning and in what it states to 'X is blue (all over at t1)'.

Not every occurrence of two negative particles in a sentence is a 'double negation', i.e. such that the negative particles cancel each other out.
Exceptions include:

1. Sentences like 'He had no money and no friends', which are to be construed as conjunctions ('He had no money and he had no friends').
2. Where the effect of a second negative particle is to strengthen, rather than to cancel, a negation, as in the English sentence 'It is not, *not* just' (as opposed to 'It is not not just') or in Ancient Greek where one order of 'nobody' and 'not' ('not nobody') strengthens the negation while the other ('nobody not') cancels it. Here the two negative particles can, and, for purposes of exposition, will be regarded as one. (Where there is a regular strengthening form as in Ancient Greek a word processor could obviously be programmed to treat them in this way.)
3. Where the negative particle takes the form 'non-' rather than 'not', and we have a term like 'non-blue' which means 'coloured and not blue'. 'It is not the case that X is non-blue' is identical in meaning not to the affirmative sentence 'X is blue' (since X can be not non-blue by not being coloured) but to the more problematic sentence 'X is blue or not coloured'.

However, the possibility of double negation has the result that any proposition/statement expressed by an affirmative sentence can also be expressed by a negative one, i.e. one containing two negative particles, and that some propositions/statements expressed by sentences containing negative particles (viz. those containing a double negation) can be re-expressed by affirmative sentences.

It obviously does not follow that the meaning of or what is stated by *every* sentence which contains a negative particle can be re-expressed by a sentence containing no negative particle. In particular it does not follow that propositions/statements expressed by uncompounded sentences containing what we can crudely call a *single* negative particle can always or ever be re-expressed by a sentence containing no negative particle. It also does not follow that the meaning of or what is stated by every or any affirmative sentence can be re-expressed by a sentence containing what can, as a first approximation, be called an *odd* number of negative particles. Let us term these, for the moment, for the sake of brevity, 'truly negative sentences'.

5.1.3   Box a

Ruling: A sentence is *truly negative* if it contains an *odd* number of negative particles (explicitly or tacitly).

Negative and affirmative sentences can have the same meaning and express the same statement(s): the meaning of, or what is stated by, every affirmative sentence can be re-expressed by a negative sentence (double negation).

It does not follow that the meaning of (or what is stated by) every negative sentence or any truly negative sentence can be expressed by an affirmative sentence nor that the meaning of (or what is stated by) affirmative sentences can be re-expressed by a truly negative sentence.

If there are propositions/statements which can be expressed only by truly negative sentences, and not by other negative sentences or by affirmative ones, the way is open to distinguishing a class of negative propositions/statements, viz. as those expressible only by a truly negative sentence. Similarly, if there are propositions/statements which cannot be expressed by truly negative sentences but only by affirmative sentences or by negative sentences which are not truly negative, then there seems no reason why we should not consider that there are affirmative propositions/statements: those which cannot be expressed by a truly negative sentence.

5.1.4 The case for claiming that propositions/statements expressed by truly negative sentences can be expressed affirmatively

(i) Ayer's case

Ayer conducted his argument against the possibility of distinguishing affirmative and negative propositions/statements by presenting examples of propositions/statements which could, he claimed, be expressed either affirmatively or negatively. Some examples were of double negations (e.g. the re-writing of 'All A is B' 'in the form of a negative existential' (nothing is both A and not B) (Ayer (1952) 1954: 36–7). But others were cases where, he argued, the same proposition/statement can be expressed by a truly negative sentence and by an affirmative one. He went on to suggest that by judicious additions to our vocabulary every proposition/statement expressed by a negative sentence, i.e. including ones with no double negation, can be re-expressed by an affirmative sentence, or, in other words, that there are no propositions/statements expressible only by truly negative sentences.

This claim seems clearly false, and in investigating it, we can see that some propositions/statements emerge as 'purely' negative (i.e. without affirmative components) while others run into the objection distinguished in 5.1.2 as C (some propositions/statements have both negative and affirmative components and are not 'purely' negative or 'purely' affirmative).

As English stands, there is no affirmative sentence with the same meaning as a negative sentence like 'X is not blue' or even like 'X is non-blue (a colour other than blue)'. Ayer considered that this absence of an affirmative mode of expression was an accidental feature of the language which could be remedied by the invention of what he called a 'predicate complementary to blue'. It must, he said,

> always be possible to find, or introduce, a predicate which is complementary to the predicate in question [e.g. blue], either, in the wide sense, as applying to all and only those occasions to which it [i.e. blue] does not apply, or, in a narrower sense, as applying to all and only the occasions of this sort that fall within a certain general range. (Ayer (1952) 1954: 48)

Thus we may invent a term like 'eulb' (i.e. 'blue' written backwards) to mean:

Eulb 1: colour other than blue (correctly applicable to everything that is coloured but not blue),
or even, if we wish, a term that means:
Eulb 2: not being blue, i.e. is correctly applicable to anything at all to which 'blue' does not apply, including, therefore, such things as qualities of character, statements, and so on.

Because Ayer's 'eulb' has two distinct meanings I shall instead employ the more easily grasped 'non-blue' for the second sense of 'eulb' mentioned in the passage quoted above (Eulb 1) and 'not-blue' in place of Eulb 2.

Ayer anticipates the obvious objection that being non-blue or not-blue is a different *kind* of property from being blue. He takes the objection to be that non-blue/not-blue things have nothing in common apart from being non-blue/not-blue, and counter-claims that the same is true of blue things, which have in common nothing but that they are blue. The most that could be urged, he argues, is that 'blue' is a little more *specific* than non-blue/not-blue. Specificity is a matter of degree, and being more or less specific is not the sort of distinction that could yield the clear-cut difference required to justify the traditional distinction between affirmative and negative. Hence, according to Ayer, the traditional distinction cannot stand.

5.1.4   Box a

Ayer: Every proposition/statement can be expressed by an
affirmative sentence if suitable terms are invented.

(ii)   Widening the discussion

The differences between 'blue' and 'non-blue' are less great than those between 'blue' and 'not-blue', but to analyse Ayer's claim properly it is necessary to turn briefly to the question of how we assign truth value to what is expressed by negative sentences, in particular 'X is non-blue' and 'X is not-blue'.

To claim that 'non-blue' and 'not-blue' are properties of the same kind as 'blue' it seems necessary to claim that where they are predicated of X we shall make the same kind of decision about ascribing truth value in their respect as we do in the case of 'X is blue' in such circumstances as radical failure of reference by 'X', X being a successfully identified object not existing at a relevant time or X being the wrong kind of thing to which to apply a term like 'blue'.

An affirmative sentence like 'X is blue' is considered not to express a truth if 'X' radically fails to secure reference ('X is blue' does not make a statement: see 2.2.2 (ix)) or if 'X' successfully identifies an object which does not exist at the time that 'is currently blue' is predicated of it ('X is blue' makes a statement which is false or fails of truth value: see 2.2.2 (ii)–(iii)) and/or if 'X' refers to the wrong kind of thing, in the case of 'blue' for example to measles (mentioned in 4.1.6 but not yet discussed in detail). A sentence like 'X is non-blue (i.e. a colour other than blue)' would generally be treated in the same way and resembles 'X is blue' in not expressing a truth in these same circumstances.

It is by no means clear that the same is true of 'X is not-blue' either as ordinarily used or in the use suggested by Ayer. Ayer tells us that 'not-blue' applies to 'all . . . those occasions' to which 'blue' does not apply, and hence it must, it seems, apply to measles, at least if 'measles' is a term securing reference and the disease it identifies currently exists, so that 'Measles is not-blue' may express a truth. We should probably not say that 'X is not-blue' expresses a truth on an occasion where 'X' fails to secure reference, although Ayer leaves it open for us to do so. And we might or might not say that 'X is not-blue' expresses a truth if X is a successfully identified object which does not currently exist. (It might seem that for instance a successfully identified but long-dead toucan cannot be said now *not* to be blue any more than it can be said now to be blue or non-blue. Or it might seem true that if it does not now exist it is not now blue, i.e. that this is an 'occasion' where 'not-blue' applies.)[3]

We shall consider problems about contradictory propositions or statements in more detail in 5.2. For the moment what is important is to note that 'X is blue' and 'X is non-blue' are not good candidates for sentences that express propositions/statements which are *contradictories*. If 'X' has the same referent and the predicates 'blue' and 'non-blue' are applied at the same time, then these two sentences cannot both express true statements, but they can both fail to express true statements.

Whether 'X is not-blue' is the kind of sentence that can express a statement which is the contradictory of a statement expressed by 'X is blue' depends, as first approximation, on whether it is ruled to express a truth *whenever* 'X is blue' is ruled not to express a truth. If it is ruled that measles and non-existent objects are not-blue then 'X is not-blue' is a sentence of a kind to express statements of the opposite truth value to those expressed by 'X is blue'. However, 'not-blue' seems a property very different in kind from 'blue'. Among other things, construed in this way, sentences of the form 'X is not-blue' follow different rules with respect to what should be said if, for instance, X is non-existent from their affirmative counterparts, since, unlike 'X is blue', 'X is not-blue' then expresses a truth. If the similarity between 'not-blue' and 'blue' is preserved by ruling that measles and/or non-existent objects are not not-blue, any more than they are blue or non-blue, then 'X is not-blue' no longer seems the right kind of sentence to express *contradictories* (as opposed to contraries) of statements expressed by sentences like 'X is blue'.

These considerations make it seem improbable that Ayer's introduction of non-blue or not-blue could serve to show that *every* proposition/statement, including the contradictories of statements made by 'X is blue', can be expressed by a sentence with the same general features as affirmative sentences like 'X is blue'.

5.1.4   Box b

The invention of terms like non-blue and not-blue either is
   not sufficient to enable sentences predicating them of X to
   express contradictories of statements expressed by 'X is
   blue' or results in sentences obeying rules different from
   those applied to affirmative sentences.

(iii)   Defects in Ayer's case

The terms Ayer selected to fill the role of supplying terms enabling propositions/statements expressed by truly negative sentences to be expressed by affirmative sentences differ in more than a relative lack of specificity from terms like 'blue' which are ordinarily regarded as positive. This is less clear in the case of 'non-blue' (which cannot play the role of predicate in sentences expressing contradictories of statements expressed by 'X is blue') than it is in the case of 'not-blue' (which might be able to play the role of predicate in sentences expressing the contradictories of statements expressed by 'X is blue') but even 'non-blue' exhibits features different in kind from purely positive terms like 'blue'.

A. Non-blue The way 'non-blue' differs from 'blue' is precisely what makes it seem proper to consider it a *partly* (although not 'purely') negative term. What it shares with blue, viz. the positive feature that it applies only to coloured things (necessarily does not apply to things that are not coloured) is what makes it seem appropriate to assign the same truth value or lack of it to what is said by 'X is non-blue' as to what is said by 'X is blue' in the event of failure of reference by 'X' or the current non-existence of X or where 'X' is the wrong kind of noun. We are not prepared to say that 'X is blue' expresses a truth in any of these circumstances, and, I have suggested, would tend to treat 'X is non-blue' in the same way, with the inevitable consequence that 'X is blue (at t1)' and 'X is non-blue (at t1)' express *contraries* and not contradictories: where 'X' makes a reference to the same object and 't1' to the same time in both sentences, the two sentences cannot both express true statements but they can both fail to express true statements.

The temptation to regard 'blue' and 'non-blue' as terms differing only in specificity, rather than in the fact that 'non-blue' has a negative component, arises as soon as we imagine a language with only these two colour terms; and we know that there are languages whose colour vocabulary is actually restricted to just two mutually exclusive and exhaustive terms. Where this is so, there are three possibilities with respect to new cases, that is, colours not hitherto assimilated into either category. They can be assimilated in fairly equal proportions to each category, they can result in the creation of a third category, or one of the existing categories can act as a 'remaindering' one, which takes in all the cases that do not fit into the other.

We can see these mechanisms where we in fact operate a vocabulary of two mutually exclusive and exhaustive terms.

Examples we have encountered in this book include 'analytic'/
'synthetic' and 'true'/'false'. In the case of 'analytic' and 'synthetic'
I invented not a third similar category to accommodate new cases
but a category of a remaindering nature ('non-analytic') which
included the original category of 'synthetic' but also whatever did
not fit into either of the two original categories. We might infer that
'synthetic' is (or I considered that it is) a positive, rather than a
remaindering term. In the case of 'true' and 'false' there has been a
constant strain as to whether 'false' is a specific category, different
from the truth value 'failing of truth value', or is equivalent to
'non-true', i.e. applies to anything which can have a truth value
and is not true. 'Non-blue' as invented by Ayer is clearly a
'remaindering' term. It applies to anything coloured which is not
blue.

One feature of remaindering terms becomes evident when we
return to a vocabulary like the English colour vocabulary, where
there are quite a large number of mutually exclusive terms: 'blue',
'yellow', 'red', green, etc. Extending Ayer's policy for expressing
the statement that something is coloured but not blue affirmatively,
to allow affirmative expression of the statements that something is
coloured but not yellow, that something is coloured but not red,
and so on, we shall require the words 'non-yellow', 'non-red', as
well as 'non-blue' ('wolley 1' and 'der 1' as well as 'eulb 1'). The
terms 'non-blue', 'non-yellow', 'non-red' differ from their counterparts blue, yellow, red not only in having a wider and, because of
their remaindering role, less determinate application but also in
not obeying rules which govern the use of positive colour terms or
their use *vis-à-vis* their own counterpart. In particular, whereas
something cannot be blue and red all over at the same time, or
blue and non-blue all over at the same time, it can very easily be
non-blue and non-red and non-yellow all over at the same time.
Similarly, if we add 'non-failing of truth value' and 'non-false' (as
well as my not infrequent 'non-true') to our truth value
vocabulary, a statement can be both non-false and non-failing of
truth value or both non-true and non-false, whereas it cannot be
both false and of the truth value 'failing of truth value', or both
true and false.

B. Not-blue Where Ayer's 'eulb' applies to anything which is not
blue (Ayer's Eulb 2), the difference between this term, my 'not-

blue', and 'blue' is very much more fundamental. While 'is non-blue' behaves similarly to 'is blue' in its predications in virtue of the positive element in its meaning, viz. coloured, and 'non-blue' things can be thought of as having something in common with each other (being coloured, visible, etc.), 'not-blue' as conceived by Ayer behaves differently, and must behave differently if it is to fill the role of supplying a means of expressing statements contradictory to those expressed by affirmative sentences like 'X is blue'. As we have seen, to operate in this way 'X is not-blue (at t1)' must express a truth at least when X is the wrong kind of thing to be blue and when X does not exist at t1.[4] Consequently, 'not-blue' applies to non-blue things and to things that are not coloured, such as diseases, poems, or numbers, and, as we have depicted not-blue, it also at any time t1 applies to anything at all that does not exist at t1.

It is impossible to see how it could be maintained that all those things that are currently not-blue (non-blue things and things that are not coloured and things that do not currently exist) have or could have anything whatever in common, apart from not being blue. 'Not-blue', as depicted by Ayer, is clearly a purely negative predicate, defined as applying, as he says, to whatever and whenever 'blue' does not apply. A sentence predicating 'not-blue' of something, as this has been depicted, cannot be considered to have any affirmative element, and hence to show that propositions/statements expressed by a truly negative sentence can be expressed by 'X is not-blue' is not to show that it can be expressed by an affirmative or even partly affirmative sentence. All that happens if we use 'Ayer's 'eulb 2', instead of my 'not-blue', is that the negative particle is transferred into a negatively defined adjective.

C. *There aren't any tigers* To prove his claim that *every* proposition/statement can be expressed by an affirmative sentence, Ayer would have had to go beyond the invention of adjectives like 'eulb 1' and 'eulb 2' to the invention of nouns like 'regit 1' and 'regit 2', i.e. non-tiger and not-tiger. Otherwise there would be no means of expressing propositions/statements such as those expressed by sentences like 'There aren't any tigers in my room' or 'There are/were/will be no tigers anywhere anytime' by affirmative sentences. By analogy with 'non-blue' and 'not-blue' a non-tiger might be considered to be any animal which is not a tiger, and a not-tiger anything which is not a tiger. (Sometimes it is less easy to make a distinction between 'non-' and 'not-' things. For example, if 'There is not a cloud in the sky' is re-expressed affirmatively by 'The sky is full of x-clouds', it is not easy to see what turns on whether 'non' or 'not' is substituted for 'x'.) The translation of 'There aren't any tigers in my room (/anywhere anytime)' seems to require not-tigers. We cannot express a statement it is used to make by saying 'There are non-tigers in my room (/anywhere anytime)' since this says that there are animals, albeit not tigers, and does not exclude there also being tigers. ('My room is full of non-tigers' suggests it is full of animals that are not tigers.) 'Non-tiger', like 'non-blue', is not a purely negative term, since it means 'animal which is not a tiger', but a partly negative one: its positive component is that it applies only to animals; its negative component is that it applies to all animals which are *not* tigers, and, like 'non-blue', it does not exclude other 'non-' terms: a zebra is a non-tiger and a non-horse and a non-elephant, and so on down the list of known and yet to be known species of the animal kingdom.

To express what is said by 'There aren't any tigers in my room (/anywhere anytime)' by an 'affirmative' sentence it seems necessary to say that my room is full of not-tigers or that there are not-tigers everywhere all the time. The full absurdity of Ayer's suggestion that by the invention of suitable vocabulary every seemingly negative proposition/statement can be expressed affirmatively becomes apparent when we consider a sentence like 'My room is full of not-tigers'. It is quite compatible with there being no tigers in my room that there are no animals in it at all. In this case it is not only full of not-tigers but also of not-pandas, not-elephants, etc. down the list of the species of the animal kingdom. These not-animals differ from animals in critical ways. We cannot for instance count them up as we do tigers and pandas and elephants, nor say how many there are in some area at some time. We are unable to do this because we cannot say what counts as one of them, nor can they be said to exclude each other from being in the same place at the same time as animals do (see 6.2, esp. 6.2.2 (iii)). There are after all supposed to be not-tigers wherever there is no tiger, not-elephants wherever there is no elephant, so that wherever there are neither tigers nor elephants, there will be not-tigers *and* not-elephants, a curious multiplication of 'entities' which seems to serve no purpose except to support the claim that every proposition/statement can be expressed without the – explicit – use of a negative particle.

5.1.4 Box c

The terms needed to express some propositions/statements affirmatively include 'non-' and 'not-' terms.

'Non-' terms are partly negative; although restricted in range of application (a positive component), each non-term applies to everything within that range that is *not* e.g. blue, a tiger. Terms like 'non-blue' and 'non-red', 'non-tiger', and 'non-horse' are not mutually exclusive (negative component).

'Not-' terms as depicted by Ayer have no positive component, and have a purely negative meaning, applying wherever a corresponding positive term does not. The concepts of 'not-blue' or 'not-tiger' differ radically from those of 'blue' or 'tiger'.

5.1.5 *Propositions/statements with both negative and affirmative components*

While Ayer claimed that propositions/statements cannot be classified as negative or affirmative because every proposition/statement can be expressed by both negative and affirmative sentences, Frege's complaint against considering propositions/statements as affirmative and negative was rather (or at least included the claim that) many propositions/statements cannot be classified as either since they contain both negative and affirmative components.

We have seen that there are some purely negative propositions/statements (those expressed by sentences of the 'X is not-blue' variety), but also that others, like those expressed by sentences of the 'X is non-blue' sort, have both negative and affirmative components. There are plenty of adjectives in, for example, English which behave like 'non-blue', including what are sometimes called 'privative' terms,[5] such as 'dead' or 'blind'.

Among the problems these cases present is that if we consider 'X is blind' (or 'X is non-blue') and 'X is not blind' (or 'X is not non-blue') it is difficult, perhaps impossible, to say which is the 'affirmative' and which the 'negative' partner. This is due to the fact that each has both a negative and affirmative component.

Example B
 a)   'X is blind (non-blue)' means/states:
'X is the sort of thing that can see (is coloured) *and* X cannot see (is not blue)'.
In other words, 'X is blind' or 'X is non-blue' expresses a *conjunction* of an affirmative and a negative proposition/statement.
 b)   'X is not blind (not non-blue)' means/states:
'Either X is not the sort of thing that can see (is coloured) *or* X can see (is blue)'.
In other words, this kind of sentence expresses a *disjunction* of a negative and affirmative proposition/statement.

The components of the sentences in Example B can be classified as negative and affirmative by the criterion that the negative components can be expressed by and only by a truly negative sentence (one with an odd number of negative particles) and the affirmative components can be expressed by and only by sentences which are not truly negative. But we cannot readily cast a) as negative and b) as affirmative or a) as affirmative and b) as negative by this criterion.

It should be noted that 'X is blind' (or 'X is non-blue') and 'X is not blind' (or 'X is not non-blue') will be contraries unless the non-existence of X results in one being true and the other not true. This supplies some incentive for casting 'X is not blind' or 'X is not non-blue' as we have treated 'not-' predicates and as the 'negative' partner if the pairs are to be treated as *contradictories*. However, wherever propositions/statements affirm or deny non-predicates, they are not purely affirmative or purely negative.

5.1.5 Box a

Propositions/statements with both negative and affirmative
components are not satisfactorily considered 'negative' or
'affirmative'. However they can be regarded as
conjunctions or disjunctions of purely negative and purely
affirmative propositions/statements and the assessments
'purely affirmative' and 'purely negative' can be restricted
to uncompounded propositions/statements.

Frege considered that even if a distinction could be drawn
between negative and affirmative propositions/statements, it was
not of great importance. A reason for this is that a proposition/
statement p and the same proposition/statement preceded by 'It is
not the case that' are contradictories whether p is affirmative,
negative, or contains both affirmative and negative components.

SECTION 2 *CONTRADICTION AND INCONSISTENCY*

5.2.1 Frege's account of contradictory statements

Frege's comment about the nature of contradictories is perfectly
correct, at least in respect of type statements, and thereby of
propositions with a meaning such that they always express the
same type statement. Prefacing any statement, whether itself
affirmative, negative, or containing components of both sorts by 'It
is not the case that', is sufficient to create a contradictory of that
statement, provided that 'It is not the case that' is treated as I have
treated 'not' predicates, i.e. as resulting in truth even if, for
example, an object which the two statements are about does not
exist at an appropriate time or if they apply a predicate to the
wrong kind of thing. There might well seem to be no more worth
saying about contradictories, apart perhaps from putting in a few
caveats, and widening the account to include inconsistencies,
whether or not contradictories.

> 5.2.1   Box a
>
> A type statement and the same type statement preceded by
> 'It is not the case that' are contradictories.

The principal caveats to be made about Frege's account of
contradictories concern what cannot be inferred from the fact that
a statement and the same statement preceded by 'It is not the case'
are contradictories.

5.2.2   *Caveats about Frege's account of contradictories*

(i)   (Caveat 1)   Contradictory statements and propositions

It does not follow for this account of contradictories that every
proposition (using 'proposition' as in 2.1.2 (iv)) and the same
proposition preceded by 'It is not the case that' results in a pair of
contradictory statements.

'He is (now) ill' and 'It is not the case that he is (now) ill' are
propositions which *could* express contradictory statements but need
not do so. Either token of 'he' could fail to refer in a radical
manner or the time in question be unclear. One token of 'he' might
refer to one person and the other to another. The times referred to
as 'now' in the two propositions might be different. 'He is ill' said
of John Smith clearly does not contradict 'It is not the case that he
is ill' said of James Jones. 'It is not the case that he is ill' said of
John Smith on Wednesday does not contradict 'He is ill' also said
of John Smith but two days or two years later. If both tokens of
'he' and 'now' secure reference but to different persons and/or
times, then the two propositions do not satisfy the condition of
expressing a type statement and the same type statement preceded
by 'It is not the case that'.

If, on the other hand, each token of 'He is ill' does express a type
statement and both express the same type statement, then, so long
as just one of them (I have suggested the statement preceded by 'It
is not the case that') is treated as true if the person referred to is
dead, the two statements clearly are contradictories. The same
might very well be said if the propositions in question are for
example 'That chair is ill' and 'It is not the case that that chair is
ill'.

When there is radical failure of reference in one or both propositions the case is more troublesome. I mentioned (5.1.4 (iii) B) that we might rule that a negative sentence expresses a truth in these circumstances and that the corresponding affirmative sentence does not but it is not easy to see how the sentences could be said to express any contradictory statements since in this event no one token of a sentence of the form 'he is ill' could be said to stand in any particular relation to any other particular token of 'he is ill' or to any token of 'It is not the case that he is ill'.

In syllogistic logic, where propositions/statements of the form 'All Xs are Y' and those of the form 'Some Xs are not Y' (i.e. It is not the case that all Xs are Y) were treated as contradictories (or sometimes contraries), the 'All' and 'Some' propositions/statements were treated as unrestricted in nature, i.e. as saying 'All Xs anywhere anytime are Y', 'Some Xs somewhere sometime are not Y'. And it should be recalled that 'All Xs are Y' and 'Some Xs are not Y' can include the restricted forms 'All the Xs in my room are Y' and 'Some of the Xs in my room are not Y'.[6] These propositions express contradictory or contrary statements only if 'in my room' secures reference in both propositions and to the same room in each.

5.2.2 Box a

A proposition and the same proposition preceded by 'It is not the case that' need not express contradictory statements.

(ii) (Caveat 2) Definitions of 'contradictory to' and 'inconsistent with'

Frege's criterion for two statements to be contradictories should not be confused with the condition often given: that two statements are contradictories if they must be of 'opposite' truth values, i.e. a) if they cannot both be true, and b) one must be true. This is a necessary condition of two statements being contradictories but it is not as it stands a sufficient condition. Any necessary truth (e.g. that 9 is greater than 7) and any statement which cannot be true (e.g. that measles is blue) satisfy condition a) that they cannot both be true and condition b) that one must be true. But such statements would not rate as contradictories. Frege's criterion that

179

contradictory statements are statements so related that one is the same statement as the other but prefaced by 'It is not the case that' (with 'It is not the case that' used as 'not' predicates were described above (5.1.3–4)) has the advantage of serving to exclude these cases.

It is less easy to see how to describe the relation of inconsistency between statements using Frege's style of criterion. Inconsistent statements include contradictory ones but also contraries, i.e. statements which cannot both be true but can both not be true. For two statements to be inconsistent it is necessary for them to satisfy the negative condition that they cannot both be true. It is not necessary for them also to satisfy the positive condition that one of them must be true. That two statements cannot both be true is not as it stands a sufficient condition for them to be inconsistent with each other since this is a condition satisfied by any two statements so long as one of them cannot be true (being for instance the statement that measles is blue) and we should not wish to say that any two statements are inconsistent with each other simply because one of them cannot in any case be true.

What we need in order to define the relation of inconsistency between statements is a condition whereby the truth of either must *result* in the non-truth of the other. There does not seem any obvious way of achieving this except by saying something like: that two statements are inconsistent with each other if they cannot (or could not) both be true even if one or both statements could not in any case be true. If we introduce a condition of this sort to delimit the relation of inconsistent statements, there seems no real reason why we should not introduce a comparable condition in the case of contradictories, that is, adding to 'they cannot both be true but one must be true' 'even if neither statement is (or were) such that it is necessarily true or necessarily not true'.

The condition in each case has to be phrased as 'even if . . .' in order to allow necessary truths and statements which are necessarily not true to be included as candidates for being inconsistent with or contradictory to each other. We should wish to include '(It is the case that) 9 is greater than 7' and 'It is not the case that 9 is greater than 7' as contradictories and to say that 'That chair is true' and that 'It is not the case that that chair is true' express contradictories if 'that chair is true' expresses the same type statement in both cases. We should probably also wish to say that 'Measles is blue' and 'Measles is non-blue' express statements inconsistent with each other.

5.2.2   Box b

Inconsistent statements: cannot (or could not) both be true
   even if one or both could not in any case be true.

Contradictory statements: cannot (or could not) both be true
   but one must be true, even if neither statement is (or were)
   necessarily true or necessarily not true.

(iii)   (Caveat 3)   Asserting and believing contradictories/ inconsistencies[7]

Certain theses sometimes put forward do not follow from the account of contradictory and inconsistent statements given in 5.2.2 (ii). In particular, it does not follow or seem to be the case either that someone cannot *assert* (say/write in the assertive style, and put forward as true) both a statement p and its contradictory (or two statements which although not contradictory are inconsistent with each other) or that someone cannot *believe* that a statement p and its contradictory (or another statement inconsistent with p) are both true.

A.   Asserting contradictories/inconsistencies   It is obvious that someone can assert a statement p and its contradictory (or a statement inconsistent with p) at different times. On Wednesday he says 'X is blue'. The next day he says 'No, I was mistaken. X is not blue', thereby contradicting what he said before. Almost as obviously, contradictory or inconsistent statements can be asserted in the same text. In one place in the text something is asserted and in another the contradictory of, or a statement inconsistent with it is asserted. Less immediately obvious but on reflection clearly so: someone can assert something and its contradictory (or something inconsistent with it) in the same breath and/or on purpose. (Politicians sometimes do the latter; it can help to further their aims.)

It is of course the case that if someone asserts a statement p and its contradictory or a statement otherwise inconsistent with p, then one of the things he asserted must be false. It is, however, worth noting that where the inconsistent statements are *contradictories*, then it is also the case that one of the things asserted must be *true*. (This can be a potent reason for politicians to assert contradictories of a not too blatant variety: they can claim to have asserted something true, whatever proves to be the case.)

B. Believing contradictories/inconsistencies Since people may not believe everything they assert (see 4.2.4), the fact that they may assert contradictory statements or statements otherwise inconsistent does not show that they can believe both of two contradictory/inconsistent statements to be true. And where someone asserts two things each apparently believed but contradictory/inconsistent with each other, there can be explanations other than that he or she held contradictory/inconsistent beliefs. For example, someone may have believed first one and then the other, or really believe one and not the other. However, it by no means follows that someone may not also believe contradictory or inconsistent statements to be true. It is easy to see how this can arise.

There is more than one possible source of a belief such as that, for instance, X has measles or that it is not the case that X has measles. For example, one sees X, hears a doctor's report or a television announcement, reads a bulletin. Different sources may supply different evidence, one lot (the doctor's report and the bulletin) leading to the belief that X has measles and the others (a television announcement that X is dead or seeing X at work) to the belief that X has not got measles (being either dead or free of the disease). No doubt if the conflicting evidence were put together, there would either be a belief that X has got measles or that he has not got measles, or no belief either way on the grounds that, although as the example is presented, one or other must be true, it is not possible to tell which it is. However, conflicting evidence is not always put together and people do in fact hold inconsistent or contradictory beliefs, not perhaps frequently on such relatively simple points as whether someone has measles, but quite often on complex matters. For example, in 5.2.6 we shall consider two common, and commonly conjoined, but inconsistent claims: (1) that a sentence has a meaning only if it can express a truth, and (2) that the meaning of some sentences is such that they cannot express truths.[8]

182

> ### 5.2.2 Box c
> It is possible for someone to assert inconsistent or
>   contradictory statements and/or to believe both to be true.

5.2.3 *Inconsistency and bad arguments*

If an argument results in a conclusion which contains a
contradiction or a pair of statements inconsistent with each other,
then the argument must be a bad argument. The conclusion *cannot*
then be true, since it must contain a statement which is not true,
and so the argument must be unsound, that is, it must either be
invalid (the conclusion not following from the premises) or one of
the premises must be false (see 1.2.1). That a contradiction or pair
of statements inconsistent with each other follows from a set of
premises is a standard way of showing that the premises of, for
example, an axiomatic system cannot all be true. One possibility is
that one of the premises is ambiguous: it expresses a truth on one
of the meanings it is given but something untrue on another which
it is also given.

> ### 5.2.3 Box a
> If the conclusion of an argument contains inconsistent or
>   contradictory statements, the argument must be unsound.

5.2.4 *'Contradictory' and 'inconsistent' as kinds of statements and propositions*

Although 'contradictory to' and 'inconsistent with' (like 'entails' or
'follows from') are conceived of as relations between statements,
the *terms* 'contradictory' and 'inconsistent' are often applied to both
statements and propositions.

The statements spoken of as '(self-) contradictory' or 'inconsistent' include ones of the form *p and not p* or *X is blue and X is non-blue*,
that is, conjunctions of statements that are contradictory to or
inconsistent with each other. But they tend to be characterized as

statements which are necessarily false or necessarily not true, and to include all statements with the feature that they cannot be true, whether or not they take the form of a conjunction of contradictory/inconsistent statements.

The *propositions* described as 'self-contradictory' or 'inconsistent' are, as one might expect, those which cannot express true statements. They include conjunctions of propositions like 'All Xs everywhere all the time are Y and some Xs somewhere sometime are not Y' which (necessarily) express a conjunction of contradictory/inconsistent statements. Conjunctions of pairs of propositions which can but need not express contradictory/inconsistent statements like 'He is ill and he is not ill' (see 5.2.2 (i)) are not contradictory or inconsistent propositions since their meaning is not such that they cannot express true statements. (With the same rigid designator (see 2.3.4) in place of 'he' they might be included.) But the category, like that of statements termed 'contradictory' or 'inconsistent', extends beyond conjunctions of propositions necessarily expressing statements contradictory to or inconsistent with each other to such propositions as 'Measles is blue' or, in general, any sentence with a meaning preventing it from expressing a truth.

While we have separate terms for propositions which must express truths on the one hand (analytic propositions) and type statements which must be true on the other (necessary truths), 'contradictory' and 'inconsistent' are used *both* for propositions which cannot express truths and for statements which cannot be true. It is important, therefore, to note that the distinctions drawn between necessarily true statements and analytic propositions are replicated in the case of contradictory/inconsistent statements and propositions. It will be recalled that I suggested in chapter 3 (see especially 3.3.1) that necessarily true statements (statements which have to be true) are statements which *can* be expressed by, although not only by, analytic propositions (propositions whose meaning obliges them to express truths). Similarly, statements which are necessarily not true seem to be distinguishable as ones which can be expressed by, although not only by, propositions which necessarily do not express truths.

5.2.5 *Varieties of contradictory/inconsistent statements and propositions*

As we might expect from the negative definitions 'cannot be true', 'cannot express truths', what for want of a better term I shall call 'internally inconsistent' statements and propositions are of many different sorts.

For an affirmative or non-style (i.e. partly affirmative) proposition to express a truth it must satisfy several conditions (cf. 2.2.2, 5.1.4 (ii)–(iii)):

a)   that every referring expression (Usage 4 – expression whose meaning does not determine what it refers to) secures reference;
b)   that successfully identified objects exist at appropriate times;
c)   that objects stand in the relations in which they are said to stand, have the properties, etc. that they are said to have.

For an affirmative (or non-style) proposition necessarily to express a truth, i.e. to be analytic, it must satisfy *all* these conditions necessarily. Satisfying one or two of the three is insufficient in the usual sense given to 'analytic' and 'necessarily true' (although not on Kripke's use of 'necessarily true: see 3.4–5; cf. also 3.3.2 (iii) b). An affirmative (or non-style) proposition fails to express a truth if it fails to satisfy any one of the conditions a), b), or c). It necessarily fails to express a truth if it necessarily fails to satisfy any one of them. 'That square circle is red' necessarily fails to satisfy a) ('that square circle' could not secure reference), while 'The number 9 is smaller than the number 7' necessarily fails to satisfy c) ('smaller than the number 7' could not apply to the number 9). These particular propositions could be characterized as respectively necessarily failing of reference and necessarily expressing a false statement, that is, of a specific kind which excludes expressing a truth. Propositions which necessarily cannot express truths include ones which cannot satisfy for instance condition b) ('That man who died on Friday is now ill with measles') or condition c) ('That chair is true') but which cannot be said necessarily to express e.g. a statement failing of truth value or a statement which must be false because they can also fail to satisfy another condition, condition a) in both these cases. A proposition like 'That stone is thinking about Vienna' necessarily fails to satisfy c) since no stone could think about anything, but it cannot be said necessarily to express a false statement since 'that stone' might fail to secure reference or a successfully identified stone not exist at the time it is said to be thinking about Vienna, in which case it has as good a claim to be said contingently not to refer to anything or to express a statement which contingently fails of truth value as it has to be said to express a statement which is necessarily false. 'That figure is round and square' necessarily fails condition c) for the slightly different reason that 'round and square', unlike 'is thinking about Vienna', could not apply to anything.

5.2.5   Box a

Propositions necessarily not expressing truths are various according to the different reasons for which they cannot express truths.

5.2.6   *Inconsistency and 'meaningless' sentences*

(i)   A problem

One of the most popular ways of distinguishing type sentences which have meaning from ones which do not is to say that type sentences which have a meaning are those which can express truths (see 2.1.2 (ii)). This excludes sentences of the kind we have just been discussing from 'having a meaning'. Since they are excluded by virtue of the fact that their *meaning* is such that they cannot express truths, there is, as I have already indicated (5.2.2 (iii) B), an inconsistency involved in the way these sentences are excluded from the realm of meaningful sentences, and thereby also, it might well seem, from expressing propositions, as we are using 'proposition' (see 2.1.2). Sometimes the resulting dilemma is resolved, or side-stepped, by speaking of such sentences as expressing propositions but ones which are meaningless. Sometimes the condition for a sentence to be said to have a meaning is altered, and a sentence is said to have a meaning if it can express a true or false (non-true) statement instead of if and only if it can express a truth. But this step is usually taken with the object of including sentences which can, even if sometimes they do not, express type statements and thereby something to which truth value can be ascribed, rather than with the intention of admitting propositions expressing inconsistencies as 'having a meaning'.

(ii)   Why there is not a simple solution

It is not easy to find any conclusive consideration for resolving the inconsistency involved in speaking of sentences whose meaning obliges them to express inconsistencies as meaningless in one direction rather than another, and arguments for treating them as having a meaning or not having a meaning are not very decisive.

For example, one might like to have a sentence and the same sentence preceded by 'It is not the case that' as always both having a meaning or always both not having a meaning. However, it is not clearly unacceptable to have them sometimes on opposite sides of the meaningful–meaningless fence, especially when one recalls that 'meaningless' is a non- rather than not- term, correctly applying only to words and sentences, and not, for instance, to chairs and toucans. It has not seemed unacceptable to logicians to say that the negation of an analytic proposition like '9 is greater than 7', i.e. 'It is not the case that 9 is greater than 7' or '9 is not greater than 7' is 'meaningless'. Similarly, it might be agreed that, although 'Measles is blue' and 'Measles is non-blue' are meaningless, this in no way prevents 'It is not the case that measles is blue' or 'Measles is not blue' from being meaningful, even very likely (negative) analytic propositions.

Again, it might be suggested that while the fact that a type sentence has a meaning such that it can express a truth is a sufficient condition of its 'having a meaning', it need not be a necessáry condition. Why not allow a sentence to be said to have meaning if its meaning is such that it can express a false or non-true statement, perhaps also if it has a meaning such that it cannot express a statement, like 'That square circle is red'? After all, such sentences pass some tests for having a meaning, for instance, that of being translatable into other languages: there is enough meaning for the meaning to be reproduced by other words. The most obvious argument against this move, which as we have noted is sometimes made, is that it might let in too much, and, in particular, grammatically ill-formed sentences like 'Toucans can brings' which might, theoretically, also be, in a way, translatable into another language; at any rate, the individual words are translatable – barring perhaps 'can' whose meaning is here not clear. It is not absolutely evident that by letting in internally inconsistent propositions, grammatically ill-formed sentences *are* let in, or that if they are, this must be letting in too much. Perhaps the line between meaningful and meaningless sentences should be drawn instead so that only sentences containing meaningless words are excluded.

Where we draw or should draw the line between sentences that have a meaning and ones which are meaningless is not as clear as it has sometimes been made to appear. It is important to recognize this, and that, therefore, wherever we decide to draw the line, the decision may well seem somewhat arbitrary. If we draw it narrowly, for instance so that only sentences which can express truths 'have a meaning', we obviously need to leave ourselves some vocabulary to discuss the varieties of meaningless sentences, so that we can for example speak of sentences with a 'meaning' such that they cannot express truths or, to mention another problematic kind of sentence (the Positivists' 'metaphysical' propositions), with a meaning such that the truth value of what they express can never be known.

5.2.6 Box a

It is not clear whether sentences whose 'meaning' is such that they cannot express truths should be considered 'meaningless'. Arguments are not decisive, and there seems to be choice as to where to put the line between sentences which have a meaning and sentences which do not.

NOTES

1. The first of these rules at least does not hold in the propositional calculus.
2. The distinction between contraries and contradictories goes back to Aristotle (see Kneale 1962: 54–6). There is a good description of the difference in Strawson 1952, ch. 1: esp. 16–18, and a brief one in Flew (1979) 1983: 75–6 and, under 'negation', 243. For pre-1952 discussions of negative propositions see e.g. Mill 1843, 1.4.2, Johnson 1921, ch. 5.
3. It is sometimes held that 'internal negation', where the negative particle occurs inside a sentence as in 'X is not-blue', puts a sentence on a par with affirmative sentences like 'X is blue', while 'It is not the case that X is blue' (external negation: the negative particle lies outside the sentence) supplies the case where a sentence expresses a

truth even if 'X' does not secure reference, etc. 'Internal' and 'external' negation clearly result in very different meanings in the case of 'Some Xs are Y' ('Some Xs are not Y' has quite a different meaning from 'It is not the case that some Xs are Y' (= 'No Xs are Y')) but it is less clear that the position of a negative particle yields such (or any) clear-cut differences in the case under discussion.

4. There is a question not yet fully discussed as to how it is to be classed if 'X' fails to secure reference, i.e. whether it should be said not to make a statement (like 'X is blue') or whether it should then be said to express a truth because 'X is blue' does not. See below 5.2.2.

5. See e.g. Aristotle (4th century BC) 1928, 1022b–1023a, Mill 1843, 1.2.6. On negative terms see also Hall 1963, Sandford 1967.

6. Cf. 1.2. (iv), n.26, 2.3.1, n.23; see also 7.1.2 (ii) C.

7. See Wolfram 1985 on views expressed in 5.2.2 (iii).

8. It is worth noting that, in arguing for the referential opacity of belief contexts, Quine took it for granted that no one could believe both of two contradictory or inconsistent statements to be true. He always assigned falsity to statements of the form 'He believes that p and not p'. See 2.4.2 (iii).

QUESTIONS

When you have read this chapter, or sections in it, you may like to try your hand at these questions, and/or to keep them in mind when doing some or all of the suggested reading. Questions are framed *primarily* on specified sections, but material from other sections may help with answers. You may also like to try the examination questions on this chapter in the Appendix.

5.1
1. Has the programme of eliminating negative propositions/ statements anything to commend it?
2. Could we have double negations and/or contradictories without purely negative terms and/or truly negative sentences?

5.2
3. Does 'contradictory' have more than one meaning?
4. Why is there a problem about whether inconsistencies are meaningless?

SOME SUGGESTED READING

For guidance on a sensible order in which to do some or all this reading, consult references in text and notes. Not all the references given in this chapter are included in the list of suggested reading, and reading can be extended by following up other references in text and notes.

W. /

Aristotle (4th century BC) (1908) 1928, *Metaphysica*, trans. L. D. Ross (vol. 8 of *The Works of Aristotle*) 1004a, 1008a–b, 10ll–1012b, 1022b–1023a.

Ayer, A. J. (1952) 1954, 'Negation' *The Journal of Philosophy* xlix (1952); repr. in A. J. Ayer, *Philosophical Essays* 1954.

Frege, G. (1919) 1952, 'Negation', trans. P. Geach 1952, in P. Geach and M. Black (eds) *Translations from the Philosophical Writings of Gottlieb Frege* 1952.

Hall, R. 1963, 'Excluders' in C. E. Caton (ed.) *Philosophy and Ordinary Language*.

Johnson, W. E. 1921, *Logic* I, ch. 5 'Negation'.

Mill, J. S. 1843, *A System of Logic*, 1.2.6 and 1.4.2.

Quine, W. V. O. 1952, *Methods of Logic*, pt 1, sec. 1, esp. pp. 1–2.

Sandford D. 1967, 'Negative Terms', *Analysis*, vol. 27 (1967).

Strawson, P.F. 1952, *Introduction to Logical Theory*, ch. 1.

Wolfram, S. 1985, 'Facts and Theories: Saying and Believing', in J. Overing (ed.) *Reason and Morality*.

Chapter 6

EXISTENCE AND IDENTITY

Existential sentences/propositions/statements, i.e. those that affirm or deny the existence of something, and those of identity, which affirm or deny that X is the same as Y, are, for different reasons, distinguished from those of subject-predicate form, i.e. sentences/propositions/statements which say about something that it is so and so. Each sort presents problems of its own.

SECTION 1 *EXISTENCE*

6.1.1 'Is 'exists' a predicate?'

Most consideration of existential sentences/propositions/statements has centred on the question of whether or when 'exists' is a predicate in sentences of the form 'Xs exist/do not exist' or 'X exists/does not exist'. For many years it was accepted, on the basis of a number of apparently decisive arguments, that although 'exist(s)' is the grammatical predicate of sentences like these, the grammatical form is misleading as to the 'logical' or real form of such sentences, and that 'exist(s)' is not really a predicate, not a 'logical predicate'. Since the 1960s, many logicians have held that there are exceptions, that in some cases 'exist(s)' is, after all, really a predicate.

(i) Standard arguments against 'exist(s)' being a predicate

Arguments for saying that 'exists' is not really a predicate are of two kinds:

A. Existing is not a characteristic One type of argument consists in saying that it is not an *attribute* or *quality* of something to exist. The Kantian type of argument along these lines is roughly that in listing the characteristics of something we shall not add 'and it exists' to a list beginning 'is furry, striped, etc.'.[1]

B. 'Exists' is not the predicate of sentences/propositions/statements[2] Most of the arguments to show that 'exists' is not a predicate from the logical point of view pointed out differences in the logic of sentences-[3] of the form 'Xs exist' and 'X exists' and sentences-which are of subject-predicate form. Three such differences are:

a) A sentence- like 'Donkeys are grey' must be construed as meaning/stating either 'All donkeys are grey' or 'Some donkeys are grey'. Similarly, 'Donkeys are not grey' means/states either 'No donkeys are grey' or 'Some donkeys are not grey'. 'Donkeys exist', on the other hand, does not mean/state 'All donkeys exist' or 'Some donkeys exist': to say that donkeys exist is not to say something about some or all donkeys but to say that there are donkeys. 'Donkeys do not exist' means/states that there are no donkeys, and not that none or some of them do not exist.

b) From a pair of subject-predicate sentences- like 'Donkeys are grey' and 'Eeyore is a donkey' we may infer 'Eeyore is grey', at least if 'Donkeys are grey' means/states 'All donkeys are grey'. But we cannot argue: Donkeys exist and Eeyore is a donkey; so, Eeyore exists.[4]

c) When someone asserts a sentence- of subject-predicate form, he affirms or presupposes the existence of the subject, and predicates something of it. If 'Tigers exist' is construed on this model, i.e. with 'tigers' as the subject and 'exists' as the predicate, it has to be said to affirm or presuppose the existence of tigers. As what it says of them is that they exist, 'Tigers exist' (it is argued) would be necessarily true, or at any rate incapable of falsity: if the subject term 'tigers' secures reference (and/or the subject exists at an appropriate time), then tigers cannot but exist.[5] Even more paradoxically, if 'Tigers do not exist' is taken to have 'tigers' as its subject and 'do not exist' as its predicate, it comes out as contradictory or inconsistent: a subject-predicate sentence- cannot make a true statement (it was argued – but see 5.1.4–5, 5.2.2 (i) on negative propositions/statements) unless the subject referred to exists, but in this case, i.e. if the subject exists, affirming the predicate 'do not exist' must result in what is said being false. In fact, 'Tigers exist' and 'Tigers do not exist' make straightforwardly contingent statements, and not ones which are in any way necessarily true or necessarily false. 'Tigers exist' expresses a truth if there are tigers, something false if there are not. 'Tigers do not exist' expresses a truth if there are no tigers, something false if there are tigers. To treat 'Tigers exist' and 'Tigers do not exist' as being of subject-predicate form would bring them out as necessarily true and false respectively (or, as is sometimes said, as referential tautologies/contradictions) in cases where it is evident that their truth or falsity depends on the state of the world; so it seems fair to infer that it is incorrect to treat them as being of subject-predicate form.

6.1.1 Box a

Arguments against 'exists' being a predicate:

A.   Existing is not an attribute of something like being furry or tame.

B.   The logic of 'X exists'/'Xs exist' is different from that of 'X(s) is/are Y'.

(ii)   Arguments for 'exists' being after all sometimes a predicate[6]

A. Existing as a characteristic   In answer to the claim that it is not an attribute or quality of something to exist, it was pointed out that there is a difference between real and imaginary things. For instance, one cannot deposit imaginary money in the bank or present imaginary tigers to the zoo, as one can real money or real tigers. Again, in games where one tries to guess whom someone is thinking of, when they live(d) is as helpful from the point of view of identifying them as most decriptions unhesitatingly accepted as qualities, attributes, characteristics. To identify a particular, such as a specific person or chair, it is vital to supply some spatio-temporal description, i.e. to say where it is at some time. This could be thought of as supplying information about where and when the particular exists.

B. *'Exists' as the predicate of some sentences-* When the wheel turned and it was argued that, after all, 'exists' might sometimes be a predicate, the cases selected were those where it seemed that a reference might succeed and something be identified, and the question yet arise whether the successfully identified item 'really' exists, still exists, existed at some particular time. It was suggested that in, for example, 'Santa Claus (Hamlet) does not exist' there is a successful reference but that it may well be true that the successfully identified object (Santa Claus, Hamlet) does not exist. And from this it was inferred that in such a case 'Santa Claus' or 'Hamlet' is the subject and 'does not exist' the predicate. Thus for instance Cartwright with respect to the example 'Dragons do not exist':

> in one sense (philosophical as well as ordinary) to predicate is to say something of or about something to which one refers; and this, I suggest, is precisely what *is* done in affirming. . . [Dragons are not real] – and hence [Dragons do not exist]. (Cartwright (1960) 1987: 29)

In discussing the difference between radical failure of reference and what I called the Neglected Case (2.2.2) I certainly supposed that the question of whether a successfully identified person or object exists at a particular time could arise as a straightforward question.

6.1.1   Box b

Arguments for 'exists' sometimes being a predicate:

A.   There is a difference between something that really exists and something that doesn't.

B.   In some cases 'X' in 'X does not exist' refers to something of which 'does not exist' says something: here 'X exists' is of subject-predicate form.

It may be agreed that statements affirming or denying the existence of successfully identified objects can be contingent. But this does not seem to settle the point at issue, namely, whether such statements should be said to affirm or deny a predicate (exists) of a subject (the identified object(s)). It is by no means clear that contingent statements concerning successfully identified objects always take the form of ascribing predicates to subjects. Whether this is so or not is part of the larger problem of how, if at all, subject-predicate statements should be distinguished from those of other forms, in particular, those of existential form.

6.1.1   Box c

The arguments for and against 'X exists' being of subject-predicate form are confusing and do not appear decisive. The discussion does not give us a grip on whether existential sentences- (see 6.1.1, n.3) form a class or kind of sentence-, and if so what is their nature.

6.1.2   Subject-predicate and existential form

(i)   The need for a distinction

Many logicians persist in believing that there is a difference of significance between sentences- of subject-predicate form, in which a predicate is ascribed to a subject, and what for convenience I shall call 'existential' form, a class made up of all, or all but a few, sentences- that affirm or deny the existence of things. This belief is displayed in the arguments denying that 'exists' is ever a predicate, and in those maintaining that *sometimes* it is. It is also to be seen in the Theory of Presupposition, and possibly the Theory of Descriptions (see 2.2.1–2). It will be recalled that the Theory of Presupposition says that *subject-predicate* sentences- presuppose the truth of *existential* statements, that is, that unless certain existential statements are true, a meaningful declarative sentence of subject-predicate form does not make a true or false statement. (It may fail to make a statement if certain existential statements are not true and/or express a statement of the special truth value 'failing of truth value' if certain (different) existential statements are not true: see 2.2.2.) But the exact difference between 'subject-predicate' and 'existential' sentences- remains problematic.

(ii)   A problem about distinguishing subject-predicate and existential form

Sentences taking the form 'Xs are/are not Ys' or 'X is/is not Y'

195

would normally be said to be of subject-predicate form while existential form is exemplified by sentences of the form 'There are/aren't Xs', 'X exists/doesn't exist', 'Xs exist/don't exist'. But there is an obvious and immediate difficulty about suggesting that sentences of these different forms differ in what they mean or state. The difficulty is similar to that alleged to exist with respect to affirmative and negative sentences (see 5.1): what is meant or stated by sentences of the two forms often appears to be identical. For example, logicians commonly translate the subject-predicate form sentence 'All Xs are Y' into a sentence of existential form 'There is nothing which is both X and not Y' (or 'There is nothing which is both X and not Y, and there are Xs'). In Russell's Theory of Descriptions, accepted by many, prototype subject-predicate sentences- like 'The King of France is wise' are 'analysed' into a conjunction of ones of existential form ('There is a King of France and . . .' (see 2.2.1)). Converse translations come equally readily to hand. The existential sentence 'There are no tame tigers' does not seem to differ greatly from the subject-predicate sentence 'No tigers are tame', nor existential sentences like 'There are tigers in Africa', 'There are five chairs in my room' from subject-predicate looking ones like: 'Africa contains tigers', 'My room contains five chairs'. 'Santa Claus (Hamlet) does not exist' or 'Dragons do not exist' seem re-expressible by sentences not containing the word 'exist': 'The world contains no such person as Santa Claus (Hamlet)/no such animals as dragons'. It is difficult to find a sentence of the one form that does not have a partner of the other form which seemingly means/states the same. If the forms of sentence indeed have indistinguishable meanings, with identical 'truth conditions' (i.e. what has to be the case for them to express a statement of the same truth value is the same), the distinction would be no more than a grammatical one, between type sentences.

6.1.2   Box a

Sentences of subject-predicate form (Xs are/aren't Y', X is/isn't Y) may mean/state the same as sentences of 'existential' form ('There are/aren't Xs', 'Xs exist/don't exist', 'X exists/doesn't exist').

In discussing whether 'exists' is a predicate, logicians suggested that *logical* form might differ from grammatical form, and it is clearly worth exploring the possibility that although English sentences of subject-predicate and existential form can frequently replace each other, nevertheless what is meant or stated by what is logically (really) of subject-predicate form on the one hand may differ from what is meant or stated by what is logically (really) of existential form on the other.

(iii)   A method of introducing a distinction between subject-predicate and existential form

One way, indeed the obvious way, of drawing a distinction between subject-predicate and existential form is to rule that subject-predicate propositions/statements do, while existential ones do not have a subject. To give more interest to the classification, subject-predicate propositions/statements might be said to be those with *one* subject, while propositions/statements with more than one subject are put into the different category of 'relational'. The problem then is to give substance to the notion of a proposition/statement having one subject, no subject, more than one subject. This requires a test for a term to be a subject term in a sentence. The test cannot be supplied by the test of ordinary English, viz. that the term comes first in the sentence (or, in other languages, is in the nominative case) due to the interchangeability in meaning between sentences of different grammatical form. But we can exploit the convention in English of putting subjects first to show the 'real' forms that a sentence like 'Jones visited the local swimming pool this morning' could have, if we can find a satisfactory (non-grammatical) test for a term being a subject term.

Example A
'Jones visited the local swimming pool this morning':
Form (i) Jones (subject) visited the local swimming pool this morning.
Form (ii) The local swiming pool (subject) was visited by Jones this morning.
Form (iii) Jones and the local swimming pool (subjects) were in the relation of visiting/being visited by.
Form (iv) There was a visit by Jones to the local swimming pool this morning.

(Form (v) This morning saw (was characterized by) a visit by Jones to the local swimming pool.)

In Example A, Forms (i) and (ii) (and (v)) depict subject-predicate form (one subject), Form (iii) depicts relational form (more than one subject) and Form (iv) existential form (no subject).

It should be noted that if such a classification can be given substance, then the categories subject-predicate, relational, existential become such that no type proposition/statement could fall into more than one of them, for the same proposition/statement could not satisfy more than one of the conditions: having one subject, having more than one subject, having no subject. The question 'Can existential propositions/statements be of subject-predicate form?' must therefore always receive the plain answer 'no' for what it asks is 'Can a proposition/statement with no subject have one subject?'. The distinct question 'Can an English type sentence of existential form express a proposition/statement of subject-predicate form?', however, would receive the answer 'Yes': a token of the type sentence 'There are five chairs in my room' might be given a meaning such that it rates as having just one subject (the room referred to as 'my room'), and its 'real' form can then be displayed by expressing it by the type sentence (not, as it happened used) 'My room contains five chairs'.

6.1.2   Box b

Subject-predicate and existential propositions/statements could be distinguished on the basis that in subject-predicate form there is one subject (term), in existential form no subject (term). This requires a (non-grammatical) way of identifying subject terms in (token) sentences.

(iv)   Two conflicting tests for subject terms[7]

There are two obvious non-grammatical tests of whether a term in a sentence is a subject term in that sentence. Each is incomplete in the sense that it would decide the matter only for certain sorts of terms, not including, for example, terms like '9'.

Test 1: Subject terms as referring expressions One test of a term being a subject term in a sentence is that it is a term whose radical failure to refer results in no statement being made. In 2.2.2 (ix) I suggested that there seemed to be good reason to treat radical reference failure on the part of *any* term used essentially in a sentence, and not just on the part of what by some prior criterion of 'subject term' is deemed a subject term, as resulting in no statement being made (since we cannot repeat the content of what has been said, express the same type statement again) (see 2.2.2 (ix)). If so, Test 1 would have the result that any term in a sentence which could radically fail to refer would rate as a subject term in that sentence, and, unless further conditions are introduced (for example, to allow terms which are not referring expressions in Usage 4 but are so in Usage 2 also to rate as subject terms: see 2.3.3 on usages of 'referring expression'), the question of the form of a sentence would be settled by how many terms it contains which could radically fail to refer. Thus 'Jones visited the local swimming pool this morning' would be of relational form, since it has more than one subject term by this test ('Jones' and 'the local swimming pool'), even if 'this morning' is not included. Sentences like 'There are (currently) five chairs in my room' (one subject term: 'my room'), 'Churchill does not exist at time 1' (subject term: 'Churchill'), 'The creatures in the story books called dragons do not exist' (subject term: 'the creatures. . .') all rate as subject-predicate, provided that the time references in the first two and 'the story books' in the last are not included for purposes of assessing form.

If this test is treated as supplying a necessary as well as a sufficient condition for a term to rate as a subject term, then only, as well as all, referring expressions (Usage 4) will rate as subject expressions. This might allow 'Tigers exist' to count as existential in form, on the grounds that 'tigers' is a term whose meaning determines the kind of animal to which it refers, i.e. is not a referring expression (Usage 4). But because it excludes '9' in '9 is greater than 7' from being a subject term, it might be thought not to supply an adequate necessary condition of subject terms in general, and to be better considered as limited in its application to some sorts of terms.

More important for our purposes than deciding this point is to see that however it is decided, Test 1 has two important consequences:

199

1. Many sentences which affirm or deny existence like 'Churchill exists at time l' rate as expressing not existential but subject-predicate propositions/statements.
2. Sentences expressing existential propositions/statements include, or perhaps consist entirely of, those which take the form 'There is (or was)/there isn't (or hasn't been) at some time something answering to the *description* "tigers" "King of France", "chair in my room", "creature in a story book called a dragon", "man called Churchill who. . ." '.

It will be recalled that these latter are the sort of existential statement the truth of which is (according to one version of the Theory of Presupposition) presupposed by token meaningful declarative sentences containing referring expressions (Usage 4): their truth is necessary in order for referring expressions used essentially to secure reference and the sentence to express a statement (see 2.2.2 (ix)). It is consistent with this that some meaningful declarative sentences used to affirm or deny existence (those classed as subject-predicate by Test 1) like 'The creatures in the story-books called dragons do not exist' presuppose the truth of existential statements, in this case that there are creatures in the story-books called dragons: if the relevant existential statement is not true, the expression 'the creatures in the story-books called dragons' radically fails to refer and 'The creatures in the story-books called dragons do not exist' fails to make a statement. Similarly, with Santa Claus or Hamlet.[8] If 'Hamlet' refers to a character in Shakespeare's play, then it must be true that there is such a character for 'Hamlet' to secure reference ('Hamlet's wife', for instance, would not, there being no such character), and for 'Hamlet does not exist' to make a statement. The truth of an existential statement is therefore presupposed (i.e. is a necessary condition of any sentence containing 'Hamlet' as a subject term to make a statement), whether the sentence is 'Hamlet wore socks' or 'Hamlet does not exist'. Test 1 may be the kind of test for subject terms, and so of subject-predicate form, which Cartwright had in mind in the passage quoted above.

6.1.2 Box c

Test 1: Referring expressions (Usage 4 – cf. 2.3.3) are subject terms.

Only sentences which do not contain referring expressions (Usage 4) contain no subject term. By this test 'Churchill exists at time 1' is of subject-predicate form while 'There is/was/will be someone answering to the description "called Churchill" and. . .' is of existential form.

It is not altogether satisfactory to have as a test of whether propositions/statements are existential or subject-predicate in form, one which puts a large section of propositions/statements that affirm or deny existence into a category other than the existential one. The object after all is to distinguish between subject-predicate and existential meaning/statements, and for the distinction to capture what is intended, statements affirming and denying existence should ideally all belong to the existential as opposed to the subject-predicate category.

Test 2: Subject terms as terms referring to objects whose non-existence leads to failure of truth value   A second test which can be used for a term to count as a subject term is that it is a term which if it successfully identifies an object and that object does not exist at an appropriate time, results in the statement made having a distinct brand of non-truth, which we can, if we wish, call failure of truth value (see 2.2.2 (iii)).

Test 2 decides the real form of a token of the sentence 'Jones visited the local swimming pool this morning' by whether the current non-existence of (the successfully identified) Jones or the (successfully identified) local swimming pool or both or neither is said to result in the statement's failing of truth value rather than being false. If the non-existence of Jones (only) has this result, we have Form (i) (subject-predicate form), if the non-existence of Jones or of the local swimming pool has this result we have Form (iii) (relational form), and if the statement rates as false if Jones is dead and if the local swimming pool has been demolished, we have Form (iv) (existential).

We have to recall that the negative statements which are the contradictories (as opposed to contraries) of affirmative statements like these rate as true when their affirmative (or partly affirmative) counterparts are not true, i.e. when these fail of truth value as well as when they are false (see 5.1.4–5). To test the status of relevant terms we have therefore to consider not a negative not-sentence like 'The creatures in the story-books called dragons do not exist' but affirmative sentences like 'The creatures in the story-books called dragons exist'.

There can be no doubt that provided that 'The creatures in the story-book called dragons' secures reference (i.e. there are such creatures in story-books), sentences like 'The creatures in the story-books called dragons exist' would be considered to express a false statement, and not one which fails of truth value if, as is the case, the creatures in question do not exist (are not real animals in the world). On Test 2, therefore, a proposition/statement like 'Dragons do not exist', construed as 'The creatures in the story-books . . . do not exist' rates as existential, and not as subject-predicate, in form. Only if the type sentence 'Dragons do not exist' is given the different meaning: 'The world contains no such creatures as those described in the story-books as dragons', where the world is the subject, could it rate as expressing a proposition/statement which is subject-predicate in form. (We can speak of different meanings, and truth conditions, since a statement made by 'The world contains no such creatures as . . . dragons' would fail of truth value while one made by 'The creatures in the story-books . . . do not exist' would be false if at some time the world did not exist; in other words, there are circumstances in which the truth values ascribed would be different.) A similar account can be given of 'Churchill, the great war leader, etc., exists at time 1', or probably any other affirmation of existence. Statements made by such propositions as these rate as false, not as failing of truth value, if the term here in the grammatical subject position refers to an object not existing at time 1. By Test 2 they are unlike the statements we are happy to class as candidates for subject-predicate form such as 'Churchill opened a bridge this morning', which, said in 1988, makes a statement to which the truth value 'fails of truth value' would readily be ascribed.

6.1.2   Box d

Test 2: Subject terms are terms in sentences such that if they
successfully refer and the successfully identified object does
not exist, the statement made (if partly or wholly
affirmative; its contradictory if the statement is negative)
fails of truth value.

By this test, 'Churchill does not exist at time 1' expresses a
proposition/statement of existential form, while 'Churchill
opened a bridge this morning' expresses one of subject-
predicate form.

The fact that Tests 1 and 2, both with something to commend
them, give different results may help to explain the persistence of
the problem as to whether 'exists' can or cannot be a predicate: for
on one, not implausible test (Test 1) it can be, while on the other,
equally plausible one (Test 2) it is extremely unlikely that it will
be. It should be noted that sentences like 'The King of France is
wise' or 'The King of France is unwise/foolish', generally treated as
paradigm examples of subject-predicate form, would normally rate
as expressing propositions/statements of subject-predicate form by
both Test 1 and Test 2, 'Jones visited the local swimming pool',
which hovers between relational and subject-predicate form, rates
as expressing a relational proposition by Test 1 but could express a
subject-predicate statement by Test 2. As in the doubtful case
'Churchill exists at time 1', which hovers between subject-predicate
and existential form, it depends on which test is used to which
category a proposition it expresses is said to belong.

6.1.2   Box e

The existence of two tests for existential vs subject-predicate
form, which can give different results for the same
proposition, may help to explain why the answer to the
question of whether or when 'exists' is a predicate appears
so problematic.

6.1.3   Real and not real

(i)   Use of 'real'

It is a commonly made point[9] that to be intelligibly used the term
'real' must qualify a noun. The question of what is 'real' cannot be
understood or answered as such. We have to ask 'Is X a real
person?' or 'Is Y a real diamond?' or 'Was Z's anger real anger?'.

In the case of some nouns, it is not easy to think what a not-real
something or other would be. But frequently, because of particular
common activities in English-speaking societies, no doubt replicated elsewhere, such as making up stories, playing games,
creating imitations, there are obvious candidates for things which
are classed as in a sense of a particular kind but not real ones or
not quite so. For example, as not real money we have 'imaginary'
money used to perform transactions in games, and also counterfeit
money, we have 'toy' tigers or cars; as not quite teeth or limbs,
false teeth and artificial limbs. We have fictitious persons, places,
and objects in plays and stories, fake diamonds, imitation furs,
synthetic fibres, pretended anger, and so on. When a kind of
object, material, etc. is created which resembles an existing one, it
may, instead of being given an entirely new name, be partially
assimilated to the kind of object it resembles (imitates), with a
distinguishing prefix indicating that, and sometimes in what way,
it is not a real F or not quite F.

If it is asked of glittering stones in a brooch of X's, or of the teeth
in X's mouth, or the dollar notes in X's hand (or these days, on his
computer) whether they are real, what is being asked is not
whether the objects referred to exist but whether they are quite or
really diamonds, teeth, money. The answer 'no' will be apposite if
the 'diamonds' are paste, the 'teeth' false ones, or the 'money' toy
or 'imaginary' money. In this setting, it would be perverse to frame
the question 'Are they real?' as 'Do they exist?'. This is, at least in
part, because the objects asked about are (except for the computer
dollars) physical objects, described in my example as known
currently to exist, and the questions are clearly questions about
their nature: whether they are diamonds, teeth, money or not really
or quite so. If we had separate terms for fake diamonds, false teeth
and toy money, say, 'monds', 'eths' and 'ney' respectively, the
question asked by 'Are those diamonds, teeth, dollar notes real (or

not real)?' would be framed 'Are those stones, things in your
mouth, notes in your hand diamonds teeth, money (or monds, eth,
ney)?'. The answer to the different questions 'Has X got diamonds,
teeth, money?' or 'Has X got monds, eth, ney?' would be partly
settled by the answer to this question. There is evidence in the
existence of the brooch, things in the mouth, notes in the hand,
that X has either diamonds or monds, either real or false teeth,
either money or ney. If the brooch is made at least partly of paste
diamonds, the teeth are at least some of them false ones, the notes
at least include toy money, then clearly X has monds, eth and ney.
If there is no (real) diamond, tooth or money among them, the
question 'Has X diamonds, teeth, money?' is not settled, either
way. These different questions could of course also be asked quite
independently, that is, without the evidence supplied by the
existence of the brooch, things in the mouth, notes in the hand, in
which case the answer could be 'no' to both questions.

6.1.3   Box a

'Real' qualifies nouns like diamonds, teeth, money, and is
opposed to classes of objects resembling (imitating)
diamonds, etc. but which are not really or not quite of the
class.

Asking whether something is (or was) a real diamond is
different from asking whether diamonds, real or fake, exist.

(ii)   Dragons and Hamlet

Questions logicians frame as questions about 'exists': 'Do (the
creatures in the story-books called) dragons exist?' or 'Does (the
character in Shakespeare called) Hamlet exist?' can be broken
down in a somewhat similar way. They can be questions about
whether what is (known to be) depicted and named 'dragon' or
'Hamlet' is a real kind of animal or a real individual person, i.e. a
species of animal or a person. The answer to this is in both cases
'no'. The objects referred to are not real (animals, persons).
Dragons are 'mals', Hamlet is a 'rson', i.e. they are fictional or
'fictitious' in the sense of occurring in stories. The questions 'Do
dragons exist?', 'Does Hamlet exist?' can also be construed on the

model of 'Has X got diamonds, teeth, money?', 'Has X got monds, eth, ney?', viz. 'Are there such animals as "dragons"?' 'Is (or was) there a person answering to the description "Hamlet, Prince of Denmark, whose mother married his uncle. . ."?' (answer, as it happens, almost certainly 'no'), or 'Are there such mals as dragons (i.e. creatures in story-books called dragons)?', 'Is there such a rson as Hamlet. . . (i.e. character in drama called Hamlet who. . .)?', to which the answer is, as it happens, known to be yes. If the questions are phrased as 'Do the creatures in the story-books called dragons exist?', 'Does (the character called) Hamlet exist?', there is already a reference to a kind of mal and to an individual rson, and the questions immediately become ambiguous and confusing. They could ask, oddly, whether the mal or rson referred to exists, or almost as oddly, whether the mal or rson referred to is an animal or person. Rephrased without already supposing that what is referred to (a dragon or Hamlet) is a mal or rson, the questions break down as above: into questions about what kind of thing something is, and whether there are characters in stories called. . ., or a species of animal or individual person which is so and so.

6.1.3   Box b

The questions 'Do dragons exist?', 'Does Hamlet exist?' can be ambiguous and sometimes confusing.

(iii)   'Real' and 'exists'

Currently existent objects (a brooch, dollar notes in the hand, etc.) can have the characteristics that make them real diamonds or money on the one hand or not real or not quite (but paste, toy, 'imaginary') diamonds or money on the other. Here we can think of a successfully identified object that exists at an appropriate time as being said to have certain characteristics. The questions as to whether there is or is not a real diamond or real money or is or is not a fake diamond or toy money are not questions about the characteristics of individual identified objects. Or if they are, the 'objects' about which the questions are are not the diamonds or monds or money or ney but the world or some other place, and the question then is, or can be construed as, a question about the characteristics of the world or some place in it, that is, whether it contains diamonds, monds, money, ney.

In the case of 'animals' or 'persons' who are real on the one hand, or not real but 'imaginary' in the sense of occurring in invented stories on the other, we do not have what could be thought of as 'currently existent objects' awaiting identification as one or the other. We could have, for example, if we had a class of robotic animals and robotic persons and the question arose of whether an individual person-like object was of this class or a real person. But fictional animals and persons are not the right kind of not real animals and persons. The nearest we can get to the picture of successfully identified objects awaiting classification is to produce descriptions or names like 'dragon', 'Hamlet', and then to make enquiry.[10] But because we normally make references to individuals of a *kind* of thing, and we have here no appropriate covering kind, the question is bound to be confusing. The existential questions also differ because 'the world' or various places in it contain persons, while it is stories, plays and so on that contain fictional species of animals and fictional individual animals and persons, set in places (which may be entirely invented or imitate real places).

6.1.3 Box c

To describe something, which is already identified, as being a real F may be to attribute characteristics to it. To say that a real F or non-real F exists is not.

(iv) Existing at different times

The possibility of distinguishing between failure of reference and non-existence at an appropriate time of something successfully referred to results from the fact that individual instances of many kinds of thing can exist at one time and not at another, and have characteristics when they exist which they are not there to have when they do not.

A question about whether something particular exists at a certain time is one about whether something successfully identified,

207

having existed at some time, exists at some specified time. Whether we should consider coming into existence at a specific time or ceasing to exist at a particular time themselves to be characteristics of the identified object is not evident. To be told when such and such object came into or went out of existence (if a person, was conceived, or born, or died) is obviously to be given information about the object, but not all information is information about characteristics, and coming into existence or going out of it are unlike other attributes in that each individual can and must have each just once. On balance, it seems better to exclude coming into and going out of existence, along with existing at time 1 and non-existing at time 2, from being characteristics, and to say, with Kant, that these do not belong to a list that starts 'striped, tame. . .'. This does not of course preclude existent stones, things in the mouth, or dollar notes in the hand from having the characteristics of real or the characteristics of not real diamonds, teeth, or money, or those that once existed from having once had them.

6.1.3 Box d

Existing at particular times is sufficiently different from other
  attributes for it to be better not to consider it a
  characteristic.

Once again, fictional items, ones in invented stories, are troublesome. They come into and go out of existence in the stories. They can also be said to come into existence in a different sense, when the stories are invented, written, published. (We could make the distinction by distinguishing when the *stories* came into existence, and maybe ultimately disappeared, and what happens at the fictional times created in them.)

SECTION 2   *IDENTITY*

6.2.1   Propositions/statements of identity

(i)   Numerical and qualitative identity

Two sorts of proposition/statement can be called propositions/
statements of identity. Each sort says that *a* is (or is not) the same
such and such as *b*. In one case, that most usually spoken of as
'identity', *numerical identity*, *a* is said to be, or not be, the very same
thing as *b*. For example, it is said of a car that it is the very same
car that you bought yesterday, or of a toucan that it is not the very
same toucan that caught cans just now. In the other case, known
as *qualitative identity*, *a* is said to be (or not to be) the same as *b* in
some, perhaps many, respects. For example, a car is said to be the
same model (or colour or make) as another car, or a toucan not the
same (in appearance, habits, etc.) as one seen last week.[11]

(ii)   Particulars and non-particulars

Discussions of identity are often confined to, or at least concen-
trated on, the identity of particulars, or, even more narrowly, on
questions about the numerical identity of material objects and
persons. So it is important to note at the outset that non-
particulars, such as diseases, colours, propositions, years, can also
be said to be the same or different in either the numerical or the
qualitative sense.[12] Thus measles can, truly, be said to be not the
same disease as chicken pox but perhaps to resemble it, for
instance in being infectious, or the proposition expressed by one
token sentence to be the very same proposition as that expressed by
another. Because non-particulars can be, and often are, referred to
(essentially) as related in a certain way to particulars, as in 'the
proposition expressed by that token sentence' or 'the disease Jones
had last week', propositions/statements of numerical identity about
non-particulars can be very like ones of qualitative identity about
particulars. For example the proposition of qualitative identity
'Smith has the same disease that Jones had last week' will express
a truth in the same circumstances as the proposition of numerical
identity 'The disease Smith has is the same disease as the disease
Jones had last week'. But it is easy to see that these are not the
very same proposition: their subjects are different and so, among

other differences, if Smith and Jones (both identified and alive) had no disease the proposition of qualitative identity about Smith and Jones would express a false statement while the proposition of numerical identity about the disease Smith has and the disease Jones had would fail to make a statement (see 2.2.2 (ix)).

(iii)   Ambiguous type sentences

Although the distinction between propositions/statements of qualitative identity and propositions/statements of numerical identity is fairly easy to see, the same type *sentence* can very readily express either: 'This is the same car as that' can mean either 'This is numerically the same car as that' or 'This is qualitatively the same car as that'. Sentences of the form 'a is the same F as b' can also express not propositions/statements of identity but rather ones which seem to belong to the subject-predicate category by either of the tests discussed in 6.1.2 (iii). For instance, the sentence 'That man who called is the same one who came collecting for charity last week' might be intended to describe the man who called, rather than to express a proposition/statement of numerical identity, or 'Smith has the same disease that Jones had' to be about Smith, rather than to express a proposition/statement of qualitative identity about Smith and Jones, that is, only 'the man who called' or only 'Smith' are treated as subject terms. Propositions of identity, whether qualitative or numerical, have two (or more) subject terms: for a sentence to express a proposition of identity it must have the appropriate meaning, which involves, among other things, that the expressions on either side of 'is the same F as' ('the man who came collecting charity last week' as well as 'the man who called', 'Jones' as well as 'Smith') must both rate as subject terms.

(iv)   The 'relation' of identity

From the point of view of the number of their subject terms, propositions/statements of identity belong to the category of relational propositions/statements.[13] However, 'being the same as' differs in important respects from most ordinary relations like 'being to the left of' or 'being the brother of'. In particular,

1.   'The same' needs completion: whether 'is the same as' is taken numerically (is one and the same as) or qualitatively (is like), 'is

the same' must be followed by an appropriate term in order to be intelligible. It makes no sense to speak of *a* and *b* as being or not being alike, the same or different in the qualitative sense, without specifying the respect in which they are, or are not, alike. Token sentence *a* cannot just be like (or not like) token sentence *b*: they have to be alike in having the same meaning or not alike in having, for instance, different typography. Similarly, and more emphasized by logicians, it makes no sense to speak of 'a' and 'b' being, or not being, numerically the same, one and the same thing, without specifying the same *what*. The expressions used to make the references to the things being said to be the same in propositions/ statements of numerical identity often contain the relevant term, as in 'This car is the same one as the car which. . .': the 'same one' in this sentence would naturally be taken to mean 'the same car'. But this may not always be so. Where it is not, the need to indicate the kind of thing of which the items referred to are being said to be one and the same instance is correspondingly greater. We should not generally say 'The author of X is the same one as the speaker last night' but rather '. . . is the same person as. . .'.

2.   Something can be 'the same as' itself. Identity is held to fit into the classifications logicians have made of relations by their properties, being reflexive, transitive, symmetrical. Although the point is less evident when 'the same as' is completed with 'such and such', I shall leave this subject aside in favour of another related point.[14] Ordinarily it is two or more things that are said to stand in a particular relation to each other. This condition is satisfied by propositions/statements of qualitative identity suitably completed: we generally, although not invariably, speak of one thing as like or unlike another thing, rather than as like or unlike itself. Propositions/statements of numerical identity, or at least affirmative ones, are different. They say of something referred to in one way that it is one and the same thing as something referred to in another way, or perhaps in the same way. 'Being the same (something or other) as itself' is a sufficiently curious relation for propositions/statements of numerical identity often to be con- sidered to form a class of their own. Kripke, for example, singled out statements of identity, or at least affirmative ones, as 'if the subjects mentioned therein exist', necessarily true, or, if true, necessarily true.[15]

6.2.1   Box a

Propositions/statements of identity refer to items and say of
them that they are (or are not) similar/the same
(qualitative identity) or one and the same (numerical
identity). They can be regarded as (a class of) relational
propositions/statements but especially in the case of
numerical identity the 'relation' is unlike standard
relations.

(v)   Completing 'one and the same'

The point that we have to speak of one *such and such*, which is
greatly emphasized in other settings in which the notion of
numerical identity is discussed, is often not stressed, and
sometimes appears to be overlooked, in discussions of propositions/
statements of numerical identity. In considering their features
logicians frequently represent such propositions/statements as 'a is
b' (or 'a is a') or even 'a = b' (or 'a = a'), although '=' generally
has more specific senses such as 'is the same number/quantity as'.
The use of 'a' and 'b', or of proper names ('Cicero is Tully',
'Kripke is Kripke') veils the point further since the expressions
treated as referring to the items being said to be the same one
contain no explicit mention of the kind of thing in question. If, as is
commonly accepted, it makes no sense to speak of *a* and *b* as just
'one and the same' but only of *a* and *b* as one and the same such
and such, then it also makes no sense to say just 'a *is* b' (or 'a is
a'): the proper form is 'a is the same such and such as b' (or 'a is
the same such and such as a').

It is important to note that if 'such and such' is not the right
noun, then a proposition of the form 'a is the same such and such
as b' (or 'a is the same such and such as a') will not express a true
statement of numerical identity. This is so irrespective of whether
there is a true (affirmative) statement of numerical identity which
could be made about *a* or about *a* and *b*. For example, if we take 'a'
to be 'that man who called' and 'b' to be 'the man who came
calling for charity last week', then the substitution of 'man' or
'person' for 'such and such' in '*a* is the same such and such as *b*'
yields a proposition which might express a true statement of

212

numerical identity, and will do so if 'a' and 'b' in fact refer to the same (living) man/person. However, taking 'a' as 'that man who called' and 'b' as 'the man who came calling for charity last week', the substitution of the following sorts of term for 'such and such' has different results, even if 'a' and 'b' do refer to the same person:

Sort 1: terms like 'weight', 'age', 'nationality', or 'truth value'. Substitution of terms like these for 'such and such' in 'a is the same such and such as b' results in a proposition which might express a true statement of qualitative identity: 'a is the same weight as b', and if *a* and *b* were in fact the same person, this particular proposition would express a truth. But the proposition is not one expressing a statement of numerical identity, or at least if it were taken as such it would be nonsense (could not express a true statement). A meaningful proposition of numerical identity of the form 'a is the same *weight* as b' requires 'a' and 'b' each to refer to a weight (for instance, 'X's weight is the same weight as the weight of this suitcase'). Given that 'a' and 'b' refer to 'the man who. . .', 'a is the same truth value as b' would be nonsense (could not express a true statement) however construed, and similarly 'a is a different truth value from b'.

Sort 2: terms like 'bicycle' or 'planet' (or, for example, 'place', 'time', etc.). Substituting terms like these for 'such and such' in 'That man who called is the same such and such as the man who came calling for charity last week' would give rise to a proposition which could not express a truth, and if 'a' and 'b' both secured reference to an existent man would express a false statement. Only if 'a' and 'b' were each expressions referring to bicycles could 'a is the same bicycle as (or: a different bicycle from) b' express a true statement.

It seems clear that far from (affirmative) propositions of numerical identity (or difference) having to express truths so long as 'the objects mentioned therein exist', many propositions of the form 'a is the same such and such as b' are incapable of expressing true statements of numerical identity (or difference). Examples of sorts 1 and 2, cited above, suggest that in order for an affirmative proposition of numerical identity to be capable of expressing a truth, the terms referring to the items being said to be one and the same such and such (or two different such and suches) must

213

contain the same noun as each other and that 'such and such' must be the same noun as both. For an affirmative proposition of qualitative identity to be capable of expressing a truth, 'such and such' has to be differently related to the terms referring to the items said to be the same. Here 'such and such' *cannot* be the same noun as the nouns referring to the items being said to be the same. It has to be a term of a kind whose meaning allows it to apply to, to name a quality of, items referred to as being the same, as 'weight' names a quality of men and 'truth value' does not. In both cases, 'a is a different such and such from/than b' behaves like 'a is the same such and such as b'. 'a is not the same F as b' often means 'a is a different F from/than b'. It can also be a purely negative proposition: 'It is not the case that a is the same F as b'. 'It is not the case that a is the same F as b' will express a truth whenever 'a is the same F as b' does not (except possibly if 'a' or 'b' fails to secure reference), i.e. if a and/or b do not (currently) exist, if 'F' is in the wrong relation to the nouns contained in 'a' and 'b', or if a is a different F from/than b (see 5.1.4, esp. (ii)).

6.2.1   Box b

The correct form of propositions/statements of identity (difference) is 'a is the same (/a different) *such and such* as b', and not 'a is (/is not) b'. The relation of the nouns (in) 'a' and 'b' to the noun standing in for 'such and such' in (affirmative) propositions of numerical identity that can express truths is different from their relations in (affirmative) propositions of qualitative identity: as a first approximation, it needs to be the same noun in the former (numerical identity), while in the latter (qualitative identity) 'such and such' needs to name an attribute a and b could have.

That the same noun should appear in or be contained in both the terms playing the part of subject terms and as 'such and such' in 'is the same such and such as' does not seem quite invariably to be a necessary condition of a proposition of numerical identity being capable of expressing a truth. This can be seen if, still taking 'a' as 'the man who called' and 'b' as 'the man who came calling for charity last week', we make another substitution:

Sort 3: terms like 'mathematician', 'lecturer', 'passenger'. It might be true that the man referred to as 'the man who called' and 'the man who came calling for charity last week' are one and the same mathematician, lecturer, and/or passenger. It is compatible with *a* and *b* being one and the same person, i.e. there being a true statement of numerical identity about them, that *a* and *b* are not the same mathematician, that is, that the person referred to as 'a' and 'b' is not a mathematician. Similarly, it can be true that *a* and *b* are different persons, but not different mathematicians (one or both not being mathematicians).

Another sort of noun poses problems for suggesting that the same noun appearing or being contained in the subject terms and as 'such and such' in 'is the same such and such as' is a sufficient condition of a proposition of numerical identity being capable of expressing a truth:

Sort 4: terms like 'thing' or 'object'. 'Person "a" is one and the same thing as person "b"' and 'Object "a" is one and the same object as object "b"' do not as they stand seem to be intelligible propositions. This is not because their meaning is such that statements of numerical identity they express must have a truth value other than true as in examples of sorts 1 and 2, but because it is not clear what the meaning, if any, is. There are similar problems about 'action "a" is the same action as action "b"' or 'Place "a" is the same place as place "b"'. Discussions of numerical identity not primarily concerned with propositions/ statements of numerical identity have been greatly concerned with the fact that it is only some nouns which are suitable to stand in for 'such and such' in 'one and the same such and such' or 'two different such and suches'. If so, only some nouns can complete 'is one and the same. . .' or 'is a different. . .' in propositions of numerical identity. As we shall see (6.2.2 (iii)), there are criteria for the use of 'one thing' or 'one object', 'action', 'place', whereby propositions like '(Object) a is one and the same object as (object) b' *can* have a meaning, but clearly they are not straightforward propositions of numerical identity.

6.2.1 Box c

Some nouns seem unsuitable as 'such and such' in 'one such
and such' or 'two different such and suches'. If so, some
sorts of noun cannot complete 'is one and the same . . .'/'is
a different. . .' in any proposition of numerical
identity/difference.

6.2.2 *Sortal terms*

(i) Supplying a principle of counting

A brief answer to the question of what kind of term is suitable to
complete 'one and the same' is that it is the kind of term which
supplies a single principle of counting things, or 'instances', of the
sort named by the term: if and only if 'such and such' is this kind
of term is it clear what counts as one and the same such and such
or two different such and suches. Terms of this kind are often
known as *sortal* terms/universals. Examples are 'car', 'toucan',
'person', 'disease'.[16]

There are sometimes said to be two kinds of general term: sortal
terms, those which supply a principle of counting, and *characterizing*
terms which supply a principle of counting only if conjoined with
or qualifying another term which supplies a principle of counting.[17]
Terms like 'red', 'small', 'true', perhaps 'real' are examples of
characterizing terms. Sortal and characterizing terms are not the
only terms with a claim to be called 'general', as opposed to
'singular'. There are many terms which are neither one nor the
other, and some which are a combination of both sorts. Among
general terms which do not fit into either class are terms which are
too general to supply a single principle of counting, terms like
'place', 'quality', 'time', 'event', 'action', 'material object', or
'thing', 'entity', 'object' (see above 6.2.1 (v), sort 4), and terms,
sometimes known as 'mass' terms, or names of 'materials', which,
like 'gold', 'butter', 'grass', or 'water', do not supply a principle of
counting unless prefaced by a more or less specific quantity word
like 'mass of', 'piece of', 'patch of', 'gram of', 'pint of'. There are
also terms which, although sortal terms in the sense of supplying a
principle of counting, do so because they include another term

which supplies the principle. 'Mathematician', 'lecturer', 'passenger', at least as most commonly used, are examples of this kind of term: one mathematician, lecturer, passenger is normally one person with certain characteristics (see above 6.2.1 (v), sort 3). Terms of this kind are sometimes called 'sortal-cum-characterizing' terms/universals. The line between sortal and sortal-cum-characterizing terms/universals is not always easy to draw.

6.2.2   Box a

A sortal term is a kind of general term which supplies a (single) principle of counting what it applies to, like the terms 'car' or 'person'.

(ii)   Nouns which are too general

Of the nouns which are what I have called 'too general' to supply a principle of counting, the terms 'thing' and 'object', the most general of all, have probably been the most discussed. It is evident that if asked to count up how many things there are in a room, or have been there in the past week, it would be impossible to give an answer. Even if 'thing' is taken as 'physical object', it is not obvious whether a desk rates as one thing, or, if it has a frame and five drawers, as six instead or as well, whether to count only a person or also each of a person's bones as one thing. The problem is compounded when 'thing' or 'object' is taken more widely so that not only people and their clothes, accessories, and bones count as things but also their smiles, utterances, finger-nails, genes, thoughts.

Hume, in the *Treatise* ((1739) 1911: 1.2.ii, 1.4.ii–vi), tried to set up a way of counting 'things' by employing the notion that only what cannot be counted as more than one thing is really one thing. As a result, he maintained that being truly one thing requires that the thing in question has no parts nor separable qualities nor any other feature which would allow it to be considered two anythings. On this basis, he claimed that most things that are counted as one something or other, for example one desk or one person, are not really one thing at all and are only mistakenly spoken of as if they were: they fail to satisfy the condition of not being countable as more than one thing.[18]

Locke had already suggested (Locke (1690) 1975, bk 2, ch. 27), and Frege later suggested (Frege (1884) 1950: parts 3 and 4, esp. secs 45–54), what is now most generally accepted, namely, that the problem of counting things, or saying what counts as one thing, arises from the fact that 'thing' is the wrong kind of noun to follow 'one and the same'. We have to speak of one *chair*, *tree*, *person*, etc., or, in other words, to follow 'one and the same' by a noun which, unlike 'thing' does allow us to count how many things of that sort there are.[19]

The general point that we cannot count 'things' or 'objects' but only instances of (certain) *kinds* of thing or object, also applies to other terms comparable in generality to 'object' or 'thing'. Just as we cannot count (physical) objects as such, so we cannot count events or actions or places or (periods of) time as such. It makes no sense to ask how many events a has witnessed this morning, how many actions b has performed, how many places c has visited, but only how many events of a certain sort a has witnessed this morning (e.g. how many accidents), how many actions of a certain kind b has performed (how many meals b has eaten, for instance), how many rooms or cities or countries c has been in.

6.2.2   Box b

Terms like 'thing', 'object', 'place', 'action' are not sortal
  terms, being too general, and 'a is one and the same object
  as b' can never be a straightforward proposition/statement
  of numerical identity

(iii)   'One object'

There are settings in which we want to re-generalize to 'one/the same object', 'one/the same place', 'one/the same time', 'one/the same act'. The dicta 'Two objects cannot be in the same place at the same time' or 'One object cannot be in different places at the same time' or 'One and the same object must have identical qualities' may not perhaps have to be accepted as they stand but they also do not have to be dismissed as total nonsense. More pertinent to some of the discussions in this book (see 2.4.2 (ii)), there is a criterion of identity for 'objects' and the rest, such that we can quite sensibly speak of saying the same of the same object(s), and thus of making the same type statement, as I have used the notion of a 'type statement'.

The most plausible criterion for 'one object' is that anything which is 'one such and such', where 'such and such' is a sortal term, is thereby also one object. Thus if, in the examples discussed above (6.1.2 (v)), 'a' ('that man who called') and 'b' ('the man who called for charity last week') refer to one and the same *person*, that is, there is *a* true statement of the form 'a is one and the same such and such as b' (where 'such and such' is a sortal term) to be made about *a* and *b*, then *a* and *b* thereby *also* count as one and the same thing or object in the wide sense of 'thing' or 'object', where these terms are not confined to physical objects. To say that 'a is one and the same object as b' is not a straightforward proposition of numerical identity. Such a proposition either makes the point that there is some true statement of numerical identity, some 'such and such' such that *a* and *b* are the same instance of it, or, if 'such and such' is already built into 'a' and 'b' as in 'Person a is the same object as person b' it says something more obscure, perhaps to the effect that a person is to be considered as a single object.

It is worth noting that 'occupant of the same place at the same time' does not, quite aside from problems about 'same place' and 'same time', rate as a sortal term and is not a suitable substitution for 'such and such' in propositions of numerical identity. It is usually included as a necessary condition of something's being one and the same 'object' that it has the same beginning and end. One purpose of this necessary condition is to exclude the possibility of a physical object and the matter/materials of which it is at some time composed from counting as 'the same object'. One way of introducing it is to treat supplying a single principle of counting over periods of time (where relevant) as part of what is meant by a term's supplying a principle of counting, and so being a sortal universal. A house and all those bricks of which at some time it is composed, or a tree and the atoms of which at some time it consists, can then clearly be seen to be different 'objects'; they do not necessarily occupy the same places at other times or begin and end at the same time.[20]

6.2.2   Box c

The most plausible way of re-introducing 'one object' is to
say that if *a* and *b* are one such and such, where 'such and
such' is a sortal term, then *a* and *b* are thereby 'one object'.
We can then speak intelligibly, for instance, of saying the
same of the same objects.

(iv)   Nouns which are too specific

The terms I referred to as 'sortal-cum-characterizing' terms, like
'mathematician' and 'passenger', are sometimes excluded from the
class of sortal terms or, at least, from being true sortal terms. The
reason for including them is that they supply an unequivocal
principle of counting. We can count how many mathematicians
there are in a room or a university at some time or over some
specified period of time, distinguish between one and the same
passenger on an aeroplane and two different ones. The reasons for
excluding them at least from being true sortal terms are less
straightforward. The most obvious is to say that the *principle* for
counting is supplied by a noun included by these terms, 'person' in
the case of mathematicians and passengers. Normally a mathematician or passenger is conceived of as a person who . . . , so that
two persons cannot be one mathematician/passenger, nor one
person two mathematicians/passengers, mathematician 'a' and
passenger 'b' may be one and the same object (= person), and so
on. To count mathematicians or passengers is to count how many
persons there are with a particular characteristic.[21]

Confusion can be caused by the fact that terms like this are not
invariably used in this way. An airline counting the passengers it
has carried in the past year probably counts the same person
travelling twice as two passengers, not as one: one 'passenger' is
one person carried for one journey. If so, we might say that one
passenger begins and ends when one person begins and ends a flight,
not when one person begins and ends, so that although a passenger
is typically constituted by a person, a passenger is not the same
kind of 'object' as a person. When a term like 'passenger' is used in
this way, it looks like a sortal term in its own right, i.e. like a true
sortal term. A symptom that it is not uncommonly used in this way

is that 'passenger' is easily extended to travellers who are not persons, such as horses in horse-transporting aeroplanes (where a count of passengers may be primarily of horses on the flight).

If 'passenger' is used sometimes to mean 'person who. . .' and sometimes in the sense just outlined, it is an ambiguous word, and which meaning it has has to be specified before we can say, for instance, how many 'passengers' an airline has really carried.

6.2.2   Box d

Some terms, such as 'passenger', generally mean 'person who. . .' and one passenger is one person who. . . . But sometimes they are true sortal terms: one (e.g. aeroplane) passenger begins and ends when one person (or etc.) begins and ends a journey (e.g. one flight). That 'a' and 'b' refer to the same person (who travels) is not, on this use, enough for them to refer to one and the same passenger.

(v)   Unequivocal principles of counting

Even terms which, with one meaning, can be said to supply a single principle of counting, like 'table' or 'person', may not do so for every case.

The principal difficulties which arise are:

(a)   when one thing of a kind can be taken apart to make two things of the same kind, or two things of a kind can be put together to make one thing of the same kind, as with a cleverly designed table that takes apart into two (complete) tables or a (compound) sentence which can be said to contain (whole) sentences;

(b)   when things of a kind are subject to fission (one becoming two of the same kind over time) or fusion (two of a kind becoming one of the same kind over time).[22]

Where any of these is unusual or brief for things of the kind in question it may pose a problem when it occurs: I do not know how many tables to say I have when I have this (these) cleverly designed table(s), you are not sure how many parties you went to as your party merged with another at midnight, she eats for two, being pregnant. But the occurrence of such occasional difficulties would not create doubts about the term naming the kind ('table', etc.) being a sortal term. However, as we saw with token sentences (2.1.2 (i)) the problem may be, as it were, endemic. In this case to count and say what is *one*, we have to introduce what appears an arbitrary ruling as to what is to be one. (To count amoebae and other living things which are subject to constant fission the notion of 'different generations' is introduced.)

It is sometimes objected to the close identification of the concept of numerical identity with that of counting that we can speak of the same such and such in the numerical sense even where there is a reason for which we cannot really count. An example sometimes given is of a material, say silver, used first to make a dish and then coins, where it is the *same* silver (exactly the same lot of it). The same water first in a pan, then poured into a coffeepot, is a similar type of example. Whether we speak of my cleverly designed table as one or two or a compound type sentence as one or more, we can still speak correctly of 'the same again' in the numerical sense. We should say in this case: the very same one (or, if you want to call it/them two, then the very same pair), or, in the case of the silver and water: the very same lot (piece or volume) of it.

6.2.2   Box e

Few terms supply a principle for counting things of the kind in *every* contingency. Where they do not, we may still be able to speak of 'the same again' by introducing the notion of the same 'however many we count them as'. Where there is a particularly common counting problem, a ruling, which can appear rather arbitrary, may be introduced to allow unequivocal counting.

(vi)   Different sorts of sortal terms

I mentioned earlier that it is the numerical identity of particulars, especially of material objects and persons which tends to be the most discussed. A symptom or consequence of this is that distinctions are drawn or 'criteria of identity' put forward which are relevant to material objects and persons but are presented as if they were generally applicable to anything which can be one and the same such and such.

A notable example is the distinction between counting or saying something is one and the same at one time and doing so over periods of time. Hume called being one at one time 'unity' (or 'simplicity'), and being one over periods of time 'identity'.[23] Sometimes principles of counting or saying something is one at one time is called 'enumeration' or 'individuation',[24] while 'identity' is used in the Humean sense, and 'principles (or criteria) of identity' are the principles employed in counting over a period of time.[25] Criteria for distinguishing one such and such from another at one time may require a different kind of description (e.g. one chair or worm is spatially continuous) from criteria for saying it is one over a period of time (e.g. it must have a continuous life history, one beginning and end, etc.).

Such a distinction is not, as it stands, wholly applicable even to different sorts of particular, such as events. Events take place over a period of time, and there cannot be said to be one (whole) performance of a symphony if it stops after five minutes but only part of one. There are non-particulars where it could be treated as having some applicability. Criteria of 'unity' for one disease such as measles or one species such as the dodo do not in the least resemble those for individual physical objects like chairs, but at least they can be described at one time (measles often has complications, dodos inhabit such and such a place) or over periods of time (measles has become less virulent, the species of dodo became extinct at such and such time). In the case of other non-particulars, like individual numbers, or type sentences or propositions, it is difficult to think of many epithets which could be applied at one time or over periods of time. We could perhaps come up with 'In the middle ages the number 9 was believed to be. . .' or 'The proposition that God exists was said to be metaphysical by the Positivists'. However, to grasp the criteria of unity/identity for such objects as type sentences or type propositions, we have to grasp not matters to do with spatial location and continuity at one time or over time but that one token sentence expresses the same type sentence as another if they have what logicians call the same typography (same words in same order, not necessarily e.g. same size or style of print) or that two token sentences express the same proposition if they have the same meaning.

6.2.2   Box f

Through the concentration on the numerical identity of material objects and persons, and consequent distinction between principles of counting at one time and over time, the term 'identity' is sometimes reserved for being one such and such over a period of time.

(vii)   'a is a'

One can fairly readily see what one is being told if told that 'the man who called is one and the same person as the man who came calling for charity last week', or that 'the token sentence you uttered has the same typography as the one I just wrote down', or that 'The number 9 is the same number/quantity as 3×3'. But it is extremely difficult to get a grip on what is stated by the examples of propositions/statements of identity particularly favoured by logicians, 'a is a', or indeed why they should be so extensively discussed. As 'a is a' is usually construed, propositions of this form would not all rate as self-evident. Self-evident propositions are normally a sub-class of analytic proposition (see 3.2.2), and where 'a' represents a referring expression in Usage 4 (its meaning does not determine to what it refers) or in Usage 3 (of a kind to refer to a particular) (see 2.3.3), 'a is a' may not express a truth, even if, when spelt out as 'a is the one and the same F as a', 'F' is the right kind of noun for the proposition to have a meaning such that it could express a true statement of numerical identity. 'a' may fail to secure reference or what it refers to not currently exist. Locke made fun of self-evident propositions of the form 'a is a' nearly three centuries ago.[26] It has lately been suggested that they should be considered 'not genuine statements of identity at all'.[27] Since there are many interesting features of propositions/statements of identity, it has not seemed necessary to discuss these certainly rather empty-looking propositions at length, although a little more will be said about them in 7.2.2 (iii).

NOTES

6.2.2 Box g

Propositions/statements of the form 'a is a' are often
discussed by logicians. But some have thought 'a is a' not a
genuine form of proposition/statement of identity. 'a is a'
need not be self-evident, even if the omitted 'same F as' is
of the right kind: 'a' may be a referring expression
(Usage 4 or 3). But as presented 'a is a' probably
resembles such propositions as 'That bald man is bald' in
that it is a proposition of a kind that cannot express a false
statement.

NOTES

1. Kant (1781) 1929, A545–602/B620–631. The argument was directed against the ontological argument for the existence of God: see 1.1.2 b.
2. See for example Russell (1918) 1956, Moore (1936) 1953, Ryle 1951.
3. For brevity 'sentences-' is used to stand for 'sentences and/or propositions and/or statements' in 6.1.1 and 2.
4. Eeyore is the name of a donkey in works of fiction by A. A. Milne.
5. The question of whether 'exists' is a predicate was most often discussed assuming Russell's Theory of Descriptions but sometimes the Theory of Presupposition analysis was adopted or taken into account, making for some difference in the way this argument was expressed. See 2.2.2 on the Theory of Descriptions and Theory of Presupposition.
6. See for example Cartwright (1960) 1987, Pears (1963) 1967, Kitely 1964, Strawson (1967) 1973.
7. On this topic see Strawson 1959, esp. ch. 5; 1974, esp. pt 2.
8. At least provided these terms (proper names) are included as referring expressions (Usage 4), cf. 2.3.3.
9. Deriving from J. L. Austin 1962 (posth.), VII: 62–77. 62–77.
10. See Strawson (1967) 1974.
11. See e.g Strawson 1959: 33–4, Carruthers 1986, 3.1: 68–76.
12. See for instance Strawson 1959: 226–34.
13. See e.g. Strawson 1959: 242–3 on the classification of statements of identity.
14. Relations are often classified according to properties which they must have, may have, or cannot have. A relation is reflexive if anything (of a relevant kind) must have this relation to itself, non-reflexive if it may or may not have it, irreflexive if nothing can have the relation to itself. It is transitive, non-transitive, or intransitive according to whether 'if a is R to b, and b is R to c, then a is R to c' is necessarily true, contingent, or necessarily false. It is symmetrical,

non-symmetrical, or asymmetrical according to whether 'If a is R to
b, b is R to a' must be true, may or may not be, or cannot be true.
On this classification, 'the same (F) as' is a transitive and
symmetrical relation. 'The same as' is normally said also to be
reflexive. But 'the same F as' can be more troublesome to fit in. See
e.g. Newton-Smith 1985, ch. 7 for a good account of these properties
of relations.

15. Kripke (1971) 1977; (1972) 1980: 97–105 (see 3.4.1); also Strawson
1974: 51–6. The view has not gone undisputed: see e.g. Sprigge 1988:
36ff.
16. See e.g. Strawson 1959: 167–73, Wiggins 1980: 7–8, 60–74, O'Hear
1985: 55.
17. Strawson 1959: 168, who re-introduced 'sortal' term (from Locke),
distinguished them in this way.
18. See Wolfram 1974: 586–93 for a detailed account of Hume's position.
19. See e.g. O'Hear 1985: 53–60 for an introduction of the point.
20. See Wiggins 1968; 1980: 68–9.
21. See Wiggins 1980: 63.
22. See Parfit (1971) 1975 for a variety of cases.
23. Hume (1739) 1911: 1.2.ii, 1.4.ii–vi; see Wolfram 1974: 586–93.
24. Carruthers 1986: 256 uses 'identification'; 'distinctness' is another
common term: see e.g. Wiggins 1980: 70.
25. See e.g. Woods 1965 for discussion. It is important to note that the
terms 'principles of enumeration' and 'principles of identity' are also,
confusingly, sometimes used to mark a different contrast: that
between counting ('enumeration'), whether at one time or over time,
and saying of something that it is one and the same ('identity'),
whether at one time or over time. See e.g. Woods 1965: 123ff.
26. Locke (1690) 1975, esp. bk 4, chs 7 and 8. See Wolfram 1978: 40–4;
1980: 89–95.
27. Sprigge 1988: 35.

QUESTIONS

When you have read this chapter, or sections in it, you may like to
try your hand at these questions, and/or to keep them in mind
when doing some or all of the suggested reading. Questions are
framed *primarily* on specified sections, but material from other
sections may help with answers. You may also like to try the
examination questions on this chapter in the Appendix.

6.1
1. Do you think the question of whether 'exists' is a predicate can
be satisfactorily resolved? If so, how? If not, why not?
2. Why does the occurrence of persons and events in fiction pose
problems?

QUESTIONS AND SUGGESTED READING

6.2
3. How would you explain the notions of qualitative and numerical identity?
4. Why is there a difficulty about the ideas of 'one thing', 'one time', 'one place'? What sense, if any, can we give to them?

SOME SUGGESTED READING

For guidance on a sensible order in which to do some or all this reading, consult references in text and notes. Not all the references given in this chapter are included in the list of suggested reading, and reading can be extended by following up other references in text and notes.

6.1 Existence

Austin, J. L. 1962 (posth.), *Sense and Sensibilia*, ch. VII.

Cartwright, R. (1960) 1987, 'Negative Existentials', *Journal of Philosophy*, vol. 57; repr. in C. E Caton (ed.) *Philosophy and Ordinary Language* 1963, and R. Cartwright, *Philosophical Essays* 1987.

Grayling, A. C. 1982, *An Introduction to Philosophical Logic*, ch. 4: 96–109.

Kant, I. (1781) 1929, *Critique of Pure Reason*, A595–602/B620–631 (Transcendental Dialectic, bk II, ch. 3, sec. 4: 500–7).

Kiteley, M. 1964, 'Is Existence a Predicate?', *Mind*, vol. 73 (1964).

Moore, G. E. (1936) 1953, 'Is Existence a Predicate?', *Aristotelian Society* Supplementary Volume 1936, repr. in A. G. N. Flew (ed.) *Logic and Language*, series 2 1953.

Pears, D. (1963) 1967, 'Is Existence a Predicate?', *Aquinas Papers* 38, 1963, repr. in P. F. Strawson (ed.) *Philosophical Logic* 1967.

Russell, B. (1918) 1956, 'The Philosophy of Logical Atomism' V: 232–41 in B. Russell (ed. R. C. Marsh) *Logic and Knowledge* 1956.

Ryle, G. 1951, 'Systematically Misleading Propositions', in A. G. N. Flew (ed.) *Logic and Language*, series 1 1951.

Strawson, P. F. 1959, *Individuals*, ch. 5: 137–79.

—— (1967) 1973, 'Is Existence Never a Predicate?, *Critica* vol. 1; repr. in P. F. Strawson, *Freedom and Resentment* 1973.

More advanced reading

Strawson P. F. 1974, *Subject and Predicate in Logic and Grammar*, pt 2.

6.2   Identity

Carruthers, P. 1986, *Introducing Persons*, ch. 3.i: 68–76.

Frege, G. (1884) 1950, *The Foundations of Arithmetic*, trans. from the original German by J. L. Austin, pts 3 and 4, esp. secs 45–54.

Hume, D. (1739) 1911, *A Treatise of Human Nature*, bk 1, pt 2, sec. ii; bk 1, pt 4, secs ii–vi, Appendix.

Kripke, S. (1971) 1977, 'Identity and Necessity', in M. K. Munitz 1971, *Identity and Individuation*; repr. in S. P. Schwartz (ed.) *Naming, Necessity and Natural Kinds* 1977

—— (1972) 1980, *Naming and Necessity*: 97–105

Locke, J. (1690) 1975, *An Essay Concerning Human Understanding*, bk 2, ch. 27.

O'Hear, A. 1985, *What Philosophy Is*: 'Identity and Individuation': 53–60; 'Personal identity': 243–53.

Parfit, D. 1971, 'Personal Identity', *Philosophical Review*, vol. 80; repr. in J. Perry (ed.) *Personal Identity* 1975.

Sprigge, T. 1988, 'Personal and Impersonal Identity', *Mind*, vol. 97.

Strawson, P. F. 1959, *Individuals*: 167–73.

Wiggins, D. 1968, 'On being in the Same Place at the Same Time', *Philosophical Review*, vol. 77.

—— 1980 *Sameness and Substance*: 60–74.

Wolfram, S. 1974, 'Hume on Personal Identity', *Mind*, vol. 83: 586–93.

Woods, M.J. 1965, 'Identity and Individuation', in R. J Butler (ed.) *Analytical Philosophy* (second series).

More advanced reading

Parfit, D. 1984, *Reasons and Persons*, pt 3.

Wiggins, D. 1980, *Sameness and Substance*, chs 1–2.

Chapter 7

ASPECTS OF MEANING

In recent years, discussion of classes of words, or more specifically, of names, has focussed on two sorts of words: proper names, such as 'London' or 'John', which are singular terms and typically the names of individual particulars, and what are commonly known as 'natural kind' terms, which are general terms and the names of certain individual kinds of things, notably of species of living things and of elements, such as gold. Logicians used to emphasize differences between general terms and proper names. Currently it is more common to stress resemblances between proper names and natural kind terms. Discussion of proper names and 'natural kind' terms raises a number of questions about the meaning of words, and is a convenient way of approaching some more general questions in this area.

SECTION 1   *GENERAL TERMS AND NATURAL KINDS*[1]

7.1.1   What is a 'natural kind'?

Despite much discussion of natural kind terms, for example as to whether they are rigid designators, and the fact that 'natural kind' is now frequently met with in logic books, generally without explanation, as if everyone knew what it meant,[2] it is not easy to be sure exactly what a 'natural kind' is, nor whether everyone understands the same by the term. It rarely receives explicit definition, and while species of living things and elements are always included as 'natural kinds', and usually also compounds like water, there are no very firm guidelines on how to extrapolate beyond these core cases, and there does not seem to be general agreement on which terms are and which are not names of natural kinds. In the terminology of earlier logicians, neither the connotation/intension (definition) nor the denotation/extension (application) of 'natural kind' is clear.

The entry, or re-entry, of 'natural kinds' (earlier, for example by Mill, alternatively called 'real' kinds: Mill 1843, bk 1, ch. 7; bk 4, ch. 7) into logic books in the last decade or two can be seen as a reaction against a view of general terms which had tended to predominate at least since Locke urged: (1) that all classification, all grouping of things into kinds, is made by man and not by nature; and (2) that all classification, including that of living things into species, is based on resemblances between things, properties they share, and that the names of kinds of things are defined in terms of specific properties.[3] Mill, although noting that there are classes of things which we can if we wish consider as 'real kinds' because they are 'distinguished by unknown multitudes of properties and not [like other classes] solely a few determinate ones' (Mill 1843, 1.7.4), still believed that the meaning of a term like 'man', which names a class of this sort, consists in whichever properties we choose to include as necessary and sufficient for something to count as a 'man', and is, as it happens, ambiguous: sometimes one property, such as rationality, is selected to define it, sometimes another, such as number of incisor or canine teeth (Mill 1843, 1.7.6). When, more than a century later, Strawson[4] distinguished particulars from non-particulars by the feature that there can be two particulars which are exactly alike except for their location in space and time, he supposed that two non-particulars could not be exactly alike since they would then be not two but one. It is a natural concomitant of this view that while no general description is necessarily satisfied by only one particular (there could always come to be another which satisfies the same general description), which *non-particular* is meant can be explained, in the Locke–Mill tradition, by giving general descriptions, those that define that kind of thing.[5]

Whatever the differences between them, current proponents of 'natural kinds' almost certainly all share the negative view that not all general names can be defined by particular properties, and that the names of species of living things and elements are among these. There seems little doubt that this negative thesis is correct. The thesis that all grouping of things into kinds proceeds on the basis of resemblances between things, and that general terms apply to things that are qualitatively similar in some respect, had an influence out of all proportion to the evidence adduced for it (one instance of the fact that what is at some time, even for several centuries, generally accepted can turn out not to be true). As we shall see (7.1.2–3), there appear to be many general terms whose meaning is not correctly rendered in this way, including those put forward as natural kind terms.

However, not being definable by specific common characteristics is not the only condition of a 'natural kind'. Natural kinds are also said to have some or all of a number of positive features. Discussions of natural kinds suggest that the following are contenders for supplying the meaning of 'natural kind' or considered to be more or less important characteristics of natural kinds:[6]

Feature 1. The 'things' which make up a natural kind have many distinctive characteristics in common, although not all members of the same kind always have all of them. (Note that natural kind terms are not necessarily sortal terms: they include e.g. terms for matter/materials such as gold and water, and 'things' must here be taken even more widely than usual.)
Feature 2. The things which make up a natural kind have a distinctive 'internal constitution' with which naming is intended to be correlated.
Feature 3. In the case of things which make up natural kinds we learn to apply the name of the kind of thing in question by means of a 'paradigm' (i.e. indisputable and/or typical) instance of the kind of thing.
Feature 4. Natural kinds are 'natural' things (things made by nature and not by man).
Feature 5. Grouping of things into natural kinds is based on 'nature'.

A difficulty that contributes to making the notion of a natural kind at present obscure, is that the addition of some or all of these positive features does not seem to be all that is meant: many classes which cannot be defined by specific common characteristics and which possess some or most of Features 1–5 are nevertheless not included as natural kinds. Moreover, it is not evident that the treatment of elements and species as the paradigm cases of natural kinds is really due to their possession of this collection of features.

7.1.1   Box a

'Natural kind term': a kind of general term, exemplified by the names of individual species of living things, e.g. 'cat', and of individual elements, e.g. 'gold', and having the negative feature that a term of this kind cannot properly be defined by specifying the common characteristics of members of the kind. Several different positive features are attributed to natural kind terms, some by one author, some by another. The notion of a 'natural kind' is not sufficiently defined for general names to be clearly divisible into 'natural' and 'non-natural' kind terms.

7.1.2   *Classifications not based on resemblance*

(i)   Variety of principles of classification

There are many general words, names of kinds of things, which correctly apply to things in virtue of characteristics or properties. Some are the names of properties, like colour terms, or terms for sizes and shapes, others are nouns, definable in the fashion that 'triangle' is defined when it is defined as a plane figure with certain properties (three sides). However, as already indicated, contrary to the Locke–Mill tradition, a great many general terms are not definable in this way, unless, and indeed even if, we extend 'property' beyond its more usual applications. These terms are very varied, and investigation of a few quickly reveals that there are many principles other than 'resemblance', strictly so called, by which classification into kinds can proceed, by no means all of which yield Features 1–5. and/or lead to these kinds being called 'natural kinds'.

(ii)   Examples

A.   Definition by function   A common way of classifying things not based on 'resemblances' is by function, i.e. what it is that things are intended to do or do do. Organs of the body are probably classified in this way: a creature's eyes are organs whereby it sees, lungs those by which it breathes.

An old model of 'definition' according to which the prototype of a definition is to supply an equivalent general description, naming necessary and sufficient properties (as in the case of 'triangle') sometimes lingers on. So it is important to note that, at the same time, many terms are considered to be definable in virtue of the fact that their meaning can be rendered in other general terms, which are not however equivalent *descriptions* that name properties. Obvious examples of definitions not consisting of equivalent descriptions are the definitions of demonstratives like 'I' or connectives like 'and'; thus, for example: ' "I" refers to the speaker' or ' "and" connects two statements such that the compound is true if and only if both constituent statements are true'. It is therefore easy to concede that a term like 'eye' is definable, without stretching the notion of properties and characteristics so that they include functions or maintaining that terms like this are definable by an equivalent general *description*. We can then make the point that 'eyes' and 'lungs', defined as 'organs of sight' and 'organs of breathing', may well have certain clusters of properties, perhaps a certain internal constitution, these being, as things are, needed for the functions in question to be performed, but that possession of particular properties is a matter of fact (not of logical necessity nor part of the meaning of 'eye' or 'lung'), and that there may be a good deal of variety of detail in the properties of eyes and lungs of different species.

Organs of the body appear to have Feature 1 (clusters of properties) and Feature 4 (made by nature) attributed to natural kinds, and on some interpretations of these features, also Feature 2 (distinctive internal constitution) and Feature 5 (grouping is based on 'nature'). In spite of this, organs of the body are not normally included in lists or examples of natural kinds. Classification of organs by functions is already one exception to the earlier doctrine that all grouping proceeds by common properties, and also supplies an example of a style of classification not based on resemblances which does not, at least clearly, yield 'natural kinds'.

Some proponents of natural kinds might be prepared to include organs of the body as natural kinds in virtue of features of the sort I have mentioned. But they would almost certainly not include every kind of thing that is distinguished by function. In particular, there are many artefacts whose names are probably defined by function – tables and chairs, pistols, watches, telephones, and the like, perhaps also institutions like companies (set up to trade) or universities (teaching and research). At least some proponents of natural kinds[7] specifically exclude artefacts, things made by man, from the realm of natural kinds, or, in other words, regard Feature 4 (that the things should be made by nature, not by man) as a necessary condition for a kind to qualify as a natural kind. It should be noted that this is not consistent with the treatment of elements as invariably natural kinds, since there are some elements (such as plutonium no. 94, or technetium no. 43[8]) which, as it happens, do not occur in nature but can be and are made by man.

B. Definition by occupation or role   There are sorts of classification other than by function that are not based on common properties and that are likely not to be regarded as giving rise to natural kinds. Occupations of people are not obviously 'properties' or 'characteristics', but terms like 'lawyer' are among those sometimes explicitly contrasted to natural kind terms. We may read, for example, that there is an 'important difference between terms like "gold", "water", and "tiger" [natural kind terms] . . . and terms like "bachelor", "sloop", and "lawyer" [non-natural or "nominal" kind terms] on the other', if with the addition that the answer to 'the deep and difficult question of which terms name natural kinds and which name nominal kinds' is often 'far from clear' (Schwartz 1977: 38, 39). Again, the division of living creatures into sexes, into 'male' and 'female', which is responsible for a substantial vocabulary in English and other languages ('men'/'women', 'stallions'/'mares', 'bulls'/'cows', etc.) is surely based on their roles in procreation, rather than on a division of properties, and the classes possess Features 1, 2, 4, and 5. Yet males and females are rarely put forward as two different 'natural kinds' of thing.

C. Closed classes   Among the most interesting exclusions from natural kinds is the tacit exclusion of many closed classes of things that in ordinary speech are often spoken of as 'kinds' of things. A 'closed' class of things (cf. 2.3.1) is a class of things so defined that there could be a time when that class could not, as a matter of logical necessity, have any more members. The class of Londoners is a closed class: if the city of London were obliterated, it could not have future members. So is the class of Victorian chairs or Regency houses: no more (real) Victorian chairs can now be made nor Regency houses built. Closed classes are opposed to 'open' classes. An open class is a class such that it is always logically possible, although it may be extremely unlikely, that there will be more members of the class. Species of living things may become extinct, like the dodo or species of dinosaur, and be most unlikely to have future members, but if the right sort of conditions were satisfied, a future creature could be a (real) dodo or Tyrannosaurus rex.

We do speak of closed classes like Victorian furniture or Regency houses as a kind of furniture or house, and furniture or architecture grouped by place and period of origin has many distinctive features. The bases of such classifications are further removed and more clearly distinct from shared properties and resemblances than functions, occupations, and roles: the times and places when things come into existence should almost certainly not be included as among their properties (see 6.1.3 (iv)). Once again, it could be said that such kinds of things are precluded from being natural kinds by the fact that the things being grouped are made by man and not by nature, that is, because they lack Feature 4.

However, the distinction between artefacts and natural things is not always a clear one. For example, breeds of animal and varieties of plants are commonly, if not invariably, brought into existence by the assistance of man, but the animals and plants themselves are not in the usual sense 'artefacts'. Or, if they were, then some species are now also artefacts, man having intervened to produce new ones. We can justify the exclusion of breeds of animals and varieties of plants from being natural kinds, if we wish, despite their possession of many of Features 1–5, simply on the grounds that they are closed classes. To be an instance of a particular breed or a particular variety it is normally necessary for an animal or plant to be descended from common ancestors. A breed or variety can die out, and while a closely resembling one could be produced again, it is exceedingly doubtful whether it would count as numerically the same breed or variety. It is a generally undeclared but almost certainly understood feature (Feature 6) of natural kinds that a natural kind must be an *open* class.

7.1.2 Box a

There are many ways of grouping things together into 'kinds' other than by common properties or resemblances, for example, by function, role, place and time of origin, descent from common ancestors. These groupings differ among themselves. Most of them exhibit some of the positive features attributed to 'natural kinds' (Features 1–5) but are not normally included as natural kinds. Sometimes exclusion is probably due to lack of another Feature, Feature 6: a 'natural kind' is an open class, i.e. it is always logically possible that there could be more members of it.

7.1.3 The case of biological species

(i) Intra-breeding groups

The classification of living things into biological species is one of the paradigm (i.e. indisputable and/or typical) cases of a division into 'natural kinds'. Locke was very much concerned to show that, perhaps contrary to appearances, this classification too rested on resemblances.[9] Biologists think otherwise. Unlike the groups considered in 7.1.2, the grouping of living things into species does not depend on members of one group sharing something other than common properties, such as the same function, descent from the same particulars, coming into existence in the same country at the same period. It depends on a relation which members of the same group have to one another, and do not have to the members of other groups. The relation is that they can interbreed among themselves, and only themselves, to produce others with the same relation to them and to each other. To quote one biologist:

> Dog is called a species because all varieties of dog can interbreed either directly or via intermediate varieties. Dog and Coyote are assigned to different species, since they interbreed seldom or not at all. All horses belong to one species and all donkeys to another; although mules are produced in large numbers in many parts of the world, these hybrids are, with few doubtful

exceptions, wholly sterile. Mankind is a single species, distinct from chimpanzee, gorilla and orang. Each of these species is a genetically closed system, and there is no gene exchange at all between the systems. (Dobzhansky 1958: 28–30)

Dobzhansky claims that 'The existence of species is perceived intuitively even by people without formal training in biology', and that the groups of animals and plants which are distinguished by name in most languages, for the most part, are those which constitute these biological species (Dobzhansky 1958: 20–1).

It certainly seems to be true in English that many common nouns for sorts of living things are the names of biological species in the Dobzhansky fashion. This is not true of *all* terms for kinds of living thing: 'bird', 'fish', or 'mammal' are not the names of individual species, and breeds or varieties within species, discussed in 7.1.2 (ii) C, may be distinguished by name. However it does seem true that there are many biological species, and that they are constituted in the way described. The classification extends beyond the members of these species to ranges of materials, foodstuffs, and so on, which are derived from them. So, for example, the names of woods (oak, and the like), of furs (mink, and so on), of fruits (lemons are the fruit of lemon trees), meats (mutton from sheep, pork from pigs, etc.), materials like wool and alpaca. There is no need to labour the point that division into species in the biologist's sense (groups of things related to each other in the specific way described) is a widely used mode of classification which proliferates a large number of general names.

7.1.3 Box a

Biological species: living things that form intra-breeding groups.

(ii)   Biological species and 'nature'

An important feature of the classification of living things into species is that 'nature' presents us with a system of discrete groups.

Members of each normally share characteristics with each other, for reasons of which there is relatively recent theoretical understanding through knowledge of genetics (deriving from the work of Mendel (1865) but ignored until de Vries's work of 1900[10]): viz. characteristics pass from parents to their young in a fairly regular and predictable pattern by the mechanism of transmitted genes.

Members of the same species also share what can be called an 'internal constitution', namely, a genetic structure. In the light of such claims as that 'Biological kinds are determined by genetic structure, and other natural kinds are similarly determined' (Schwartz 1977: 28), that is, have Feature 2 of natural kinds (see 7.1.1), it is important to note that it is a contingent, and not a necessary, matter that all the members of the same species share a genetic structure. What is essential for, for instance, a creature from another planet to rate as of the same biological species as our cats, and so to have a right to the species name, is that it can interbreed with our cats, in the same way that our cats can interbreed among themselves. Because groups of creatures related in this way have been found to share the same genetic structure (i.e. one qualitatively similar in many respects), that new creatures can interbreed with ones already known is good evidence that their genetic structure will be similar. Conversely, if x has a relevantly similar genetic structure to y, the chances are that x and y will be able to interbreed, that is, are members of the same species. However, genetic structure is not the determinant of membership of the same species in the sense of having any logical connection with it: it is the capacity to interbreed, and not identity of genetic structure, which is necessary and sufficient for creatures to belong to the same species.

Although the recent focussing of attention on 'natural kinds', at the expense of other sorts of classification may not have been altogether profitable, it is worth dwelling for a moment on the role of 'nature' in the classification of living things into species. There is no doubt that 'nature' plays a greater role in this classification than it does in classifications based on 'resemblances'.

(a)   Classification into species is dependent on certain facts   Whereas we could always find some resemblances or differences as a basis for grouping things, the possibility of classifying living creatures into species in the biologist's sense depends on certain definite and specific features of the world. It has to be the case that any one living creature can interbreed with only some and not all living

creatures, that those living creatures with which any one living creature can interbreed are able to interbreed with each other and only one another, that their offspring are able to interbreed with and only with them, and so on. Were nature not as by and large it is in these respects, if living creatures did not on the whole fall into distinct groups in this way, they *could not* be classified into species in the biological sense. It is difficult to imagine a world with no similarities or differences, but perfectly easy to think of one in which creatures do not reproduce in the manner in which in fact they do to form biological species. There being the groups called 'species' is a matter of how 'nature' happens to be.

(b)   The intra-breeding criterion yields only one set of groups   If we decide to group things by resemblance, we retain the choice of *which* sort of resemblance or difference to use, for instance, level of rationality, colour, shape, nature of teeth, and even when we have decided on, for example, teeth or colour, we are left with a choice about where to fix the boundaries of one kind of teeth or one colour. The intra-breeding criterion differs in that once we have decided to adopt it as our principle of classification, we no longer have this sort of choice. The intra-breeding criterion yields only *one* set of groups of living creatures, and the determination of which creatures to assign to the same group and which to different groups is no longer in any sense a matter of choice but only of discovery.

(c)   Members of the same species are likely to share many characteristics   For reasons already mentioned, viz. the facts of genetics, members of the same species are likely to have many common properties, including possession of similar genes. This makes classification into species a particularly useful classification. If we know that a creature is a cat, we can be fairly sure of many of its characteristics. This is due to natural laws being the way they are. Were this not so, the classification could still be made but it would be of much less interest and utility.

There is clearly no harm done if species of living things are therefore distinguished from many other kinds by calling them 'natural' kinds. However, since nothing but living creatures could fall into groups of this particular kind, that is, into intra-breeding groups,[11] extension of the notion of 'natural' kinds to other sorts of things, even to the other favoured paradigm case of elements, is confusing, unless it is decided which of the characteristics of species is to be selected as necessary and sufficient for a kind of thing to count as 'natural', as opposed to non-natural.

7.1.3   Box b

The existence and nature of groups distinguished as biological species depends on certain specific facts, which can justify distinguishing them as 'natural' kinds. But to extend the notion of a 'natural' kind it has to be decided which characteristics of species are necessary and sufficient for other kinds of things also to be classed as 'natural'.

(iv)   The logic of species names

In 7.1.2 I pointed out that where kinds are distinguished by such features as function or role, their names may be considered to be definable, in terms of the relevant function or role: the notion of the definition of a term extends beyond that of supplying equivalent *descriptions* and naming necessary and sufficient *properties*.

As species have been described, it is by no means obvious that their names can be defined. On the contrary, there is reason to suppose that they cannot. This results in problems about how the *meaning* of a term like 'cat' or 'man'/'*homo sapiens*' can be rendered, and also about the way in which a particular species such as that of cats can be identified.

To say that 'cat' is the name of a *species* of animal is to supply a partial explanation of its meaning. Anyone understanding the nature of grouping into species knows that it follows that 'cat' is the name of a specific intra-breeding group. For some purposes, or in some cases, knowing this much is to be said to know the meaning of the relevant word. If I know that some term is the name of some obscure species of insect or of a species of bird found in South America, it would be a harsh judgement to say that I did not know what the word meant. However, in other cases, such as that of 'cat' in societies where cats aré common domestic pets, more stringent conditions tend to obtain for 'knowing the meaning of the name': we should normally be required to know not just that 'cat' is the name of *a* species, but also of *which* species. The problem which arises is somewhat similar to that which arises with proper names (discussed in 7.2), viz. that a name applies to a definite individual (a definite species in the case of species names, a definite particular in the case of proper names) which can be identified in a variety of ways, not however including merely satisfying a general description.

It should be added that it is not clear that the same problem would arise if it were the case that the nature of a creature's genetic structure determined of what kind it was. It is probable that elements, unlike species of living things, are distinguished from each other by a structure. If so, the meaning of the name of an element could be rendered by describing this structure. Kripke's claim that it is a necessary truth that gold is the 79th element seems correct, but not particularly startling: each element receives its number in the periodic table by the number of protons in the nucleus of its atom, and 'gold' is the name of the element with 79 protons.[12]

There are several ways in which an individual species, such as that of cats, can be identified:

(a) via a 'paradigm' instance (Feature 3 of natural kind), that is, an individual creature which is of that species, i.e is a cat; any creature able to interbreed with this one is a member of the same species, and thus also a cat.

(b) via characteristics, for example, the nature of teeth, or shape, or voice, or genetic structure typical of cats. 'Cats', it may be said, are the species which. . . .

(c) via a place in an evolutionary table or table of genetic structures, as the element meant can be indicated by its place in the periodic table.

(d) via the place/time where the species in question arose, was first observed, or etc.

It is not obvious that any one of these methods of identifying which species is meant is more correct or more fundamental than the others. Even more troublesome, no one of them appears in itself foolproof: the wrong creature could be taken as a paradigm instance, or the wrong genetic structure be inadvertently selected, or the characteristics chosen not actually be shared by all the members of the species meant, an error have occurred over who discovered the species or where or when it arose.

Short of setting up an agreed standard cat, as agreed lengths and weights are set up by using a single case as the 'paradigm' (i.e. indisputable) metre or gram, there seems no way of resolving the problem that identification of individual intra-breeding groupings can be, although as things are generally is not, prone to error. The setting up of an agreed standard cat would introduce a certain means of identification: any creature able to interbreed with this one would be, indubitably, a cat, the species 'cat' consisting of all those creatures that belong to numerically the same intra-breeding group as the standard cat.

If 'cat' is indeed the name of a biological species, and a biological species is an intra-breeding group of the sort described, then there will be few analytic propositions or necessary truths concerning cats. 'A cat is a living creature', 'A cat is an animal', 'Cats are a species of animal' appear analytic, and the truths they express necessary. However, there are no characteristics which can be said to be necessarily possessed by all the members of a group defined as an individual intra-breeding group, nor, unless we introduce the standard cat, is there any creature of which it could be said that it is *necessarily* a cat. This is because if, as I have suggested, 'cat' is the name of a species of animal, it is not also *definable* – unless it should be that we introduced one or another of (a)–(d) as the standard mode of identifying individual species. This would be a new introduction: we do not appear actually to use one method as opposed to another with any great regularity. It seems therefore purposeless to argue about how 'cat' or other species names identify the species they do. The claim that 'cat' is a rigid designator, i.e. a term which, with the same meaning, cannot designate anything else but what it does (see 2.3.4) must, it seems, be construed to make the fairly harmless claim that 'cat' is a term which applies to one individual species, and which cannot with the same meaning apply to anything else, such as a numerically different species.

7.1.3 Box c

The names of biological species are not definable in general terms. There is no one method for identifying which intra-breeding group is meant, but several different methods, none, however, necessarily free from error. (The missing error-free method could be introduced by the device of the 'standard' cat.) This feature of names of biological species is not shared by the other favourite example of 'natural kinds', the names of elements. These are defined and distinguished from each other by a feature of their 'internal structure' (the number of protons in the nucleus of the atoms of the element).

SECTION 2 *PROPER NAMES*

7.2.1 Questions about proper names

The category of 'proper names', unlike that of 'natural kinds', is not an invention of logicians. English speakers for example are familiar with the notion, and in possession of such pieces of information as that in English proper names are written with a capital letter or that certain 'words' such as 'Mary' or 'James' are common names of persons. In discussing proper names we are therefore dealing with an existing category of word, which already has some kind of definition and range of application in ordinary English.

As a first approximation, and as they are most commonly thought of, proper names are the names of individual particulars, such as individual persons, cities, mountains, universities, or battles.[13] The problem most commonly raised about them is whether they have a meaning. Logicians have been divided. Proper names have been said to be 'unmeaning marks' (by Mill 1843, 1.2.5), to have 'sense' as well as 'reference' (by Frege (1892) 1952), to be rigid designators, like natural kind terms (by Kripke (1971) 1977, (1972) 1980). Dictionaries and spell-check programs vacillate about whether to include them, and if they include some, vary greatly in which they choose to include. There seem to be some reasons for saying that they do have meaning, some for saying that

243

they do not. For example, we do not really want to say that because it contains a proper name, the sentence 'Churchill opened a bridge this morning' is a meaningless sentence. The validity and invalidity of numerous inferences, such as 'If a is ill, then a is ill' or 'If a is ill, then b is ill' seem to rest on a use of 'a' and 'b' approximating to that of proper names. On the other hand, not knowing who or what is called by what proper name, while possibly very crass ignorance, does not, at least always, seem to be exactly ignorance of a *language*. My French may be defective if I do not know that 'Londres' is the French for 'London'. But not knowing where London is, who Charlemagne was, or Gorbachev is seem gaps in geographical, historical, or general knowledge, rather than in knowledge of the English language.

We have already seen (5.2.6) that there is a problem about where to draw the line between having a meaning and being meaningless in the case of sentences. Proper names furnish an example of an analogous, and possibly similarly insoluble, problem in the case of words.

The arguments can perhaps be summed up by seeing how proper names feature in two different classifications of words:

1. Proper names vs general names

Proper names have been contrasted to other sorts of names, especially those grouped together as 'general' names.[14] General names were earlier thought to be typified as each definable by an equivalent description (set of properties) (see 7.1.1). Most logicians were and are agreed that a proper name cannot be defined by an equivalent description. This was a reason for saying that they had no 'meaning'. However, the claim that 'natural kind' terms, such as the names of biological species, which are included as terms with a meaning, are equally indefinable, and resemble proper names in how they acquire their referents, seems to re-open the question of whether proper names were rightly excluded from having a meaning on the grounds of indefinability.

2. Proper names as referring expressions

We saw earlier (2.3) that proper names are included as (one sort of) 'referring expressions' in Usage 2 (terms for referring to definite individuals (2.3.3)). Referring to something by *name* (general or proper) is one way of referring to a definite individual; other ways are by demonstratives, possessives, definite descriptions.[15] In another use of 'referring expression' (Usage 3 (2.3.3)), referring expressions are confined to expressions referring to *particulars* (or perhaps closed classes of them). The names of particulars are proper names, and proper names are one way of referring to individual particulars, others being supplied by demonstratives, definite descriptions, and so on. The latter kinds of expressions can be defined – except in so far as definite descriptions often *contain* proper names, like 'France' in 'the King of France'. It seems indisputable that proper names can at any rate *refer* to individual particulars and occur in sentences that can make the same type statement as sentences not containing them. (Example: 'Churchill opened a bridge this morning', 'The man we just spoke of opened a bridge this morning'). On the other hand, proper names seem to differ from 'natural kind' terms in being names of individual particulars (or closed classes) and not of kinds or open classes of things;[16] and perhaps this difference should, after all, exclude proper names from having, in at least a full sense, a 'meaning'.

7.2.1 Box a

As a first approximation, 'proper names' are names of individual particulars. Proper names differ from general names (names of non-particulars or classes of things) but have also been compared with names of 'natural kinds' in the way they name individuals (e.g. not being 'definable'). Proper names are also contrasted to other means of referring to particulars.

There is an old, intractable problem as to whether proper names have a 'meaning'.

To consider the question of the 'meaning' of proper names further, and other problems that proper names pose, we need to look more fully at their features.

7.2.2 Features of proper names

(i) Improving the description

The description of a proper name as the name of an individual particular is only a first approximation, and as it stands it is not quite accurate.

To be a 'name' of an individual, a term must ordinarily apply to the individual so long as it is the same one. When a word applies to an individual *particular* so long as it is the same one, the word appears to be a proper name of the particular. (I use 'a' instead of 'the' proper name because a particular can have more than one name.) However, to apply to an individual particular a proper name must be the name of one such and such (see 6.2.1(v), 6.2.2), and the sortal term (e.g. 'dog') which plays the part of 'such and such' is thus a term which must also always apply to the particular so long as it is the same one.[17] Other terms may of course happen to do so too. My dog Fido for instance was male, had a white nose, etc. throughout his existence.

The immediately obvious difference between the sortal term 'dog' and the proper name 'Fido' is that 'Fido' applies to *one* particular dog, whereas 'dog' applies to any dog. So it might seem that proper names can be distinguished from sortal terms as being the name of one and *only one* individual such and such, where 'such and such' names a kind of particular.

Any English speaker knows that typographically the same proper name can often correctly apply to many different particulars. This has been and is a substantial problem for logicians. The trouble is not that there can be a 'Battle of Waterloo' as well as 'Waterloo Station', but that many particulars of the same kind may have the same proper names. For example many people in England have the same forename(s) and/or surname. Quite often, for instance, in the treatment of proper names as rigid designators (a 'rigid designator' cannot apply to something different so long as it has the same meaning – see 2.3.4) or in the use of 'a' and 'b' by logicians (so that 'a' and 'b' cannot both apply to the same thing and neither can apply to more than one (see 7.2.2 (iii))) proper names are treated as if they were at any rate intended to satisfy, or 'really' satisfied the convention that each applies to only one particular. Typographically the same name 'Mary' will then be said to have different 'meanings' if it is a name of two different people.

There are systems of proper names which approximate to this model because typographically the same name may not be given to two different particulars. For example, in the UK two different racehorses may not have the same name. In some societies the name of one person may not ever be given to another. However, there are also systems of proper names which do not work like this, where it is part of the system that typographically the same names are commonly used as the names of many different particulars.

One type of case occurs where forenames of people are chosen from a pool of terms set aside for the purpose: as there are far fewer terms in the pool than people, large numbers of people are likely to have the same one. Here, it is often said, each 'use' of typographically the same name for a different person, is a use of the name with a different 'meaning' or at any rate a different 'use' of the name, resembling typographically identical words of other sorts which are ambiguous, like 'can' (see 2.1.1).

The other type of case fits even less plausibly into the model that each proper name properly applies to just one particular. This is where typographically the same name applies to a set of particulars bound together by a relation between them. An obvious example is where surnames of people are transmitted from one person to another by a rule such as that a child has its parents' surname. Other examples come to hand from the closed classes considered in 7.1.2 (ii) C. Sometimes, as with the names of individual varieties of plant (e.g. 'Queen Elizabeth rose') or breeds of animal ('Siamese cat'), the names are not considered the proper names of each member of the variety or breed, but rather the proper name of the variety or breed. Sometimes, as with surnames or the names of shops, the names are also the names of individual particulars: a surname is not only the name of a family but also that of individual members of it; 'Woolworths' is not only the name of a shop with many branches but also of each branch of it. It seems less plausible to say that where 'Smith' is the name of father and son or 'Woolworths' the name of a shop in my town and a shop in yours, this is an instance of different meanings or 'uses' of a name than to say that pool names like 'Mary' and 'James' have many different meanings or uses.

We can certainly note that a term which names an open class or all its members will not rate as a 'proper' but as a 'general' term. This is sufficient to distinguish 'proper' names from 'general' names, including names of 'natural kinds': we have seen (7.1.2 (ii) C) that it appears to be an absolute bar on a term counting as a 'natural kind' term that it applies to a closed class. However, the fact that proper names do not accord closely with the model that one proper name applies to one particular (or one closed class) means that proper names do not have quite the role in reference that is sometimes assigned to them.

7.2.2 Box a

Not every word that correctly applies to a particular so long as it is the same one is a proper name: there is also at least one sortal term, and may be other terms. A single proper name cannot be thought of as applying to just one particular, or doing so with the same 'meaning': many proper names normally apply to many different individuals, sometimes by virtue of a rule.

(ii) Proper names and reference

A considerable mystique has developed around the question of how proper names are acquired and used correctly.[18]

A. *Acquiring a proper name* There are many different ways in which a particular or closed class can acquire a name. The name may be chosen, and given, with or without ceremony. For example, a child's parents may choose its forenames; authors, founders, inventors may choose the titles of books, institutions, products; governments the names of countries. There may generally be a ceremony: 'I name this ship. . .', or rarely be one: adults do not normally attach ceremony to the naming of their cat. A name may be registered with a suitable authority, as forenames of people or racehorses are registered in many countries, or it may not. The name may be acquired as the result of rules, as children inherit a surname or an Englishwoman's surname changes to her husband's at marriage. Or a name may just happen, as the local field gets called something or other, or someone acquires a nickname:

someone perhaps starts it, and it catches on. Ordinary words, i.e. those that are not proper names, come into the language in similar ways, but many of them arrive with *definitions*, which explain their meaning, whereas proper names and names of biological species specifically enter as *names* of individual things, whether particulars, closed classes of them, or kinds. It is this bestowal that gives the name a reference. Hence the common view that it is not through its *meaning* (definition by general terms/properties) that it refers to something, and also the view that a bestowed term necessarily refers to what it is bestowed on.

It is important to note that because a proper name is the name of an individual particular or closed class, what is necessary, to know to what or whom it applies, is which particular or closed class it applies to. There are many fashions in which particulars can be identified, none of which seems superior to the rest, nor quite foolproof. Among them is meeting the particular or an instance of the closed class, knowing its place in some pattern (e.g. fifth son of the Archbishop of Canterbury), knowing some property or set of properties nothing else currently has, knowing some place and time when it originated or ceased to exist or performed some activity, which is sufficiently circumscribed for there not to be another particular of the same sort in the 'same' place at the 'same' time. (We have been through a somewhat similar list with biological species: see 7.1.3 (iv).) Once a particular or closed class is identified, what is needed to re-identify it on another occasion depends on the criteria of identity for the kind of particular or closed class in question (see 6.2.2 (vi)).

It is often but not always the case that when a bestowal has taken place, it is correct to use the name of the same particular before the time of bestowal (Examples: My kitten was given the name 'Muon' when three months old; it is correct to say 'Muon was born in August'. Mary Jones becomes Mary Smith at marriage. It is not correct to say that Mary Smith was born in August without the qualification 'as she later became'.)

7.2.2   Box b

A proper name is the name of an individual particular or closed class if the name is given to the particular/closed class. There are many ways of giving names, including by a rule.

B.   Referring by proper names   If a particular typographical word has not been allotted to anything by one or another method, then a sentence containing it used to try to state something fails to make a statement (provided it is used essentially: see 2.2.2 (viii)–(ix)). The methods of bestowal do not preclude the same particular from acquiring two or more typographically different names simultaneously, as parts of a compound name (Mary Smith) or as alternative names (a pen or pet name as well as a 'real' name) or as successive names (Miss Jones/Mrs Smith). There may then be two or more different ways of referring to the same individual particular by name. The methods of bestowal also do not preclude mistakes such as bestowing a name on a non-existent particular or on two in the belief that they are one (for example, because a definite description believed to be satisfied by one thing is satisfied by nothing or by two things).

If, as we have seen is common, typographically the same name is (quite correctly in each case) bestowed on different particulars, then, whatever the cause of the plurality of individual particulars having the same name, reference to a particular by this name will fail unless supplementary individuating facts (ones which distinguish the particular referred to as 'Mary' from others also called 'Mary') are added explicitly or implicitly. That a proper name has been bestowed on a particular (correctly) is therefore not enough for the name (by itself) necessarily to refer to that particular. The name (by itself) successfully refers to that particular only if as a matter of fact no other particular has typographically the same proper name.[19] The idea, incorporated in the notion that proper names are 'rigid designators', that proper names are a superior, foolproof mode of reference to particulars seems misleading.

7.2.2   Box c

If a proper name has not been given to anything, it cannot
   successfully refer to anything. That a proper name has
   been given to something does not ensure successful
   reference, unless it has been given to only one thing.
   Reference to a particular by means of a proper name is no
   more assured of success than any other mode of reference.

(iii)   'a' and 'b'

Logicians often use 'a' and 'b' ambiguously. Sometimes 'a' stands for one name (or other expression) and 'b' for a typographically different name (or other expression). In this case a token of 'a' may refer to nothing or two tokens of 'a' to two different things, while a token of 'a' and a token of 'b' may both refer to the same thing: it may not be true that 'a is (the same F as) a' (a token of 'a' may fail to refer or the first token of 'a' refer to a different thing from the second token) or may be true that 'a is (the same F as) b' (the names 'a' and 'b' both refer to the same thing). However, it is equally common for logicians to use 'a' and 'b' so that 'a' cannot refer to two different things, nor 'a' and 'b' to the same thing, and perhaps also to add in that both 'a' and 'b' secure reference. The adoption of this convention can be useful for displaying the forms of arguments. But it important to note that 'a' and 'b' do not then also represent one (type) name each (or one each of some other type words) as names or other expressions are normally employed.

7.2.2   Box d

'a' and 'b' as used by logicians sometimes represent type names, but sometimes are employed with the convention that 'a' refers to one thing, 'b' to another.

(iv)   Proper names and dictionaries

The non-appearance of proper names in most dictionaries and spell-check programs may not reflect on their status as meaningful words but be due simply to the large number of entries which would result. The *Oxford English Dictionary*, which follows the Locke–Mill tradition of supposing biological species to be defined by properties, lists large numbers of names of biological species, sometimes merely as 'species of bird found in South America', sometimes more fully. Were it to add proper names and their applications, it would be even longer than it is. Proper names, and their referents, are of course listed, as in geographical atlases, catalogues of plants or books, indexes of journals, dictionaries of biography, and the like. Whether proper names should or should not be said to have a 'meaning' seems largely a matter of choice, of how we like to use the word 'meaning'.

7.2.2 Box e

Whether proper names are to be said to have a 'meaning' seems a matter of choice.

SECTION 3 *QUESTIONS ABOUT MEANING*

7.3.1 *General questions about meaning*

Logicians are interested in many different questions about meaning, among them some very general and extremely difficult ones, like the following: What is necessary and sufficient for there to be a language? Is the function or notion of communicating something by words/sentences more basic than there being rules or conventions governing the uses and combinations of words/sentences which determines what they can communicate? Or is it the other way about, the former being dependent on the latter? How can someone who knows the meaning of no words or sentences in any language, or in some language, come to learn the meaning of any? Is it words or sentences which are the primary units of language/meaning? How, in general, can one distinguish what has and what has not 'meaning' in the sense of 'meaning' in which words and sentences can have a meaning? In what way(s) does 'mean' in the case of words and sentences differ from 'mean' in 'Those spots mean measles' or 'That means rain'?

Such fundamental questions are obviously both interesting and important, and the answers are likely to affect the ways in which more specific topics like those we have been considering are approached.[20] However, extensive debate, stretching back over centuries, cannot be said to have settled them, brief discussion could not do them justice, and, once engaged in such discussions, it is not easy to return to the more immediately useful, and equally important, task of disentangling particular problems that have arisen about the nature of particular sorts of words and sentences. It has seemed better therefore to omit consideration of such general questions about the nature of meaning, and to concentrate on questions which, if not always easy to resolve, can be grasped and profitably discussed by those relatively new to the subject. (Induction, to which Mill devoted more than two-thirds of his *A System of Logic* (1843 et seq.) has also been omitted. This is another vast area, currently largely studied under the aegis of Philosophy of Science.)

7.3.2 Pulling some threads together

Many of the questions discussed in this and preceding chapters can be seen as relating to aspects of the meaning of words and sentences. By the end of chapter 6, the reader will have noted that '(type) proposition', as I have used the term, is a sortal term, naming a kind of non-particular. Some of the topics considered in the course of this book concern ways in which numerically different propositions may resemble or differ from each other. We have seen, for example, that some propositions have a meaning such that they always express the same type statement, while others have a meaning allowing them to express different type statements on different occasions, or, again, that propositions differ among themselves in whether their meaning is such that they must, may, or cannot express truths. We have looked at the somewhat neglected question of the difference between wholly affirmative and purely or partly negative propositions, and also at the classification of propositions, according to whether they have one, no, or more than one subject. Some propositions contain terms of a kind to refer to definite objects; others are general (All Xs) or what used to be called 'particular' (Some Xs). Such features of propositions have interested logicians because they affect the part propositions can play in arguments and inferences, within and outside formal systems. In passing, we have seen that the reasons for which some declarative sentences, or a certain class of words, may be considered 'meaningless' are various, and that there are quite simple and mundane reasons for which the line between a sentence, or a word, having a meaning and not having a meaning is not easy to draw in practice.

Because some type propositions can express more than one type statement, and numerically the same type statement (saying the same of the same objects) can be expressed by different propositions, whether an argument is sound or unsound, valid or invalid, consistent or not, cannot always be discovered by considering the propositions of which it is made up. Studies of reasoning must extend beyond the meaning of sentences to what meaningful sentences state (or on occasion may fail in stating). The separation of propositions and statements (as I have employed these terms), discussed at an early stage, adds complexity to the exposition of some questions, but also assists in resolving some confusing and relatively intractable problems such as those discovered by Quine in the area of necessary truth.

A good deal of attention has been given to individual terms of concern to logicians, such as 'true' and 'false', 'necessary' and 'contingent', 'exists', 'the same', and other more technical terms like 'referring expression', 'rigid designator', 'sortal term', 'natural kind'. We have also, apart from considering the word 'word' itself, looked at some classifications of words made in logic, for example, into positive and negative words, into words that supply principles of counting and ones which do not, into ('general') names of kinds, 'natural' and 'non-natural', and 'proper' names, into words that are 'names' and words that refer to things otherwise than by name.

Logicians are not grammarians, trying to systematize a language. Apart from not intending to limit themselves to some language in particular, their interest lies in features apt to cause confusion and to inhibit sound argument. Nevertheless, it is noteworthy how theories and controversies tend to congregate around, not always well-defined, particular specimens, such as 'natural kinds', proper names, or propositions/statements of numerical identity, while their background, the wider landscape of words or their uses, is left relatively uncharted, the concern perhaps of grammarians or the 'Philosophy of Language'. The effect is untidy, and not very systematic. I have tried to indicate how consideration of one feature relates to that of another, and sometimes engaged in a little more general mapping, but it is certainly beyond the scope of an introductory book to go far outside already charted territories. We can justify its procedures better if we think of philosophical logic as aiming not so much to chart territories or build systems as to resolve difficulties, or, more generally, to create a kit of tools which can be used as need arises, here to resolve a problem, there to root out a specious argument, avert a confusion, smooth the path of innovative thought.

NOTES

1. Some of the argument in 7.1 appears in a different form in Wolfram 1987.
2. See e.g. Wiggins 1980: 77, O'Hear 1985: 56–7, Devitt and Sterelny 1987: 67.
3. Locke (1690) 1975, bk 3, esp. chs 3 and 6. See Wolfram 1987 for exposition of Locke's arguments on these points, and criticism of (2).
4. See especially Strawson 1959: 25–30, 180–6, 230–4.
5. See Quine (1969) 1977 on the close association of 'similarity' to 'kind'.
6. See e.g. Mackie 1976: 86–8, 99–100, 105, Putman (1970) 1977, (1973) 1977, Schwartz 1977: 26–34, Wiggins 1980, esp. ch. 3, O'Hear 1985: 56–60, 252, Devitt and Sterelny 1987: 67–80.
7. E.g. Mackie 1976: 99, Wiggins 1980: 86–99, Devitt and Sterelny 1987: 67–79.
8. Also e.g. berkelium no. 97, the post-actinide elements nos 104–5. See any account of the periodic table. I owe the information to Stephen Wolfram.
9. Especially Locke (1690) 1975, 3.6; see Wolfram 1987: esp. 83–6, on Locke's arguments about biological species.
10. See Wolfram 1987a: 40, 156 n.11A for a brief history.
11. Diseases, which are sometimes included as natural kinds, in some cases share a feature of biological species: if caused by particular viruses or bacteria, which reproduce, although not by sexual means, and giving rise to infectious diseases, we might think of one such disease as caused by one such set of viruses or bacteria. However, the mode of reproduction differs, and not all diseases are thought to be infectious ones, and the classification of diseases is clearly not exactly like that into species
12. Kripke (1972) 1980: 123–5. It was of course a discovery that the substance known as 'gold' has 79 protons, or more generally that what had been distinguished as different elements in terms of other characteristics differed systematically in the number of protons in their nucleus. But by now the number of protons probably is the defining characteristic of each element. The terms already in use (for elements already known) should probably be said to have changed their meaning, although, in so far as classification in terms of distinctive characteristics had led to the same groupings, not their application.
13. See Strawson 1974: 42–50, also on which particulars tend to have names.
14. See e.g. Mill 1843: 1.2.5.
15. See, for example, Searle (1958) 1967, Strawson 1974: 42–51, Evans 1982, ch. 11, O'Hear 1985: 154ff.
16. 'Class' must be so used that it includes biological species, i.e. a class of things must not be confined to a group of things sharing certain *characteristics*.

17. It should be noted that sometimes one particular is a temporal slice of another, and the slice, say a king or queen, has a different name from the particular (in this case, person) of which it is a temporal slice, but as with 'passenger' (6.2.2 (iv)) usage is apt to shift between the slice (reigning sovereign) and the person, so that e.g. 'George VI' which is the name of a King of England can sometimes be treated as if it were the name of a person.
18. For discussions see Kripke (1971) 1977, (1972) 1980, Evans (1973) 1977, 1982, ch. 11, Strawson 1974: 42–51, O'Hear 1985: esp. 161–9, Devitt and Sterelny 1987, chs 3–4.
19. Strawson 1974: 57–60.
20. See suggested reading on 7.3 for some reading.

QUESTIONS

When you have read this chapter, or sections in it, you may like to try your hand at these questions, and/or to keep them in mind when doing some or all of the suggested reading. Questions are framed *primarily* on specified sections, but material from other sections may help with answers. You may also like to try the examination questions on this chapter in the Appendix.

7.1
1. Is the concept of 'natural kinds' useful?
2. If you were dividing general terms into kinds how would you proceed?

7.2
3. Is it important that two particulars may have one name or one particular two names?
4. Why is it so difficult to decide whether proper names do or do not have meaning?

7.3
5. Why should it matter how we learn the meaning of words?
6. What do you think is the most important question about meaning?

SOME SUGGESTED READING

For guidance on a sensible order in which to do some or all this reading, consult references in text and notes. Not all the references given in this chapter are included in the list of suggested reading, and reading can be extended by following up other references in text and notes.

(7.1)

Kripke, S. (1972) 1980, *Naming and Necessity*, Lecture III: 116–29.
Locke, J. (1690) 1975, *An Essay Concerning Human Understanding*, bk 3, esp. chs 3 and 6.
Mackie, J. 1976, *Problems from Locke*, ch. 3. secs 5–10: 88–106.
Mill, J. S. 1843 et seq., *A System of Logic*, bk 1, chs 7 and 8; bk 4, ch. 7.
Putman, H. (1970) 1977, 'Is Semantics Possible?', in H. E. Kiefer and M. K. Munitz (eds) *Language, Belief and Metaphysics*, repr. in S. P. Schwartz (ed.) *Naming, Necessity and Natural Kinds* 1977.
—— (1973) 1977a, 'Meaning and Reference', in *Journal of Philosophy*, lxx; repr. in S. P. Schwartz (ed.) *Naming, Necessity and Natural Kinds* 1977.
Quine, W. V. O. (1969) 1977, 'Natural Kinds', in N. Rescher (ed.) *Essays in Honour of C. G. Hempel*; repr. in S. P. Schwartz (ed.) *Naming, Necessity and Natural Kinds* 1977.
Wiggins, D. 1980, *Sameness and Substance*, ch. 3.
Wolfram, S. 1987, 'Locke and "Natural Kinds"', *The Locke Newsletter*, no. 18.

(7.2)

Evans, G. (1973) 1977, 'The Causal Theory of Names', *Aristotelian Society Supplementary Volume* xlvii; repr. in S. P. Schwartz (ed.) *Naming, Necessity and Natural Kinds* 1977.
Kripke, S. (1971) 1977, 'Identity and Necessity', in M. K. Munitz (ed.), *Identity and Individuation*; repr. in S. P. Schwartz (ed.) *Naming, Necessity and Natural Kinds* 1977.
—— (1972) 1980, *Naming and Necessity*: esp. 90–105, 134–46.
Mill, J. S. 1843 et seq., *A System of Logic*, bk 1, ch. 2, sec. 5.
O'Hear 1985, *What Philosophy Is*: 58–9, 154–73.

Searle, J. R. (1958) 1967, 'Proper Names', *Mind* (1958), vol. 67; repr. in many places including P. F. Strawson (ed.) *Philosophical Logic* 1967.

Strawson, P. F. 1974, *Subject and Predicate in Logic and Grammar*, ch. 2: 42–65.

(7.3)

Austin, J. L. (1940) 1961 (posth.), 'The Meaning of a Word', ch. 2 in J. L. Austin (posth.) *Philosophical Papers* 1961; repr. in C. E. Caton (ed.) *Philosophy and Ordinary Language* 1963.

Blackburn, S. 1980, *Spreading the Word*, ch. 1.

Grice, H. P. 1957, 'Meaning', in *Philosophical Review*, vol. 66; repr. in P. F. Strawson (ed.) *Philosophical Logic* 1967.

Peacocke, C. 1983, *Sense and Content. Experience, Thought, and their Relations*.

Ryle, G. (1957) 1963, 'The Theory of Meaning', in C. A. Mace (ed.) *British Philosophy in Mid-Century*; repr. in C. E. Caton (ed.) *Philosophy and Ordinary Language* 1963.

Waismann, F. (1965) (posth.), *The Principles of Linguistic Philosophy*, chs 5–12.

Wittgenstein, L. (1945) 1953, *Philosophical Investigations*, pt 1.

APPENDIX: EXAMINATION QUESTIONS

These questions come from examination papers on philosophical logic set for the BA Honours or the BPhil (graduate) degree examinations at the University of Oxford. The majority are from papers set in the last five years, all from papers set in the last decade. They are arranged in chapters: readers of a chapter should be able to provide answers. Answering questions on later chapters may require knowledge of the topics of earlier chapters, and those on earlier chapters may be improved by reading later chapters. It should be noted that it is permissible to object to a question or some part of it: questions may deliberately be ambiguous, wordy, ill-framed, etc. to test skill and comprehension.

CHAPTER 1

1. Why is it important to distinguish between proof and valid argument?

CHAPTER 2

2. How would you set about proving or disproving that there are sentences, statements and/or propositions as well as utterances?
3. Are there any grounds for rejecting Russell's theory of Definite Descriptions?
4. 'Referring is something that speakers do, not something that words do.' 'Speakers can refer only by using words that refer.' Assess these rival claims.

5. Can a singular term have a semantic value when it lacks a reference? BPhil.
6. Do we need more than two truth-values?
7. Are all, some, or no uses of definite descriptions, uses of referring expressions?
8. Is the notion of 'context' a useful philosophical tool?
9. Do 'I see myself' said by Jones, and 'He sees himself' said of Jones, say the same thing?

CHAPTER 3

10. Could there be a community for whom it was true that $2 + 2 = 5$? If not, why not?
11. 'No interesting sentences are analytic, so it is uninteresting whether there are analytic sentences.' Discuss.
12. Are logical truths true by convention?
13. Is the appearance of referential opacity in natural language veridical?
14. Are all analytic truths necessary, and vice versa?
15. Do we need the terms 'necessary' and 'contingent' as well as 'analytic' and 'synthetic'?
16. Isn't it time we dropped the dogma that no useful purpose is served by distinguishing analytic from synthetic propositions?
17. Is there a non-arbitrary distinction between the analytic and the synthetic?
18. Is convention the mother of necessity?

CHAPTER 4

19. Is it philosophically important whether 'true' is treated as a property of sentences or propositions or statements?
20. It may be claimed that, when the word 'true' is used in the sense in which we speak of true statements,

    (i)   All uses of 'true can be paraphrased by uses of 'it is true that';
    (ii) All uses of 'it is true that' are logically superfluous.

    Which of these claims is the more doubtful?
21. What makes an utterance an assertion?

22. 'To say of what is that it is and of what is not that it is not, is true' (Aristotle). Can we hope for anything better as an account of truth?
23. Is there a version of the correspondence theory of truth which is both clear and defensible?
24. What, if anything, does coherence have to do with truth?
25. 'I know that Jones has a red Porsche.' 'I know that $2 + 3 = 5$.' Is there a single analysis of knowledge appropriate to both these cases?

(with 6.1):

26. Is there any better reason for regarding truth as a predicate, than existence?

CHAPTER 5

27. Are there negative facts?
28. 'A: The number 5 is perpendicular.
    B: The number 5 is *not* perpendicular.
    A: Oh yes, it is.
    B: Oh no, it's not.'

    What, if anything, is wrong with each of these four utterances?
29. 'We are unable to affirm and to deny one and the same thing: this is a subjective empirical law not the expression of any "necessity" but only of an inability' (Nietzsche). Discuss.
30. Is it more difficult to explain falsity than to explain truth?
31. Is there anything wrong with regarding every grammatical utterance as meaningful?
32. Might one understand a certain proposition or sentence without understanding its negation?

CHAPTER 6

33. Is 'exists' ever a predicate?
34. 'Brasenose College exists.' Is this a sort of tautology, which can be used to convey information?
35. If Pegasus does not exist, how can he be a winged horse?
36. Is the time when someone dies a property of his?
37. Are there different types of identity?

38. 'No entity without identity.' How do you interpret this
    slogan? What are its consequences?
39. Can two things be in the same place at the same time?
40. Can there be contingent identity statements?
41. Could we arbitrarily decide to call the earlier stages in the
    history of object a and the later stages of an object b stages in
    the history of one object?

CHAPTER 7

42. What if anything is distinctive of a 'natural kind'? Why do
    colours, women, measles, or alsations count/not count as a
    natural kind?
43. 'The giraffe is a quadruped.' Could we refute this by finding a
    deformed or damaged giraffe with only three legs?
44. 'Our theory can be summarized by saying that words like
    "water" have an unnoticed indexical component: water is
    stuff that bears a certain similarity to water around here'
    (Putnam). Comment on this claim.
45. 'Natural kinds are not the products of nature, but the
    artefacts of language.' Discuss.
46. What do natural kind terms have in common with proper
    names?
47. Is there anything to be said for the view that proper names
    are the names of particulars?
48. Is there any difference between a proper name and a
    candidate's examination number?
49. 'If we know of anyone that he is called John, we know that he
    is almost certainly a male member of an English-speaking
    community; this shows that there is no clear distinction to be
    made between proper names and ordinary descriptive terms.'
    Does it?
50. 'To understand a proper name is to know which object it
    stands for.' Is this correct? Does it follow that if I understand
    a name I can distinguish its bearer from all other objects?
51. Do names have meanings?

BIBLIOGRAPHY
OF WORKS REFERRED TO

Where reference is to a later edition, original date of publication is given in brackets.

Aristotle (4th century BC) (1908) 1928, *Metaphysica*, trans. from the original Greek by L. D. Ross (vol. 8 of *The Works of Aristotle*), Oxford: Clarendon Press.

Austin, J. L. 1961 (posth.), *Philosophical Papers*, ed. J. O. Urmson and G. J. Warnock, Oxford: Clarendon Press.

—— (1940) 1961, 'The Meaning of a Word', in Austin 1961, reprinted in Caton 1963.

—— 1962 (posth.), *Sense and Sensibilia*, reconstructed, by G. L. Warnock, from manuscript lectures at Oxford (1947–59), Oxford: Clarendon Press.

Ayer, A. J. (1936) 1946, *Language, Truth and Logic*, London: Gollancz.

—— (1952) 1954, 'Negation', *The Journal of Philosophy* xlix, no. 26, reprinted in Ayer 1954.

—— 1954, *Philosophical Essays*, London: Macmillan.

Baker, G. P. and Hacker, P. M. S. 1984, *Language, Sense and Nonsense. A Critical Investigation into Modern Theories of Language*, Oxford: Basil Blackwell.

Barnett, S. A. (ed.) 1958, *A Century after Darwin*,. London: Heinemann.

Blackburn, S. 1980, *Philosophical Logic*, Milton Keynes: Open University Press.

—— 1984, *Spreading the Word. Groundings in the Philosophy of Language*, Oxford: Clarendon Press.

Brotman, H. 1956, 'Could Space be Four Dimensional?', in Flew 1956.

Butler, R. J. (ed.) 1962, *Analytical Philosophy* (First series), Oxford: Basil Blackwell.

—— 1965, *Analytical Philosophy* (Second series), Oxford: Basil Blackwell.

Carruthers, P. 1986, *Introducing Persons. Theories and Arguments in the Philosophy of Mind*, London: Croom Helm.

Cartwright, R. (1960) 1987, 'Negative Existentials', *The Journal of Philosophy* 57, reprinted in Caton 1963, and Cartwright 1987.

BIBLIOGRAPHY

—— (1962) 1987, 'Propositions', in Butler 1962, reprinted in Cartwright 1987.

—— (1968) 1987, 'Some Remarks on Essentialism', *Journal of Philosophy*, vol. 65 (1968), reprinted in Cartwright 1987.

—— 1987, *Philosophical Essays*, Mass: MIT.

Caton, C. E. (ed.) 1963, *Philosophy and Ordinary Language*, Urbana: University of Illinois Press.

Davidson, D. (1967) 1985, 'Truth and Meaning', *Synthese* 17, 1967, reprinted in Davidson 1985.

—— (1969) 1985, 'True to the Facts', *Journal of Philosophy*, vol. 66 (1969), reprinted in Davidson 1985.

—— (1979) 1985, 'Moods and Performances', in Margalit 1979, reprinted in Davidson 1985.

—— 1985, *Inquiries into Truth and Interpretation*, Oxford: Clarendon Press.

Descartes, R. (1636) 1912, *Discourse on Method*, trans. from the original French by J. Veitch, Everyman edition 1912, London: Dent.

—— (1641) 1912, *Meditations of the First Philosophy*, trans. from the original French by J. Veitch. Everyman Edition 1912, London: Dent.

—— (1644) 1912, *Principles of Philosophy*, trans. from the original French by J. Veitch. Everyman Edition 1912, London: Dent.

Devitt, M. and Sterelny, K. 1987, *Language and Reality. An Introduction to the Philosophy of Language*, Oxford: Basil Blackwell.

Dobzhansky, T. 1958, 'Species after Darwin', in Barnett 1958.

Donnellan, K. (1966) 1977, 'Reference and Definite Descriptions', *Philosophical Review*, vol. 75, 1966, reprinted Schwartz 1977.

Dummett, M. (1959) 1978, 'Truth', *Proceedings of the Aristotelian Society*, vol. 59, reprinted in Dummett 1978.

—— 1978, *Truth and Other Enigmas*, London: Duckworth.

Euclid (*c*.300 BC) 1908, *Elements*, trans. from the original Greek by J. L. Heath as *The Thirteen Books of Euclid's Elements*, Cambridge.

Evans, G. (1973) 1977, 'The Causal Theory of Names', *Aristotelian Society Supplementary Volume* xlvii (1973), reprinted in Schwartz 1977 and Evans 1985.

—— 1982, (posth.), *The Varieties of Reference*, ed. J. McDowell, Oxford: Clarendon Press.

—— 1985, (posth.), *Collected Papers*, Oxford: Clarendon Press.

Feigl, H. and Sellars, W. 1949, *Readings in Philosophical Analysis*, New York: Appleton-Century-Crofts.

Flew, A. G. N. (ed.) 1951, *Logic and Language* (First series), Oxford: Basil Blackwell.

—— 1953, *Logic and Language* (Second series), Oxford: Basil Blackwell.

—— 1956, *Essays in Conceptual Analysis*, London: Macmillan.

—— (1979) 1983, *A Dictionary of Philosophy* (Second revised edition 1983), London: Pan Books.

Frege, G. (1879), *Begriffschrift (eine der arithmetischen nachgebildete Formelsprache des reinen Denkens)*. Halle, ch. 1 trans. from the original German by P. T. Geach in Frege 1952.

—— (1884) 1950, *The Foundations of Arithmetic. A Logico-mathematic Enquiry*

BIBLIOGRAPHY

into the Concept of Number, trans. from original German (*Die Grundlagen der Arithmetik*, Breslau 1884) by J. L. Austin (1950) (reprinted 1980), Oxford: Basil Blackwell.

—— (1892) 1952, 'On Sense and Reference' ('Uber Sinn und Bedutung'), trans. from the original German by M. Black (1952) in Frege 1952.

—— (1919) 1952, 'Negation', trans. from the original German by P. Geach (1952), in Frege 1952.

—— (1919) 1967, 'The Thought: A Logical Inquiry' ('Die Gedanke'), trans. from the original German by A. and M. Quinton, *Mind*, vol. 65 (1956), reprinted in Strawson 1967.

—— 1952, ed. P Geach and M. Black, *Translations from the Philosophical Writings of Gottlieb Frege*, Oxford: Basil Blackwell.

Garner, R. T. 1970, 'Lemmon on Sentences, Statements and Propositions', *Analysis*, vol. 30 (1970).

Geach, P. T. 1965, 'Assertion', *Philosophical Review*, vol. 74 (1965).

Grayling, A. C. 1982, *An Introduction to Philosophical Logic*, Brighton: Harvester Press and New York: Barnes & Noble.

Grice, H. P. (1957) 1967, 'Meaning', *Philosophical Review*, vol. 66, reprinted in Strawson 1967.

Haack, S. 1978, *Philosophy of Logics*, Cambridge: Cambridge University Press.

Hall, R. 1963, 'Excluders', in Caton 1963.

Harman, G. and Davidson, D. (eds) 1972, *Semantics and Natural Language*, Dordrecht: Reidel.

Hodges W. 1977, *Logic*, London: Penguin Books.

Honderich, T. and Burnyeat, M. 1979, *Philosophy As It Is*, London: Penguin Books.

Hume, D. (1739) 1911, *A Treatise of Human Nature*, Book 1. Citations are from Everyman edition of 1912, London: Dent.

—— (1748) 1894, *An Enquiry Concerning Human Understanding*. Citations are from the edition by L. A. Selby-Bigge, reprinted from the posthumous edition of 1777.

Johnson, W. E. 1921, *Logic*, Part I. Cambridge: Cambridge University Press.

Jones, O. R. 1968, 'In Disputation of an Undisputed Thesis', *Analysis*, vol. 28 (1968).

Joseph, H. W. B. (1906) 1916, *An Introduction to Logic*, Oxford: Clarendon Press.

Kant, I. (1781) 1929, *Critique of Pure Reason* (first translated into English 1838). Trans. from the original German by N. Kemp Smith 1929, following the second edition of 1787, London: Macmillan.

Keynes, J. N. 1884, *Studies and Exercises in Formal Logic, Including a Generalization of Logical Processes in the Application of Complex Inferences*, London: Macmillan.

Kiteley, M. 1964, 'Is Existence a Predicate?', *Mind*, vol. 73 (1964).

Kneale, W. and M. 1962 *The Development of Logic*, Oxford: Clarendon Press.

Kripke, S. (1971) 1977, 'Identity and Necessity', in M. K. Munitz (ed.)

1971, reprinted in Schwartz 1977 (and Honderich and Burnyeat 1979).

—— (1972) 1980, *Naming and Necessity*, first published in Harman and Davidson 1972 (some excerpts in Moser 1987).

Leibniz, G. W. (1720 in German posth.) 1898, trans. by R. Latta, *The Monadology*, Oxford: Clarendon Press.

—— (1765 in French posth.) 1981, trans. and ed. P. Remnant and J. Bennett, *New Essays on Human Understanding*, Cambridge: Cambridge University Press.

Lemmon, E. J. 1965, *Beginning Logic*, London: Nelson.

—— 1966 'Sentences, Statements and Propositions', in Williams and Montefiore 1966.

Locke, J. (1690) 1975, (ed. P. H. Nidditch from 1700 edition), *An Essay Concerning Human Understanding*, London. 1st edition, usually cited as 1690 (in fact December 1689); 2nd edition 1694; 3rd edition 1695; 4th edition 1700. The edition cited here (for brevity (1690) 1975) is the 4th edition, ed. P. H. Nidditch 1975, Oxford: Clarendon Press.

Macdonald, M. 1954, *Philosophy and Analysis*, Oxford: Basil Blackwell.

Mace, C. A (ed.) 1957, *British Philosophy in the Mid-Century*, London: Allen & Unwin.

Mackie, J. 1976, *Problems from Locke*, Oxford: Clarendon Press.

Margalit, A. 1979, *Meaning and Use*, Dordrecht: Reidel.

Mill, J. S. 1843 et seq., *A System of Logic ratiocinative and inductive. Being a connected view of the principles of evidence and the methods of scientific investigation*, London: Longmans.

Moore, G. E. 1903, *Principia Ethica*, Cambridge: Cambridge University Press.

—— (1936) 1953, 'Is Existence a Predicate?', *Aristotelian Society Supplementary Volume* 1936, reprinted in Flew 1953.

Moser, P. K. (ed.) 1987, *A Priori Knowledge*, Oxford: Oxford University Press.

Munitz, M. K (ed.) 1971, *Identity and Individuation*, New York: New York University Press.

Newton-Smith, W. H. 1985, *Logic. An Introductory Course*, London: Routledge & Kegan Paul.

O'Hear, A. 1985, *What Philosophy Is. An Introduction to Contemporary Philosophy*, London: Penguin Books.

Overing, J. (ed.) 1985, *Reason and Morality*, London: Tavistock.

Parfit, D. (1971) 1975, 'Personal Identity', *Philosophical Review*, vol. 80 (1971), reprinted in Perry 1975 and Honderich and Burnyeat 1979.

—— 1984, *Reasons and Persons*, Oxford: Clarendon Press.

Peacocke, C. 1983, *Sense and Content. Experience, Thought, and their Relations*, Oxford: Clarendon Press.

Pears, D. F. 1953, 'Incompatibilities of Colours', in Flew 1953.

—— (1963) 1967, 'Is Existence a Predicate?', *Aquinas Papers*, 38, Aquin Press, reprinted in Strawson 1967.

Perry, J. (ed.) 1975, *Personal Identity*, Berkeley: University of California Press.

Pitcher, G. 1964, *Truth*, New York: Prentice-Hall.

Putman, H. (1970) 1977, 'Is Semantics Possible?', in H. E. Kiefer and
 M. K. Munitz (eds) *Language, Belief and Metaphysics*, reprinted in
 Schwartz 1977.
—— (1973) 1977a, 'Meaning and Reference', in *Journal of Philosophy* lxx
 (1973), reprinted Schwartz 1977.
Quine, W. V. O. 1952, *Methods of Logic*, London: Routledge & Kegan
 Paul.
—— 1953, *From a Logical Point of View*, Cambridge, Mass.: Harvard
 University Press.
—— (1953a) 1987, 'Two Dogmas of Empiricism', in Quine 1953,
 reprinted in many places including Moser 1987.
—— 1953b, 'Reference and Modality', in Quine 1953.
—— (1953c) 1966, 'Three Grades of Modal Involvement', *Proceedings* of
 the XIth International Congress of Philosophy, Brussels 1953, reprinted
 in Quine 1966.
—— (1956) 1966, 'Quantifiers and Propositional Attitudes', reprinted in
 Quine 1966.
—— 1960, *Word and Object*, Mass: MIT.
—— 1966, *The Ways of Paradox and Other Essays*, New York: Random
 House.
—— (1969) 1977, 'Natural Kinds', in Rescher 1969, reprinted in Schwartz
 1977.
Ramsey, F. (1927) 1931, 'Facts and Propositions', *Aristotelian Society
 Supplementary Volume*, vol. 7, 1927, reprinted in Ramsey 1931.
—— 1931, *The Foundations of Mathematics and other Logical Essays*, London:
 Routledge & Kegan Paul.
Rescher, N. (ed.) 1969, *Essays in Honour of C.G. Hempel*, Dordrecht:
 Reidel.
Russell, B. (1905) 1956, 'On Denoting', *Mind* N.S., vol. 14 (1905),
 reprinted in Russell 1956.
—— (1918) 1956, 'The Philosophy of Logical Atomism', reprinted in
 Russell 1956.
—— 1919, *Introduction to Mathematical Philosophy*, London: Allen & Unwin.
—— 1956,(ed. R. C. Marsh), *Logic and Knowledge. Essays 1901–1950*,
 London: Allen & Unwin.
Ryle, G. 1951, 'Systematically Misleading Propositions', in Flew 1951.
—— 1954, *Dilemmas* (The Tanner Lectures 1953), Cambridge: Cambridge
 University Press.
—— (1957) 1963, 'The Theory of Meaning', in Mace 1957, reprinted in
 Caton 1963.
Sandford, D. 1967, 'Negative Terms', *Analysis*, vol. 27 (1967).
Schwartz, S. P. 1977, *Naming, Necessity, and Natural Kinds*, Ithaca and
 London: Cornell University Press.
—— 1977, Introduction, in Schwartz 1977.
Searle, J. R. (1958) 1967, 'Proper Names', *Mind* (1958), vol. 67, reprinted
 in many places including Strawson 1967.
—— 1969, *Speech Acts. An Essay in the Philosophy of Language*, Cambridge:
 Cambridge University Press.

Sloman, A. 1965, ' "Necessary", "A Priori" and "Analytic" ', *Analysis*, vol. 26 (1965).

Sprigge, T. 1988, 'Personal and Impersonal Identity', *Mind*, vol. 97 (1988).

Stebbing, L. S. 1943, *A Modern Elementary Logic*, London: Methuen and New York: Barnes & Noble.

Strawson, P. F. 1949, 'Truth', *Analysis*, vol. 9 (1949), reprinted in Macdonald 1954.

—— (1950) 1971, 'On Referring', *Mind*, vol. 59 (1950), reprinted in many places including Strawson 1971.

—— (1950) 1964, 'Truth', *Aristotelian Society Supplementary Volume* (1950), reprinted in Pitcher 1964.

—— 1952, *Introduction to Logical Theory*, London: Methuen.

—— (1957) 1971, 'Propositions, Concepts, and Logical Truths', *Philosophical Quarterly*, vol. 7 (1957), reprinted in Strawson 1971.

—— 1959, *Individuals. An Essay in Descriptive Metaphysics*, London: Methuen.

—— (1964) 1971, 'Identifying References and Truth Values', *Theoria* xxx (1964), reprinted in Strawson 1971.

—— (1964a) 1971, 'A Problem about Truth', in Pitcher 1964, reprinted in Strawson 1971.

Strawson, P. F. (ed.) 1967, *Philosophical Logic*, Oxford: Oxford University Press.

—— (1967) 1973, 'Is Existence Never a Predicate?', *Critica*, vol. 1 (1967), reprinted in Strawson, P. F. 1973.

—— (1969) 1971, 'Meaning and Truth', Oxford Inaugural Lecture 1969, reprinted in Strawson 1971 and Honderich and Burnyeat.

—— 1971, *Logico-Linguistic Papers*, London: Methuen.

—— 1973, *Freedom and Resentment, and Other Essays*, London: Methuen.

—— 1974, *Subject and Predicate in Logic and Grammar*, London: Methuen.

Swinburne, R. G. (1975) 1987, 'Analyticity, Necessity and Apriority' *Mind*, vol. 84 (1975), reprinted in Moser 1987.

Tarski, A. (1944) 1949, 'The Semantic Conception of Truth', *Philosophy and Phenomenological Research* 4 (1944), reprinted in Feigl and Sellars 1949.

Waismann, F. 1965 (posth.), *The Principles of Linguistic Philosophy*, ed. R. Harré, London: Macmillan and New York: St Martin's Press.

Wiggins, D. 1968, 'On Being in the Same Place at the Same Time', *Philosophical Review*, vol. 77 (1968).

—— 1980, *Sameness and Substance*, Oxford: Basil Blackwell.

Williams, B. and Montefiore, A. 1966, *British Analytical Philosophy*, London: Routledge & Kegan Paul.

Wittgenstein, L. 1922, *Tractatus Logico-Philosophicus*, London: Routledge & Kegan Paul.

—— (1945) 1953, *Philosophical Investigation*, trans. E. Anscombe, Oxford: Basil Blackwell.

Wolfram, S. 1974, 'Hume on Personal Identity', *Mind*, vol. 83 (1974).

—— 1975, 'Quine, Statements and "Necessarily true" ', *Philosophical Quarterly*, vol. 25 (1975).

—— 1978, 'On the Mistake of Identifying Locke's Trifling-Instructive

Distinction with the analytic-synthetic distinction', *The Locke Newsletter*, no. 9 (1978).

—— 1980, 'Locke's Trifling-Instructive Distinction – a Reply', *The Locke Newsletter*, no. 11 (1980).

—— 1985, 'Facts and Theories: Saying and Believing', in Overing 1985.

—— 1987, 'Locke and "Natural Kinds" ', *The Locke Newsletter*, no. 18 (1987).

—— 1987a, *In-Laws and Outlaws. Kinship and Marriage in England*, London: Croom Helm and New York: St Martin's Press.

Woods, M. J. 1965, 'Identity and Individuation', in Butler 1965.

GLOSSARY

The glossary is intended for quick reference, and the meanings given are approximate only. Section numbers refer to the sections where a term is principally discussed. * indicates that there is an entry under this term.

affirmation   saying that something is the case (5.1.1).
affirmative   (of sentences) containing no negative particle (5.1.1); (of propositions/statements) can be rendered without the use of a negative particle (5.1.3).
ambiguous, ambiguity   (of words, sentences) with more than one meaning (2.1.1).
analytic   (of proposition) with a meaning such that it must express a truth in any circumstances (3.3.2).
Analyticity Argument   (coined) argument by which Quine sought to show that 'analytic' is not a viable concept (3.3.2).
a posteriori   (of knowledge) requiring experience of the world, acquired by observation (3.1, 4.3.2). See *empirical.
a priori   (of knowledge) can be acquired without observation of the world (3.1.1, 4.3.2).
asserting   saying or writing declarative sentence, putting something forward as true (4.2.1, 4.2.4).
assertion   (*token) asserted declarative sentence, (*type) that which is said/written and put forward as true (4.2.1).
attributive   (of use of expression) expression used *essentially so that if nothing answers to it reference fails (2.2.2). See also *referential.
axiom   decreed true and serving as premise of a system of arguments (1.1.1).

causally *sufficient (*necessary) condition   condition sufficient (necessary) to bring something about (1.2.2).

characterizing   (universal, term): adjective or noun not supplying a principle for counting what falls under it (6.2.2).

closed class   class such that there could be a time when it could not have any more members (2.3.1, 7.1.2).

coherence theory   (of truth) the view that being true is a matter of cohering with other truths (4.3.1).

conjunct   one term in a conjunction, e.g. p in 'p *and* q' (1.1.1).

conjunction   (sentence/proposition/statement) of the form 'p and q': true if both p and q are true (1.1.1).

consistent   (of argument) possible for conclusion to be true if premises true (1.2.1, 5.2.2); (of proposition/statement) possible for it to express truth/be true (5.2.3).

context (of utterance)   surrounding circumstances, specifically: speaker(/writer), hearer, place, time, etc. of utterance (2.4.2).

contextually dependent   (of expressions): referent of expression depends on *context of utterance (2.4.2).

contingent   (of statements) truth value depends on state of world (3.1.1, 4.3.2).

contradictory, contradiction   (relation between statements) if either true, the other is false (even if neither necessarily true/false); (loosely): inconsistent; (of propositions/statements) sometimes prefaced by 'self-': cannot be true in any possible world/state of the world (5.2).

contrary   (relation between statements) cannot both be true but can both be false (5.1.1).

conventionalism   name given to theories of necessary truth whereby necessary truth derives from meaning of words (3.1.2, 3.2).

correspondence theory   (of truth): the view that being true consists of corresponding with facts (4.3.1).

declarative   (of sentences) of a kind to express a truth, 'convey information' (2.1.2).

definite description   expression of the form 'the man round the corner', 'the King of France' (2.3).

definite reference   referring to a definite individual (2.3.1–2).

demonstrative   'this', 'that', and terms containing them (2.3.2).

deny, denial   saying that something is not the case (5.1.1).

designator   term referring to an individual (2.3.4).

disjunct   one term in a disjunction, e.g. p in p *or* q (1.1.1).

disjunction   sentence/proposition/statement of the form p or q. Inclusive use of 'or': true if p or q or both are true; (exclusive: true if p or q but not both are true) (1.1.1).

double negation   'not not p'; generally restricted to case where two negative particles cancel each other out so that the result is affirmative (5.1.3).

empirical   (of knowledge): acquired by observation of world (3.1, 4.3.2).

equivalence   relation between p and q when p implies q and q implies p: p and q (always) have same truth value (1.1.1, 4.1.3).

essential   1) (of use of expression): if there is nothing answering to the expression, reference fails (2.2.2); 2) = *necessary (3.1.2).

essentialism   name given to theory whereby there are necessary truths about 'things' and/or not deriving from the meaning of words (3.1.2, 3.4).

existential   (of sentences, propositions, statements) those that affirm or deny that there are Xs (6.1).

formulated   (of statement): expression of a statement by a declarative sentence (4.1.5).

general   (of sentences, propositions, statements): of the form 'All Xs are Y': 'restricted' if all Xs form a *closed class; 'unrestricted' if all Xs are an *open class (all Xs anywhere anytime) (1.2.1); (of terms): applicable to (open) class of things (7.2.1–2).

identifying reference   reference by an expression which could pick out what the speaker wishes to refer to but where he also has other expressions in mind (expression used *inessentially) (2.2.2).

identity, identical   being the same. Often used in sense of numerical identity (one and the same thing); may include qualitative identity (being similar) (6.2.1). See *principles/criteria of identity.

implication   relation between p and q where p implies q: p cannot be true without q also being true. Often distinguished into kinds, e.g. 'material implication' (holding so long as p is not true and q false), 'strict'/'logical' implication (if p then q is necessarily true), etc. (1.1.1).

inconsistent   (as a relation between statements) cannot be true together (1.2.1, 5.2.2); (of propositions, statements) cannot express truth/be true (5.2.3).

indefinite reference   referring to *a* something or other (2.3.1).

indexical   (2.2.2). See *contextually dependent.

individual   one of a kind of thing (2.3.3).

inessential 1) (of use of expression): if expression fails to refer, failure is non-radical, the speaker having another mode of reference in mind (2.2.2); 2) = non-*necessary.

invalid (of argument): premises are (/or may be) true and conclusion false (1.2.1).

Logical Positivism doctrines of group of philosophers known as Vienna Circle, centred on Vienna University in 1920s–1930s (for brevity generally referred to here as Positivism).

logical truth a form of necessary truth held to owe truth to meaning of logical constants only (3.2.2).

metaphysical (of propositions – usage of Logical Positivists) truth value cannot be known whatever the state of the world (2.1.2).

modal (of propositions, statements) term covering necessarily, not necessarily, possibly, not possibly true (2.4.2, 3.3.1).

mutually exclusive (of terms) not more than one can apply to the same thing.

mutually exhaustive (of terms) at least one must apply to each thing.

natural kind class of thing exemplified by species of living things and elements; variously defined (7.1).

necessary (of truths) true in any possible world/state of the world (3.1).

necessary condition A is a necessary condition of B if there cannot (in fact or necessarily) be B without A (1.2.2).

Necessity Argument (coined): argument by which Quine sought to show that truths cannot be necessary as such (3.3.1).

negation not-p is the negation of p, and vice versa: one statement is the negation of another if it is (strictly) the *contradictory of that statement, (loosely) if it is *inconsistent with it (5.2).

negative (of sentences) containing a negative particle (5.1.1); (of propositions, statements): cannot be rendered without the use of a negative particle (5.1.3); (of terms) require negative particle in their definition (5.1.4). (see also *truly negative and *purely negative).

Neglected Case (coined) where a predicate which can apply only to existing things is applied to something not currently existent (2.2.2).

non-particular individual that is not a particular (see *particular): there cannot be two that are indistinguishable except for their location in time and space.

non-radical failure of reference term actually used does not in fact refer to anything specific but speaker (and hearer) can identify intended referent through another mode of reference (2.2.2).

nonrigid designator   (coined by Kripke) term that could apply to different individuals than it does (2.3.4); see also *rigid designator.

numerical identity   the same in the sense of one and the same thing (6.2.1).

ontological argument   (particular) argument to prove the existence of God (1.1.2).

open class   class of things which could always have more members (2.3.1, 7.1.2).

Oxford linguistic philosophy   name given to philosophy flourishing in Oxford after World War II, concentrating on analysis of words/concepts.

paradigm case   typical and/or indisputable case.

particular   individual such as material object, event, person: distinguished from non-particulars by feature that there can be two particulars which are indistinguishable except for their location in time and space (1.1.1).

positive   (of terms) can be defined without the use of a negative particle (5.1.4).

possessive   appertaining to someone or something, e.g. 'my', 'your', 'its', 'his' (2.3.2).

predicate   (1) what is said about the subject of a sentence/proposition/statement; (2) term of a kind to be predicate in sense 1) (1.1.1, 6.1).

predicate calculus   system of formal logic, developed in late nineteenth–early twentieth century, concerning predicates, 'some', 'all', etc. (1.1.1).

presupposition   (1) use of expression presupposes existence of what it refers to: if it refers to nothing, there is a failure of reference; (2) (technically) statement p presupposes statement q if the falsity of q leads to p being neithr true nor false (2.2.1–2).

principle/criteria of identity   that whereby *identity is established; sometimes confined to identity over time (6.2.2).

principle/criteria of individuation   that whereby *identity is established; sometimes confined to identity at one time (6.2.2).

privative   (of terms) a privative term has a negative and affirmative component, usually, like 'blind', applying to something of a kind that normally has a quality (seeing) but in this instance lacks it (5.1.5).

pronoun   stands in for a noun, e.g. 'he', 'she' (2.3.2).

proper name   (approx.) name of *particular (7.2).

proposition   (varied usage). Here used of sentences with a meaning and so that two token sentences with the same meaning express the same proposition (not necessarily the same *statement) (2.1.2 (iv)).

propositional attitude   (of sentences/propositions/statements) of the form 'he believes, knows, hopes, etc. that p' (2.4.2).

propositional calculus   system of formal logic developed in late nineteenth and early twentieth century concerning relations of propositions/statements (1.1.1).

purely affirmative   (coined): no negative component (5.1.4).

purely negative   (coined): no affirmative component (5.1.4).

qualitative identity   the same in the sense of having (some of) the same qualities (6.2.1).

quantifier   terms like 'all', 'some', which indicate how many of a kind are in question (1.1.1).

radical reference failure   failure of reference such that nothing can be said to have been referred to (2.2.2).

redundancy theory   (of truth): view that saying of a statement that it is true says no more than the statement itself and that 'true' is not needed (4.1–2, 4.3.3).

reference failure   (of use of terms, of speaker): terms/speaker fail(s) to refer to anything. See also *non-radical and *radical reference failure (2.2.2).

referent   that which is referred to.

referential   (of use of expression) an expression used inessentially, the speaker having another in mind (2.2.2). See also *attributive.

referential opacity   the phenomenon that a change in the mode of reference to something may lead to a change in truth value (2.4.2).

referentially opaque   (of sentences, statements, contexts, etc.): such that a change in the mode of reference may lead to change of truth value (2.4.2).

referring, reference   speaking of something so as to pick it out (2.2.2–3).

referring expression   (variously) expression referring to subject, individual, and/or particular, such that its meaning does not determine to what it refers (2.3.3).

relational   (of proposition, statement) with more than one subject, affirming or denying a relation between them (6.2.1).

rigid designator (coined by Kripke) expression which cannot without a change of meaning refer to anything different from what it does refer to (2.3.4). See also *nonrigid, *strongly rigid designator.

scepticism disputing accepted doctrine. As name of view about *necessary truths according to which there are none or cannot be known to be any (3.1.2, 3.3).

self-contradictory see *contradictory

self-evident (of proposition, truth) such that anyone knowing the meaning of the terms must know that it expresses a truth/is true (a sub-class of *analytic propositions/*necessary truths) (3.2.2).

semantic theory (of truth): view according to which 'true' is a predicate of sentences (4.3.3).

sentence (varied usage) here used of series of *words bounded by full stops, etc. and distinguished into *token (one instance), *type (all with the same typography) (2.1.2).

singular (of sentences, propositions, statements): about an individual thing; (of terms): refers to single thing (1.1.1).

sortal universal *general term which supplies a principle for counting what falls under it (6.2.2).

sound (of argument): premises true and argument *valid (1.2.1).

statement (varied use). Here used of what is stated by a meaningful declarative sentence, all the expressions in which secure reference and so that the same (*type) statement says the same of the same objects (2.1.3, 2.4).

strongly rigid designator (coined by Kripke) expression which with the same meaning must apply to what it does (2.3.4). See also *rigid, *non-rigid.

subject (expression) what a sentence, proposition, statement is about (1.1.1, 6.1.2).

sufficient condition A is a sufficient condition of B if whenever there is A then there is (in fact or necessarily) B (1.2.2).

syllogism (usually) three propositions (of form 'all. . .', 'some. . .') of which, if valid, one can be derived from the other two (1.1.1).

synonymy, synonymous (words, sentences): with the same meaning (2.1.1–2).

synthetic (of propositions) class of propositions expressing contingent statements (often used as equivalent to non-analytic, i.e. applied to meaningful sentences which are not *analytic) (3.5).

tautology has to be true (pejorative sense): self-evident, uninformative (3.2.2).

Theory of Descriptions   (Russell) theory by which subject-predicate propositions are analysable into a conjunction of *existential propositions, one of which states that the *subject exists (2.2.1).

Theory of Presupposition   (Strawson) theory by which subject-predicate proposition presupposes existence of *subject and does not express true or false statement unless subject exists (2.2.1).

token   (word, sentence, proposition, statement) individual instance of a word, etc., a *particular (e.g. one utterance of 'cat')(2.1.1–2).

token-reflexive   (expression) expression refers tacitly or explicitly to the *token sentence in which it occurs (e.g. 'here') (the place where this is said/written) (2.4.2).

truly negative   (coined) (of sentences): containing an odd number of *negative particles (5.1.3).

truth conditions   conditions in which a sentences/propositions/statements are true or false (2.4.3).

truth value   term covering 'true', 'false', 'not true', etc.

type   (word, sentence, proposition, statement) – opposed to *token – one type word, etc. is the same word, etc. (e.g. 'cat') whenever it occurs, all instances (=*tokens) counting as the same (*non-particular) word, etc. (2.1.1–2).

unsound   (of arguments): argument which does not prove its conclusion either because a premise is false or because the argument is *invalid (1.2.1).

valid   (of arguments): conclusion must be true if premises are true (a valid argument may not be *sound) (1.2.1).

word   may be used for *token or *type word (one instance of 'cat', any instance of 'cat'): the same (type) word has the same typography; (sometimes, not invariably, required to have the same meaning as well as or instead of same typography) (2.1.1).

INDEX

a posteriori see empirical
a priori 14, 80-93, 106, 117, 125, 153-5
action 74, 146-9, 156-7, 159, 181-2,
  215, 216, 218; asserting as 74, 146-9,
  156-7, 159, 181-2
affirmation 162, 191-203; of existence
  191-203; *see also* affirmative,
  assertion
affirmative 162-77, 188, 191-203,
  211-14, 253; component 167, 171-7;
  existential 191-203; propositions
  162-77, 185-6; purely 167, 253;
  sentences 163-77, 179; statements
  162-77, 211
'all' 4, 6, 10, 11-12, 14, 24, 86, 91-3,
  126, 153-4, 192, 196, 253; *see also*
  general
ambiguity 4, 6, 10, 14, 29-31, 33-4, 73,
  75-6, 83, 86-8, 93, 124, 142, 145, 183,
  206, 210, 220-1, 230, 246-7, 251;
  lexical 73; semantical 73; of sentences
  34-5, 75, 83, 86-8, 124, 145, 210;
  structural 73; syntactical 73; of words
  29-31, 33-5, 73, 75-6, 142, 220-1,
  230, 246-7
analytic 8, 9, 70, 80-90, 94-115, 118-26,
  133, 148, 153-5, 172, 184, 185, 224-5,
  242; attacks on 102-10; avoidance of
  103, 111, 119-20; coined 104, 112,
  124, 125; definitions of 104-10;
  sub-classes of 88-90, 224-5
Analyticity Argument 102-10
'and' *see* conjunction
Anselm, St 7
application 230, 243, 246, 249, 251, 255
argument 1, 10-15, 23-4, 64, 96, 183,
  192-3, 244, 251, 253-4; bad 13-15,

183; conclusion of 10-15, 162, 183;
consistent 1, 11-13, 23-4, 152, 253-4;
defects of 13-15; good 13-15;
inconsistent 1, 10-13, 23-4, 163,
180-1, 183-4, 253-4; invalid 1, 10-15,
23-4, 162, 183, 244, 253-4;
ontological 7-8, 225; premises of
10-15, 23-4, 162, 183; sound 1,
12-15, 23-4, 253-4; unsound 1,
12-15, 23-4, 96, 183, 253-4; valid 1,
10-11, 23-4, 96, 152, 162, 244,
253-4
Aristotle 23, 188-9
artefact 233-4, 235; *see also* object
assertibility conditions 156-7, 159
assertion(s) 52, 70-1, 73, 74, 76, 106,
  115, 134-6, 139-49, 156-9, 181-3,
  192; as action 146-9, 156-7, 181-2;
  and ascribing truth 134-6, 142-4,
  156-8; assertive style 139-45, 148-9,
  159, 181; and belief 144-8, 159,
  182-3; conditions of 134-6, 139-41,
  142-4; counting of 140-1, 147;
  contradictions/inconsistencies 106,
  159, 181-3; and giving information
  148-9; identity of 142; justifying
  148-9, 156-7, 159; purposes of 74,
  146-9, 156-7, 159, 181-2; sign 140-1,
  143; sincere 76; and statements 52,
  65, 70-1 134-6, 139-49, 156-8; token
  140-1, 147, 148; type 140-1, 148
attribute *see* predicate, property
attributive 48-9, 74; *see also* reference,
  referential
Austin, J. L. 93, 225
axiom(s) 1-4, 9, 21, 22, 151, 153, 183;
  and proof 21; in propositional

278

calculus 2-4; and systems 9, 21, 151, 153, 183
Ayer, A. J. 89, 124, 158, 163, 167-75

Baker, G. P. 23, 40, 75, 76, 159
basic particular *see* particular
belief 70, 76, 139-40, 142, 144-7, 148, 159, 182-3, 189; and assertion 144-8, 159, 182-3; in contradictions/inconsistencies 181-3, 189; reasons for 147, 159, 182; *see also* propositional attitude
biological species 62, 199, 223, 229-32, 235-43, 249, 251, 255; *see also* kinds
Blackburn, S. 22, 73
Brotman, H. 124

Carruthers, P. 24, 225, 226
Cartwright, R. 73, 126, 194, 200, 225
causally necessary condition 20; *see also* necessary condition
causally sufficient condition 20; *see also* sufficient condition
certainty 14-15, 88-93, 107; *see also* uncertainty
characterising term 216-17; *see also* term(s)
characteristic *see* property
class 52, 55, 74, 114, 116, 126, 136, 143-4, 230-43, 245, 247, 248-9, 255; closed 52, 55, 74, 116, 136, 143-4, 234-7, 245, 247, 248-9; open 74, 114, 126, 136, 235-43, 245, 255; *see also* classification, general
classification 59-60, 80-2, 94-6, 101-2, 107, 116, 121-5, 145, 162, 163-4, 166, 176-7, 191-207, 211-12, 225-6, 229-45, 247, 253-5; into biological species 230-2, 236-43, 255; into breeds 235, 237, 247; by common descent 235-6; of diseases 59-60, 255; into elements 229, 231-2, 234, 241, 243, 255; into families 116; of forms 253-4; by man 230; by nature 231; of propositions 80-2, 101-2, 107, 121-5, 145, 162, 166, 176-7, 191-203, 211-12, 253-4; of relations 211-12, 225-6; of sentences 121-4, 145, 163-4, 166, 195-8; of statements 80-2, 94-6, 101-2, 121-4, 145, 162, 166, 195-203, 211-12; into varieties 235, 237, 247; varieties of 232-43, 255; of words 229, 243-5, 254;

see also definition, kinds
closed class *see* class
coherence theory of truth 150-7; *see also* truth
commands 32, 34-5, 73, 148
common notion 22
compound: sentences 32, 71, 139-41, 145, 175-7, 221-2, 233; chemical 229; names 250
conclusion *see* argument
conditional 71; *see also* implication
conjunction 2-4, 41-3, 90, 165, 176-7, 183-4, 196, 233; conjunct 41-3, 176-7, 233
connotation 230
consistency 11-13, 151-2
context 38, 66-8, 71, 75-6, 189; of utterance 38, 66-8, 71, 75-6; contextually dependent 66-8, 76
contingent 8, 18-21, 80-96, 115, 117, 122-4, 151-7, 159, 185-6, 193-5, 225-6, 238, 254
contradiction, contradictory 58, 85, 104, 106, 159, 163, 169-71, 176-89, 192-3, 201-2; asserting 106, 159, 181-3; believing 181-3, 189; blatant 181-2; propositions 178-9, 183-8; as relation 179-81, 183; self- 58, 85, 104, 183-6; statements 169-71, 177-86, 189, 201-2; *see also* inconsistency
contrary 163, 170-1, 176-7, 179, 180, 188-9, 201-2; *see also* inconsistency
conventionalism 82-94, 96, 99-100, 112, 116, 120-4; modified 100, 120-4; Positivist version 82-94, 96, 99, 112, 116, 120, 122-4
correspondence theory of truth 150-7; *see also* truth
counting 5, 26-31, 36-8, 54, 174, 215-26, 254; assertions 140-1, 147; and identity 215-26; objects 54, 211, 215-20; at one time 220-3; over time 219-23; possibility of 5, 54, 174; principles of 216-26, 254; problems about 215-22; propositions 34-8, 63-5; sentences 31-5, 63-5, 140-1, 221-2; and sortal terms 174, 216-26, 246, 254; statements 36-8, 63-6, 68-9, 135-6, 140-1; words 26-31; *see also* identity

Davidson, D. 75, 158
Descartes, R. 7-8, 23, 92

declarative sentence 32-3, 71, 73, 85, 139-41, 145, 147-9, 159; *see also* sentence

definite description 5, 52-5, 115, 245

definite reference *see* reference

definition 2, 7, 8, 14, 22, 38, 89, 103, 105, 108, 164, 173, 229-38, 240-5, 249, 251, 255; by equivalent properties 230-8, 240-4, 249, 255; by function 232-4, 240; negative 164, 173, 184-5; not possible 240-5; by occupation 234; by role 234, 240; and species 236-7, 240-3, 251, 255; true by 108

demonstrative 5, 53-4, 125, 233, 245

denial 39-40, 73, 104, 105-6, 139, 162, 191-203; act of 105-6; of existence 191-203; *see also* contradiction, negation

denotation 230

De Vries 238

description 52-5, 115, 200-1, 206, 207, 230-43, 245; answering to 200-1, 206; definite 52-5, 115, 245; in definitions 230-43; general 230-6, 240-3; indefinite 52-3

designator 60-3, 66, 95, 97, 98, 109-10, 115-16, 119, 121, 184, 229, 242-3, 246, 250, 254; nonrigid 60-3, 66, 95, 97, 109-10; rigid 60-3, 109, 115-16, 119, 121, 184, 229, 242-3, 246, 250, 254; strongly rigid 60-3, 97, 98, 109 115-16

Devitt, M. 158, 159, 255, 256

dictionary 3, 27-31, 38-9, 243, 251-2

difference: statements of 209-25; *see also* identity

diseases 59-60, 209-10, 255

disjunction 2-4, 90, 176-7; disjunct 176-7; of negative and affirmative 176-7

distinctness 266

Dobzhansky, T. 236-7

Donnellan, K. 48-9, 61, 74

double negation 165-7; *see also* negation

Dummett, M. 158, 159

element 229, 231-2, 234, 241, 239-40, 243, 255

empirical 8, 14-15, 21, 24, 80-93, 106-7, 117, 125, 148-50, 152-7, 159, 182, 239; empiricism 83; evidence 8, 14-15, 85, 92-3, 149-50, 153-5, 182;

investigation 87-8, 91-3, 148, 239; knowledge 14-15, 80-93, 117, 125, 152-5, 159; and propositions/ statements 86, 106-7; subject 21; and uncertainty 14-15, 24, 83, 86, 91-3, 106-7, 149-50, 153-7

entail *see* implication

entity *see* object

enumeration 223, 226; *see also* counting, identity

epistemology 9, 14, 91

equivalence 2, 17, 46, 74, 75, 129-38, 141-7, 157, 158; of *p* and *p is true* 46, 74, 75, 129-39, 141-7, 157, 158; and propositions 134, 136-9; and statements 132-4, 141-4

error 92-3, 106, 113, 150, 241-3, 249, 250

essential: property 84, 111; use of expression 48-52, 54, 61-2, 73-4, 135, 138, 199-200, 209, 250; *see also* necessary truth, reference

essentialism 82-4, 110-22; meanings of 112-16; *see also* necessary truth

eternal sentence 159; *see also* sentence

Euclid 21, 22, 89

Evans, G. 255, 256

event 5, 9, 54, 55, 216, 218, 221, 223; *see also* object, particular

exclamations 32

existence 6, 7-8, 39-40, 42-52, 62-3, 97-8, 105, 115-17, 119, 121, 130, 137-9, 153, 169-71, 173, 176-8, 191-208, 214, 219, 224-5, 234-6, 241, 254; current 44-7, 98, 137, 169-71, 173, 176-8, 191-2, 194, 201-8, 214; 'exists' 6, 7-8, 191-208, 254; failure of 39, 40, 42-52, 105, 130, 138-9; of God 7-8, 40, 225; necessary 47, 62-3, 97-8; past 44-7, 194; as predicate or not 191-5, 203, 225; not necessary 8, 47, 98, 105, 115-17, 119, 121, 137-9, 153, 224-5; at particular time 194, 207-8, 219, 234-6, 241; of particulars 115-17, 207-8; *see also* existential

existential 6, 7-8, 40-7, 117, 126, 167, 191-203; form 191-203; import 6, 126; negative 117, 167, 191-203; propositions 41-3, 191-203; quantifier 4; sentences 191-203; statements 8, 40-7, 191-203; *see also* form

expression *see* term

INDEX

extension 230, 239-40
external world 14 *see also* world

fact 9, 18-21, 88-90, 92, 124, 151-2, 238-40; classification dependent on 238-40; matter of 9, 18, 21, 88-90, 92, 124; *see also* contingent
falsifiable 33, 86, 106-7, 144-6
falsity 12-15, 33, 46-7, 50, 80, 85-6, 92, 98, 106-7, 123-4, 130-2, 137-8, 149-56, 158, 172, 183-6, 189, 192-3, 201-5, 210, 224-5, 254; ambiguity of 130-2, 172; contingent 80, 151-2; and failed reference 50, 98, 192-3; incapable of 98, 185-6, 192-3, 224-5; kinds of 46-7, 150-2; necessary 80, 85-6, 92, 123-4, 137-8, 153-6, 158, 183-6, 189, 192-3, 225-6; predicating 129-31, 136-9; of premises 12-15, 183; proof of 14-15, 33, 86, 92, 106-7, 149-50, 153-6; of teeth 204-5
fiction 140, 145-6, 194, 196, 199-200, 202, 204-8
fission *see* identity
Flew, A. G. N. 22, 23, 24, 73, 158, 188
form 4, 6, 10-12, 14-15, 24, 39-52, 55-9, 70, 86, 93-7, 99, 104-5, 114, 125-6, 130, 133, 135-6, 142, 144-6, 149-50, 153-5, 162-77, 179, 189, 191-203, 209-25, 253; affirmative 162-77; existential 191-203; general 14, 24, 52, 86, 91-3, 114, 126, 153-5, 179, 192, 196, 253; grammatical 191, 195-8; identity 209-25; logical 195-8; modal 70, 94-7, 99, 125; negative 162-77; particular 4, 6, 10-12, 14-15, 92, 135-6, 154, 179, 189, 192; real 197; relational 197-203, 210-12; subject-predicate 4-6, 39-52, 55-9, 104-5, 130, 133, 142, 144-6, 149-50, 191-203, 210
formal logic 1-6, 9-12, 21, 22-3, 41, 89, 90, 158, 188, 253; as branch of logic 1, 9, 22-3, 253; and everyday thinking 2-4; predicate calculus 1, 4-6, 10-12, 21, 22-3, 34; propositional calculus 1-4, 9, 12, 21, 22-3, 41, 90, 158, 188; relation to philosophical logic 1-6, 9, 22-3; syllogistic logic 4, 162, 179
formulated statement 134-6, 143-7; *see also* statement

Frege, G. 22, 73, 76, 159, 162, 177-81, 218, 243
function 131-2, 134, 136, 232-4, 240; definition by 232-4, 240; truth value of *p is true* as 131-2, 134, 136
fusion *see* identity
future *see* tense

Garner, R. T. 73
Geach, P. T. 76
general 9, 10-12, 14, 24, 86, 91-3, 126, 135, 153-5, 192, 196, 216, 229, 244, 247-8, 253; description 230-6, 240-3; term 9, 216, 229-43, 244, 247-8, 254; restricted 14, 24, 52, 91-3, 179; unrestricted 14, 86, 91-3, 126, 153-5, 179, 192, 196, 253
genetics 237-9, 241
grammatical 191, 195-7, 202, 254
Grayling, A. C. 22, 73, 158, 159
group: discrete 237-9; intra-breeding 236-43; *see also* class, classification
grouping *see* classification

Haack, S. 22, 23, 24, 73, 75, 76, 158, 159
Hacker, P. M. S. 23, 75, 76, 159
Hall, R. 189
Hodges, W. 23, 73
Hume, D. 8, 9, 23, 83, 92, 124, 217, 223

identification 38, 47-54, 59-60, 66-7, 193, 207-8, 248-9; by paradigm 231, 241-3; of particulars 38, 47-54, 66-7, 193, 249; of species 240-3
identifying reference *see* reference
identity, identical: 5, 26-38, 51, 54, 59-60, 68-9, 73, 74, 76, 86-8, 90, 94-6, 108-10, 113, 115, 117-23, 129-39, 141-4, 158, 162-8, 172, 178-81, 191, 195-7, 206-26, 230, 235, 240-3, 246, 249, 251, 253-4; and counting 215-26; criteria of 5, 68-9, 222-4, 226, 249; and fission 221; and fusion 221; of meaning 29-31, 34-5, 60-5, 68-9, 72, 73, 86, 90, 108-9, 121, 132, 141-2, 164-8, 195-7, 211; of non-particulars 5, 59-60, 209-10, 213-14, 216, 223-6, 230, 235, 240-3, 253-4; numerical 209-26, 242, 253-4; of objects 36-7, 51, 54, 63-5, 68-9, 108-9, 163, 211, 215-20, 246, 251; of particulars 5, 209-26, 230; of

281

propositions 34-5, 38, 63-5, 86, 134, 137-9, 195-7, 209-10, 223-4, 253; propositions of 34-5, 117-21, 209-25, 254; qualitative 204-7, 209-224; qualitative in classification 230-43; questionable propositions/statements of 117, 224-5; of reference 51, 64, 68-9, 73, 76, 108-9, 118, 251; as relation 210-12; self- 117, 211-12, 224-5; of sense 73; of sentences 31-3, 63-5, 140-1, 221-2, 223-4; of statements 36-8, 51, 63-9, 94-6, 120-3, 132-4, 141-4, 158, 162-6, 178-81, 195-6, 218-9, 253; statements of 110, 113, 115, 117-21, 191, 209-25, 254; over time 219, 222-4, 246, 249; of truth value 74, 129-39, 141-2; of typography 26-34, 86-8, 223-4; and unity 223; of words 26-31; *see also* individual, necessary identity
'if. . .then' *see* implication
iff 17; *see also* equivalence
imaginary 193, 204-8
implication 2-4, 12, 15-21, 90, 152, 162, 183; paradoxes of material 12
inconsistency 1, 10-13, 33, 58, 106, 152, 159, 163, 177-89, 192-3; asserting 106, 159, 181-3; believing 181-3, 189; internal 33, 58, 183-6; as relation 179-81, 183
indefinite reference 52-3, 58, 135-6
indexical 75; *see also* context
individual 4-5, 23, 53-60, 63, 68-9, 114-15, 120, 135, 199, 207, 223-4, 229, 240-53; non-particular 5, 23, 59-60, 223, 240-5, 253; particular 5, 23, 55-60, 114-15, 120, 229, 243-52
individuation 223; *see also* identity
induction 253
inessential use of expression 48-9, 60-1, 74, 75, 135; *see also* reference
inference 1-7, 20-1, 192, 244, 253
informal logic 9; *see also* philosophical logic
information 8, 32-3, 74, 83, 87-90, 148-9, 155, 193-4, 207-8; mis- 148, 155, 207-8; new 148-9; about world 8, 83, 87-8
instructive 87, 89, 125
intension 230
internal: constitution 231-3, 238, 241-3; inconsistency 33, 58, 183-6

invalidity 10-15, 23-4, 162, 183, 244, 253-4
item *see* object

Johnson, W.E. 22, 158, 159, 188
Jones, O.R. 158
Joseph, H.W.B. 22, 73
judgment 104, 112

Kant, I. 8, 9, 23, 84, 124, 104-5, 112-13, 192, 225
Keynes, J.N. 23
kind(s) 4-5, 9, 23, 52, 55, 62, 68-9, 74, 80-2, 94-5, 101-2, 107, 114-16, 121-5, 136, 143-5, 152, 162, 166, 168-73, 176-7, 191-205, 204-7, 210-24, 229-55; biological species 62, 199, 223, 229-32, 235-43, 249, 251, 255; breeds 235, 237, 247; chemical compound 229; closed class 52, 55, 74, 116, 136, 143-4, 234-7, 245, 247, 248-9; common descent 235-6; distinction of 107; elements 229, 231-2, 234, 241, 243, 255; of knowledge 80-2; of individual 4-5, 23, 68-9, 114-15, 199, 207, 223-4, 229, 246, 249-53; of name 229-52; natural 9, 62, 229-43, 244-5, 248, 254, 255; need to specify 204-5, 210-24, 246; nominal 234; non-natural 232, 234, 254; not quite of a 204-7; of property 168-73; of proposition 80-2, 101-2, 107, 121-5, 145, 162, 166, 176-7, 191-203, 211-12, 253-4; real 230; of statement 80-2, 94-5, 101-2, 121-4, 145, 162, 166, 176-7, 195-203, 211-12; of truth 80-2, 152; variety 235, 237, 247; of word 229, 243-5, 254; *see also* class, classification, definition
Kitely, M. 225
Kneale, W. and M. 22, 23, 188
knowledge 8, 9, 14-15, 80-93, 106-8, 112, 115, 117, 125, 148, 152-7, 159, 240-4, 249, 252; *a priori* 14, 80-93, 106, 117, 125, 153-5; empirical 8, 9, 14, 80-2, 86, 88-93, 117, 153-7, 159; of meaning 88-90, 108, 112, 240-4, 252; of names 244; *see also* certainty, uncertainty
Kripke, S. 60-3, 75, 84, 109, 110-20, 121, 126, 153, 159, 211, 226, 241, 243, 255, 256

language 28, 30, 33, 34, 83-4, 187-8, 244, 252-4; conventions of 83-4, 252; philosophy of 252-4; translatable into another 34, 187-8
Leibniz, G. W. 124
Lemmon, E. J. 22, 23, 73, 75, 76
Locke, J. 8, 9, 23, 86, 89, 93, 105, 113, 116, 124-5, 226, 230, 232, 236, 251, 255
logic 1-15, 21-3, 89-90, 151, 253-4; formal 1-6, 9-13, 21, 89, 90, 151, 253; philosophical 1-9, 13-15, 21-3, 254
logical constant 90
Logical Positivism 40, 83-96, 105, 111, 114, 116, 120, 122-4, 154, 188; and necessary truth 83-93, 105, 111, 114, 116
logical truth 88-90, 125
logically possible 87, 235-6; see also necessary truth

Mackie, J. 255
mass term see term
material implication see implication
material object 55, 75, 93, 204-5, 207, 209, 215-19; see also object
materials 216, 219, 222, 231, 237
mathematics 8, 89-90, 151
matter of fact see fact
meaning 5, 24, 27-35, 38-40, 42-3, 55-65, 68-9, 72-5, 85-6, 88-90, 93-8, 104-5, 108-9, 112, 115-16, 118-19, 121-4, 132, 134, 137-8, 141-2, 145, 148-50, 157, 162-77, 178-9, 182, 184-8, 195-7, 199, 211-16, 224-5, 229-32, 240-55; determining reference 55-63, 74, 75, 97, 109, 115-16, 118-19, 199, 250; not determining reference 55-63, 93-8, 105, 109, 115-16, 118-19, 125, 134, 178-9, 199, 224-5, 250; difference of 29-31, 34-5, 246-7, 255; general questions about 24, 252-3; having 27-9, 32-3, 39-40, 42-3, 85, 121-4, 148, 182, 186-8, 212-16, 243-5, 251-4; knowing 88-90, 108, 112, 240-4, 252; identity of 29-31, 34-5, 60-5, 68-9, 72, 73, 86, 90, 108-9, 121, 132, 141-2, 164-8, 195-7, 211; lack of 27-9, 32-3, 38-40, 85-6, 121, 124, 137-8, 145, 148, 182, 184-8, 212-16, 243-5, 251-3; negative 162-77; of proper names 5, 28, 57, 60, 75,

243-52; of propositions 64-5, 85-6, 121, 123-4, 149-50, 157, 182, 184-8, 195-7, 253; of sentences 24, 32-3, 38-9, 42-3, 104, 108, 121-4, 132, 137-8, 145, 148-50, 157, 164-6, 184-8, 212-16, 244, 252-4; theories of 149-50, 252-4; of words 27-31, 89-90, 104, 108,187-8, 229-32, 240-5, 244, 251-5; see also ambiguity, propositions, sentences, synonymy
meaningful see meaning, having
meaningless see meaning, lack of
Mendel, G. 238
mention see reference
metaphysics 9, 33, 40, 84, 85-6, 107, 154, 188
middle term 4; see also term
Mill, J. S. 22, 84, 124, 113, 188-9, 230, 232, 243, 251, 253, 255
misdescription 47, 49
mispredication 33, 44-7, 85, 129-31, 136-9, 142, 149-50, 157-8, 169, 171, 173, 177, 185-6
modal 70, 94-6, 99, 125; see also necessary truth
Moore, G. E. 7, 23, 225
moral philosophy 7
mutually exclusive 13, 85, 123, 171-2, 174-5
mutually exhaustive 85, 123, 171-2

name 5, 9, 28, 53, 57, 58, 60, 62, 75, 110, 115, 116, 118, 212, 225, 229-52, 254, 256; acquiring 248-50; family 246, 247; general 229-49; of materials 237; of species 229-32, 235-43; proper 5, 9, 28, 53, 57, 58, 60, 62, 75, 110, 115, 116, 118, 212, 225, 229, 240, 243-52, 254, 256; see also term, word
natural kind 9, 62, 229-43, 244-5, 248, 254, 255; negative features 230-2; obscurity of 229-40; positive features 232, 235-6; see also kind
nature see world
necessary condition 15-21; causally 20; contingently 18-21; logically 18-21; see also sufficient condition
necessary identity: of reference 73, 76, 108-9, 251; of truth value 129-38
necessary truth 7-8, 9, 14, 18-21, 70, 80-126, 133, 152-5, 159, 179-81, 184-5, 192, 211, 224-6, 238, 242, 254; and analytic 80-90, 93-102, 120-2,

125; and certainty 91-3, 152-5;
conventionalist theories about
80-114, 120-6; essentialist theories
about 110-22; and existence 7-8,
116-17, 153, 192; knowledge of
80-93, 106, 117, 125, 152-5, 159;
Kripke's redefinition 116-17, 121,
126, 152, 159, 185, 211; and logical
truth 88-90, 125; and non-analytic
94-102, 120-5; about objects 94-6,
110-11,113-20; and reference 93-9,
105, 109-10, 116-20, 123-4; and
referential opacity 70, 93-6;
scepticism about 93-110; and
self-evidence 88-90, 93, 105, 117,
125, 224-5; about species 238, 242;
subclasses 88-90; and synthetic 9,
80-90, 95, 104, 111-12, 122-4; *see also*
analytic
Necessity Argument 94-103, 111,
118-19, 121, 125
negation 2, 9, 39-40, 163, 165-7, 188-9;
double 165-7; external 188-9;
internal 188-9; *see also* contradiction,
inconsistency, negative
negative 107, 162-78, 184-5, 188-9,
191-203, 209, 214, 230, 253;
arguments against 162-5, 167-8,
175-7; arguments for 166, 168-77;
component 171-7, 253; definition 164,
173, 184-5; existential 191-203;
neglect of 163; non- and not 165-77,
187; particle 163-6, 173-6, 188-9;
predicate 167-77; proposition 107,
162-77, 192-3, 201-2, 214, 253;
purely 167, 171, 173, 176-7, 214;
sentence 163-78, 188-9, 192-3,
201-2, 214; statement 107, 162-77,
192-3, 201-2, 209, 214; term 163-77,
254; traditional view 162, 168; truly
166-7, 173, 176-7; view 230
Neglected Case 43-7, 50, 194-5, 201-3
Newton-Smith, W.H. 23, 73, 226
'no' 14
nominal kind *see* kind
non-analytic 94-102, 120-5, 172
non-natural kind *see* kind
non-particular 5, 62, 72, 59-60, 110,
115, 209-25, 230, 245, 253-4; identity
of 209-25; *see also* particular
non-radical failure of reference *see*
reference
nonrigid designator *see* designator

'not' *see* negative
noun 33, 85, 129-31, 136-9, 142,
149-50, 157-8, 169-71, 173-5, 177,
185-6, 204-7, 209-25; negative
173-5; and 'real' 204-7; and 'same'
209-25; wrong 33, 85, 129-31, 136-9,
142, 149-50, 157-8, 169, 171, 173,
177, 185-6, 212-16, 218
number 62-3, 75, 97, 122-3, 125, 198-9,
212, 223
numerical identity *see* identity

object 36-7, 44-8, 50-1, 53-60, 62-5,
68-9, 71-2, 75, 84, 88, 93-6, 97, 98,
105, 108-11, 113-23, 125, 130, 133,
135, 137-9, 141-2, 155-6, 163,
169-71, 173-4, 176-8, 185, 191-5,
198-9, 201-9, 211-12, 215-26, 231-5,
243, 246, 250-1, 256; action 146-7,
215-16, 218; artefact 233-4, 235;
event 5, 54, 55, 216, 218, 221, 223;
material 55, 75, 93, 204-5, 207, 209,
215-19, 222-4; as material 231;
multiplication of 71-2, 174; natural
231-5; necessary truths about 110-11,
113-17; and current existence 44-7,
98, 105, 115-21, 137-9, 169-71, 173,
176-8, 191-5, 201-8, 214, 224-5;
number 62-3, 75, 97, 122-3, 125,
198-9, 212, 223; person 55, 155-6,
204-8, 209, 211, 215, 217, 219, 222-4,
243, 256; identity of 36-7, 51, 54,
63-5, 68-9, 108-9, 163, 211, 215-20,
246, 251; successfully identified 48,
50, 54, 64-5, 75, 130, 135, 137-8,
141-2, 185, 192-5, 201-8, 250-1;
usage 54, 113-15, 215-20; *see also*
non-particular, particular
'only if' 7, 15-21; *see also* necessary
condition
O'Hear, A. 22, 23, 158, 159, 226, 255,
256
ontological argument 7-8, 225
open class *see* class
'or' *see* disjunction
organs of body 87-8, 232-3
Oxford linguistic philosophy 83-94

paradigm case 231, 236, 239, 241-2;
identification by 241-3
Parfit, D. 226
particular 5, 23, 54-60, 72, 75, 93, 110,
114-16, 120-1, 155-6, 193-4, 204-5,

207-26, 229, 230, 243-54, 256; basic
75; definition of 23, 55, 75, 114-15,
230; event 5, 54, 55, 216, 218, 221,
223; existence of 207-8, 115-16,
193-4; identity of 5, 209-26, 230, 246;
material object 55, 75, 93, 204-5, 207,
209, 215-19; names of 116, 229,
243-52, 256; necessary truths about
114-16, 120-1; non-5, 59-60, 72, 110,
115, 209-26, 230, 245, 253-4; person
55, 155-6, 204-8, 209, 211, 215, 217,
219, 222-4, 243, 256; and proper
names 57, 60, 115-16, 119, 229,
243-52, 254; references to 59-60,
114-15, 244-52; as 'some' 4, 6, 10-12,
14-15, 92, 135-6, 153-5, 179, 189,
192, 253; see also object
Pears, D. F. 124, 225
perception 14-15, 92-3, 155
person 55, 155-6, 204-8, 209, 211, 215,
217, 219, 222-4, 243, 256; fictitious
204-8, 209; see also object
physical object see material object
philosophical logic 1-9, 13-15, 21-3,
254; as branch of logic 1, 21-3; and
formal logic 1-6, 9; and grammar
254; in own right 8-9; and philosophy
6-8, 9; uses of 254
philosophy: of science 253; and
language 252-4; and logic 6-8, 9
place 24, 51, 54, 55, 63, 75, 76, 115, 149,
155-6, 181, 193-4, 204-7, 215, 216,
218, 219, 223, 235-6, 241, 249; and
assertion 181; fictitious 204-7; and
identity 223, 241; and particulars 55,
75, 115, 193-4, 219, 223, 249;
problem in counting 54, 76, 215, 216,
218; reference to 51, 63, 115; as
subject 206-7; and verification 149,
155-6
positive term 170-7; see also term
Positivism see Logical Positivism
possessive 53-4, 245
possible 19, 70, 80, 87, 92, 152-5;
knowledge 152-5; logically 87, 235-6;
world 19, 80, 108;
postulate 3, 22, 89; see also axiom
predicate 5-6, 7-8, 9, 33, 44-7, 56, 85,
104-5, 112, 129-39, 142, 144-7,
149-52, 155-8, 167-77, 185-6,
191-208, 225; complementary 167-8;
contained in subject 9, 104-5, 112;
'exists' as 6, 8, 191-208, 225;

grammatical 191; inappropriate 33,
44-7, 85, 129-31, 136-9, 142, 149-50,
157-8, 169, 171, 173, 177, 185-6;
logical 191-5; negative 167-77; real
191-5; tensed 44-5, 149-50, 155-6;
'true' as 129-39, 144-6, 150-2, 157-8;
see also form, subject-predicate
predicate calculus 1, 4-6, 10-12, 22-3,
34; see also formal logic
premise see argument
presupposition 42-52, 74, 192-3, 195,
200, 225; failure of 42-52, 74, 192-3;
Theory of 42-52, 192-3, 195, 200,
205; types of 43-52, 200
principle of identity 226; see also identity
privative term 175-7
pronoun 5, 53, 74
proof 14-15, 21-2, 33, 86, 91-3, 106-8,
149-57, 183, 195-6; difficulties of
14-15, 21-2, 33, 86, 149-57; by
observation 14-15, 21, 91-3; from
axioms 21, 152, 183; of falsity 14-15,
86, 92, 106-8, 149-57, 183; of truth
14, 106-8, 149-57, 195-6; see also
knowledge, uncertainty
proper name 5, 9, 28, 53-4, 57, 58,
60-1, 62, 75, 110, 115, 116, 118-20,
212, 225, 229, 240-1, 243-52, 254,
256; acquiring 248-9; alternative 250;
compound 250; and general terms 9,
62, 244-8; meaning of 5, 28, 57, 60,
75, 243-52; in reference 53-4, 57-8,
60, 75, 115, 212, 225, 244-51; rules
about 53, 57, 60, 243, 246-9;
successive 250; see also name
property 7-8, 84, 111, 167-77, 191-5,
204-8, 214, 216-18, 220-1, 224-5,
230-44, 249, 255; and classification
204-8, 230-6, 255; clusters of 231-3,
237-9; in definition 230-44, 249;
essential 84, 111; 'exists' 7-8, 191-5,
207-8; of natural kinds 230-43;
negative 167-77; of relations 224-5;
unique set 249; see also predicate
proposition 1-6, 8-14, 24, 32-6, 38,
39-52, 55-9, 63-5, 69, 72-4, 80-93,
95-112, 117-26, 130, 133-4, 137-9,
142, 144-6, 148-50, 155-7, 159,
162-79, 183-8, 191-203, 208-25,
253-4; affirmative 162-77, 185-6;
analytic 80-90, 96-110; contradictory
104, 178-9, 183-8; counting of 3-38,
63-5; definitions of 3, 34-5, 39-41,

73; existential 41-3, 191-203; failure to express 32-3, 124; 186-8; general 14, 86, 91-3, 126, 179, 192, 196, 253; identity of 34-5, 63-5, 86, 134, 137-9, 195-7, 209-10, 223-4, 253; of identity 34-5, 117-21, 209-25, 254; inconsistent 10-13, 106, 159, 178-9, 183-6, 192-3; informative 8, 32-3, 74, 83, 87-9, 148-9, 193-4, 208; instructive 87, 89, 125; making more than one statement 35-6, 52, 63-5, 97-8, 122-4, 133-4, 145, 178-9, 184, 224-5, 253; meaningful 85-6, 121, 123-4, 149-50, 157, 184-8, 213-14; negative 107, 162-77, 192-3, 201-2, 214, 253; in propositional calculus 1-4; qualities of 162; self-evident 9, 88-90, 93, 105, 117, 125, 224-5; subject-predicate 4-6, 39-52, 55-9, 104-5, 130, 133, 142, 144-6, 149-50, 192-203, 210; synthetic 9, 80-93, 95, 103-4, 111-12, 122-4, 172; token 34-6, 72; trifling 89, 125; truth conditions of 24, 72, 76, 108, 149-50, 155-7, 186-8, 196, 202, 209-10; and truth value 65, 69, 134, 157; type 34-6, 86, 99-102, 223-4, 253-4; uninformative 8, 83, 87-90, 104, 148-9; *see also* sentences, statements
propositional attitude 70, 76, 139-40, 142, 146-7, 189
propositional calculus 1-4, 9, 12, 21-3, 41, 90; *see also* formal logic
punctuation marks 31-2, 140-1
purely affirmative *see* affirmative
purely negative *see* negative
Putman, H. 225

qualitative identity: (6.2.1); *see also* identity
quality: of propositions 162; *see also* property
quantifier 4-5, 135; existential 4; universal 4; quantify over 4-5, 135
quantity 5, 216, 22
questions 32, 73, 134-5, 137-8, 148
Quine, W. V. O. 23, 64, 69-70, 73, 76, 83-4, 93-110, 125-6, 113, 118-19, 121, 189, 254, 255

radical reference failure *see* reference
Ramsey, F. 158
real 63, 191-5, 197, 204-7, 230, 233;

existence 194; form 197; and imaginary 193; kind 230; number 63; predicate 191-5
reasoning 1, 13, 22; *see also* argument
recalcitrant experience 106-8
redundancy theory of truth *see* truth
reference 9, 26, 43-69, 73-5, 83, 93-9, 105-21, 123-4, 129-30, 135, 137-9, 141-3, 146, 158-9, 163, 169, 171, 178-9, 192-5, 199-209, 229, 212, 225, 240-51, 254; definite 52-62, 73-4, 114-15, 135, 199, 240-5; and designators 60-3, 66, 95,97, 98, 109-10, 115-16, 119, 121, 184, 229, 242-3, 246, 250, 254; and mention 53-9, 68-9, 74 , 116-19, 121, 146; essential 48-52, 54, 61-2, 73-4, 135, 138, 199-200, 209, 250; failure 43-52, 55-60,63-4, 74-5, 105-15, 124, 138-9, 142-3, 158, 169, 171, 178-9, 185-6, 188-9, 194, 199-201, 250-1; knowing 66-8; identifying 48, 240-3, 248-9, 250; identity of 51, 64, 68-9, 73, 118-19, 129-30, 251; indefinite 52-3, 58, 74; inessential 48-9, 60-1, 74, 75, 135; necessary failure of 159, 185; necessary identity of 73, 76, 108-9, 251; necessary success of 59-63, 74-5, 97, 109, 115-16, 118-19, 199, 249-51; and necessary truth 93-9, 105, 109-10, 116-20, 123-4; non-radical failure 47-9; primary 75; proper names in 53-4, 57-8, 60, 75, 115, 212, 225, 244-51; radical 49-52, 63-4, 74-5, 98, 124, 138-9, 142-3, 158, 169, 171, 178-9, 185-6, 188-9, 194, 199-201, 250-1; secondary 75; success of 48, 50, 54, 64-5, 75, 130, 135, 137-8, 141-2, 185, 192-5, 201-8, 250-1; *see also* referring expression
referential: opacity 70, 93-6, 125, 189; tautology 192-3; use of expression 48, 49, 74; *see also* necessary truth, reference
referring expression 50-1, 55-60, 61-2, 63, 66-9, 75, 95, 97, 98, 109-10, 125, 185, 199-201, 224-5, 244-5, 254; different uses 55-9
reflexive *see* relation
relation, relational 129-44 151-2, 183-4, 197-203, 209, 210-12, 225-6, 236-7, 247; classification of 211-12, 225-6; in classification 236-7; of

coherence 151-2; of
contradiction/inconsistency 179-81,
183; of correspondence 151-2; form
197-203; of ideas 124; of identity
210-12; of *p* and *p is true* 129-44;
properties of 211-12, 225-6
remaindering term 171-5; *see also* term
resemblance *see* identity, qualitative
rigid designator *see* designator
Russell, B. 22, 40-1, 73, 196, 225
Ryle, G. 23, 225

'same': and nouns 219-25; *see also*
identity
Sandford, D. 189
scepticism 14-15, 82-4, 93-110, 150
Schwartz, S. P. 234, 238, 255
science 8, 21
Searle, J. 75, 255
self-contradiction 58, 85, 104, 183-6; *see
also* contradiction
self-evident 9, 88-90, 93, 105, 117, 125,
224-5
semantic theory of truth 157; *see also*
meaning, truth
sense 73, 243; *see also* meaning
sense perception *see* perception
sentence 4-6, 24, 27-9, 31-52, 55-9,
63-9, 71, 72-6, 83, 85-90, 97-9,
104-6, 108-9, 112, 121-4, 130, 132-5,
137-42, 144-50, 155-7, 159, 163-79,
182, 184-9, 191-203, 209-16, 221-5,
233, 243-5, 250-4; affirmative
163-77, 179; ambiguous 34-5, 75, 83,
86-8, 124, 145, 210; bounds 31-3,
140-1, 221-2; compound 32, 71,
139-141, 145, 175-7, 221-2, 233;
contextually dependent 66-8;
counting 31-5, 63-5, 140-1;
declarative 32-3, 71, 73, 85, 139-41,
145, 147-9, 159; eternal 159;
existential 191-203; about future
155-6; grammatically ill-formed 32,
73, 85, 187-8; grammatically
well-formed 33, 139; making more
than one statement 35-6, 52, 63-5,
97-8, 122-4, 133-4, 145, 178-9, 184,
224-5, 253; knowing meaning 88-90,
108, 112, 252; making no statement
39, 42-4, 49-52, 63-4, 74, 98, 124,
137-9, 179, 195, 199-201, 209-10,
224-5, 250; making same statement
58-9, 64-9, 74, 97-8, 132-4, 177, 179,
195-6; meaningful 27-9, 32-3, 39-40,
42-3, 85, 121-4, 148, 182, 186-8,
212-16, 244, 251-4; meaningless
27-9, 32-3, 38-40, 85-7, 124, 137-8,
145, 148, 182, 184-8, 212-16, 243-5,
251-3; negative 163-78, 188-9,
201-2, 214; about other minds 24,
149, 155-6; about past 24, 149-50,
155-6; simple 32, 166, 175-7;
-statement distinction 35-9, 73;
subject-predicate 4-6, 39-52, 55-9,
104-5, 130, 133, 142, 144-6, 149-50,
191-203, 210; synonymous 34-5,
64-5, 86, 90, 108-9, 121, 132, 141-2,
164-8, 195-7, 211; token 31-9, 90,
106, 121, 124, 134-5, 138-41, 159,
178-9, 209-11, 221-2; and 'true'
39-40, 65-7, 69, 149-50, 155-7, 159,
186; and truth conditions 24, 72, 76,
108, 149-50, 155-7, 186-8, 196, 202,
209-10; truth-functional 32, 139-40,
145; type 31-6, 86-8, 90, 99, 106,
149-50, 186-8, 195-8, 210, 223-4;
uttering/writing 27, 66-8, 71, 134-5,
139-41, 146-9, 157, 159; *see also*
proposition, statement
singular term 4-5, 74, 216, 22
Sloman, A. 124
'some' 4, 6, 10-12, 14-15, 92, 135-6,
153-5, 179, 189, 192, 253
sortal term 174, 220-1, 216-26, 231,
246, 253-4, 256; -cum-characterizing
215, 216-17, 220-1; true 220-1; *see also*
term
sound *see* argument
spatio-temporal location 5, 23, 55, 59,
75, 115, 193-4, 219, 230; *see also*
place, time
species *see* biological species, kind
specificity 168-71
speech episode 134-5, 139-41, 146-7,
159
statement 4-6, 8, 14, 19, 24, 36-52,
55-9, 63-72, 74-6, 80-2, 85-102,
104-8, 110, 113-15, 117-26, 129-58,
162-7, 169-71, 176-89, 191-203,
205-7, 209-25, 230-40, 245, 253-4;
affirmative 162-7, 253; argument
about 64-72; and ascribing truth
value 44-7, 65, 69-70, 131-47,
149-55, 186; and assertion 52, 65,
70-1, 134-6, 139-50, 156; about belief
70, 76, 139-40, 145, 189; contingent

94-6, 122-4, 151-7, 185-6;
contradictory 85, 104, 163, 169-71,
177-86, 189, 201-2; contrary 163,
170-1, 176-7, 179, 180, 188-9, 201-2;
counting 36-8, 63-6, 68-9, 135-6,
140-1; established 107, 155-6;
existential 7-8, 191-203; failing of
truth value 39, 42-7, 63, 98, 124,
131-2, 137-8, 145, 154, 169, 171-2,
185-6, 192-3, 195, 201-3, 224-5;
failure to make 50-2, 74, 124, 130,
137, 209-10, 254; formulated 134-6,
143-7; identification of 70-1, 130-1,
135, 143; identity of 36-8, 57, 63-9,
94-6, 120-3, 129, 132-4, 141-4, 158,
162-6, 178-81, 209-10, 218-19, 245,
253; of identity 110, 113, 115, 117-21,
191, 209-25, 254; inconsistent 106,
152, 163, 169-71, 177-89; knowing
truth value of 152-6; made by more
than one sentence/proposition 36, 51,
64-8, 75, 94-102, 118-19, 120-3, 135,
235; necessarily false 123-4, 154, 158,
183-6, 192-3; necessarily not true
104, 130, 137-8, 154, 158, 183-6,
179-81, 183-6, 192-3, 213, 253;
necessarily true 80-2, 93-102, 120-3;
negative 107, 162-77, 192-3, 201-2,
209, 214; not necessarily true 81, 99,
145, 154-5; presented 74, 140-1,
144-7, 150; and presupposition
42-52, 74, 192-3; relational 197-203,
210-12; of restricted generality 14, 24,
52, 91-3, 179; subject-predicate 4-6,
39-52, 55-9, 104-5, 130, 133, 142,
144-6, 149-50, 192-203, 210; token
36-7, 71, 134-6, 140-1, 144, 155-6;
and truth conditions 72, 76, 108, 196,
202, 209-10; type 36-8, 39, 64-9,
86-8, 94-102, 114, 115, 120-4, 129,
140-1, 148-50, 155-8, 177-81, 183-4,
218-19, 220, 245, 253-4; of
unrestricted generality 14, 86, 91-3,
126, 153-6, 179, 192, 196, 254; about
world 8, 14, 83, 87, 93, 113, 121, 124,
125, 151-7, 196; see also proposition,
sentence, truth
Sprigge, T. 226
Stebbing, L. S. 73
Sterelny, K. 158, 159, 255, 256
Strawson, P. F. 23, 42-4, 48, 50-1, 55,
59-60, 62, 73, 75, 93, 125, 158, 159,
188, 225, 226, 255, 256

strongly rigid designator see designator
subject 4-6, 9, 33, 39-52, 55-9, 85, 98,
104-5, 112, 129-31, 133, 137-9, 142,
144-6, 149-50, 157-8, 169-71, 173,
176-8, 185-6, 191-210, 253;
containing predicate 9, 104-5, 112;
existence of 44-7, 98, 105, 137-9,
169-71, 173, 176-8, 191-5, 198-208;
grammatical 191, 197-8, 202;
inappropriate 33, 44-7, 85, 129-31,
136-9, 142, 149-50, 157-8, 169, 171,
173, 177, 185-6; none, one or more
197-203, 210, 253; -predicate 4-6,
39-52, 55-9, 104-5, 130, 133, 142,
144-6, 149-50, 191-203, 210; with no
referent 39, 40, 45-52, 105, 130,
138-9; and referring expression 50,
55-8, 192-3, 199-201; test of 197-203
sufficient condition 15-21; causally 20;
contingently 18-21; logically 18-21; see
also necessary condition
Swinburne, R. G. 126, 159
syllogistic logic 4, 162, 179; see also
formal logic
symbolic logic see formal logic
symmetrical see relation
synonymy 29-31, 34-5, 60-5, 68-9, 72,
73, 86, 90, 108-9, 121, 132, 141-2,
164-8, 195-7, 211
synthetic 9, 80-93, 95, 103-4, 111-12
122-4, 172; necessary truth 83, 87-8,
91, 111, 123-4

Tarski, A. 159
tautology 88, 91, 192-3
tense 44-5, 75, 149-50, 155-6; future
155-6; past 149-50, 155-6; of
predication 44-5, 149-50, 155-6; of
verbs 75
term 4-6, 9, 28, 52-63, 66-8, 74, 75,
110, 115-16, 118, 163-77, 185-6,
191-5, 212, 215-17, 220-1, 215-26,
229-54, 256; characterizing 216-17;
contextually dependent 66-8; general
9, 216, 229-43, 247-8, 254; mass 216;
middle 4; name 5, 9, 28, 53, 57, 58,
60, 62, 75, 110, 115, 116, 118, 212,
225, 229-52, 254, 256; natural kind
229-43; necessarily securing reference
59-63; negative 163-77; not
necessarily securing reference 52-63;
positive 170-7; predicate 5-6, 191-5;

proper name 5, 9, 28, 53, 57, 58, 60, 62, 75, 110, 115, 116, 118, 212, 225, 229, 240, 243-52, 254, 256; privative 175-7; remaindering 171-5; self-contradictory 58, 185-6; singular 4-5, 74, 216, 229; sortal 174, 220-1, 216-26, 231, 246, 253-4, 256; sortal-cum-characterizing 215, 216-17, 220-1; subject 45-6, 51-2, 55-6, 197-203; see also designator, reference, subject, predicate, word
theoretical identification 110
Theory of Descriptions 40-3, 46, 51, 138, 158, 192-3, 195, 196, 225
Theory of Presupposition 42-52, 192-3, 195, 200, 225
thing see object
time 3, 24, 44-7, 51, 54, 55, 63, 75, 76, 115, 146-7, 149-50, 155-6, 163, 178, 181, 182, 193-4, 199, 206-8, 215, 216, 218, 219, 223, 226, 234-6, 241, 249, 256; and assertion 146-7, 181; and belief 147, 182; of existence 44-7, 178, 193-4, 207-8; and identity 223, 226, 241, 249; and particulars 55, 75, 115, 193-4, 206-8, 219, 223, 249, 256; problem in counting 54, 76, 215, 216-18; in propositional calculus 3; references to 51, 63, 115, 163, 178, 199; restricting class 24, 234-6; and verification 149-50, 155-6
token: assertion 140-1, 147-8; proposition 34-6, 72; sentence 31-9, 90, 106, 121, 124, 134-5, 138-41, 159, 178-9, 209-11, 221-2; statement 36-7, 71, 134-6, 140-1, 144, 155-6; word 26-31, 72, 90, 109-10, 118, 223-4, 251
token-reflexive 40, 75
transitive see relation
transparent 76; see also referential opacity
trifling 89, 125
truly negative see negative
truth 9-15, 24, 32, 33, 72, 73, 76, 80-96, 105-11, 113, 115, 117, 119, 122-6, 129-59, 172-201, 224-5, 238, 254; ascriptions of 80-96, 105-8, 129-39, 141-52, 156-9, 254; and assertibility 134-6, 139-49, 156-9; coherence theory of 150-7; of conclusions 10-15; conditions 24, 72, 76, 108, 149-50, 155-7, 186-8, 196, 202, 209-10;

contingent 8, 18-21, 80-96, 115, 117, 122-4, 151-7, 159, 185-6, 193-5, 225-6, 238, 254; correspondence theory of 150-7; by definition 108; established 107-8, 155-6; of fact 124, 151-2; -functional 32, 139-40, 145; kinds of 80-2, 150-2; logical 88-90, 125; no matter what 105, 106-8, 113, 119, 122; non- 172-201; as predicate 129-39, 144-6, 150-2, 157-8; of premises 10-15; proof of, difficulties in 14-15, 33, 106-8, 149-56; of reason 124; redundancy theory of 73, 129-39, 140-7, 157-9; self-evident 9, 88-90, 93, 105 117, 125, 224-5; synthetic-necessary 83, 87-8, 91, 111, 123-4; theories about 150-8; in virtue of meaning 108-10; see also necessary truth, truth value
truth conditions see truth
truth value 33, 39-40, 42-7, 63, 65-70, 74, 85-6, 98, 107, 124, 129-59, 163, 168-75, 177-89, 192-3, 195, 201-3, 214, 224-5; ascriptions of 44-7, 65, 69-70, 131-47, 149-55; discovery of 152-7; failure of 42-7, 63, 98, 124, 131-2, 137-8, 145, 154, 169, 171-2, 185-6, 192-3, 195, 201-3, 224-5; gap theory 44; identity of 74, 129-38, 141-2; necessary difference of 163, 169-71, 177-86; necessary identity of 133-4; necessary lack of 136-9, 169-71; and negative statements 168-75, 201-2, 214; opposite 163, 169-71, 177-86, 188-9, 201-2; and propositions/sentences 39-40, 65-9, 149-50, 155-7, 159, 186-8; and referential opacity 70, 93-6, 189; third 43-7, 98, 131-2, 142, 145, 172, 195, 201-3; unknowable 33, 40, 85-6, 107, 149-50, 152-6, 188; see also contradiction, necessary truth, truth
type: assertion 140-1, 148; proposition 34-6, 86, 99-102, 223-4, 253-4; sentence 31-6, 86-8, 90, 99, 106, 149-50, 186-8, 195-8, 210, 223-4; statement 36-8, 39, 64-9, 86-8, 94-102, 114, 115, 120-4, 129, 140-1, 148-50, 155-8, 177-81, 183-4, 218-19, 220, 245, 253-4; word 26-31, 72-3, 90, 109, 243, 250-1, 253
typography 26-31, 86, 211, 233-4, 246-7, 250

uncertainty 14-15, 24, 83, 86, 91-3, 106-8, 149-50, 153-7
uninformative 8, 83, 87-90, 104, 148-9; *see also* informative
unity *see* identity
universal 219; *see also* general term, non-particular
unrestricted generality *see* general
unsound *see* argument
utterance 27, 66-9, 71, 134-5, 139-41, 146-9, 157, 159; circumstances of 66-9; context of 38, 66-9, 71, 75-6

vacuous 150-1, 154; *see also* metaphysical
validity *see* argument
variable 4
verifiable 33

Waismann, F. 124
Wiggins, D. 226, 255
Wittgenstein, L. 73
Wolfram, S. 70, 76, 124-5, 159, 189, 226, 255
Woods, M. 226

word 26-31, 66, 72-3, 87-90, 108-10, 112, 118, 142, 163-77, 187-8, 220-1, 223-4, 230, 240-7, 249-54; ambiguous 29-31, 33-5, 73, 87-8, 142, 220-1, 230, 246-7; counts 26-31; kinds of 229, 243-5, 254; knowing meaning of 88-90, 108, 112, 240-4, 252; meaningful 27-31, 243-5, 251-3; meaningless 27-30, 188, 243-5, 251-3; negative 163-77; spoken 27, 66; synonymous 29-31, 33-4, 72, 90, 108-9; token 26-31, 72, 90, 109-10, 118, 223-4, 251; type 26-31, 72-3, 90, 109, 243, 250-1, 253; written 27, 66; *see also* name, term
word processor 26-31, 32, 38-9, 121, 140-1, 165; spell-check program 27-8, 251-2
world 8, 14, 19, 80, 85-6, 87, 88-90, 108, 113, 114, 121, 124, 125, 193, 196, 202, 205-7, 230-40; information about 88-90; investigation of 81-2, 86; 'nature' 230-40; possible 19, 80, 108; statements about 8, 14, 83, 87, 93, 113, 121, 124, 125, 151-7, 196; as subject 202, 206-7